Beginning Silverlight 5 in C#

Fourth Edition

Robert Lair

Apress®

Beginning Silverlight 5 in C#

ISBN-13 (pbk): 978-1-4302-3461-6

ISBN-13 (electronic): 978-1-4302-3462-3

President and Publisher: Paul Manning
Lead Editor: Ewan Buckingham
Technical Reviewer: Todd Meister
Editorial Board: Steve Anglin, Ewan Buckingham, Gary Cornell, Louise Corrigan, Morgan Ertel, Jonathan Gennick, Jonathan Hassell, Robert Hutchinson, Michelle Lowman, James Markham, Matthew Moodie, Jeff Olson, Jeffrey Pepper, Douglas Pundick, Ben Renow-Clarke, Dominic Shakeshaft, Gwenan Spearing, Matt Wade, Tom Welsh
Coordinating Editor: Jennifer L. Blackwell
Copy Editor: Roger LeBlanc
Compositor: Bytheway Publishing Services
Indexer: SPI Global
Artist: SPI Global
Cover Designer: Anna Ishchenko

Distributed to the book trade worldwide by Springer Scie nce+Business Media New York, 233 Spring Street, 6th Floor, New York, NY 10013. Phone 1-800-SPRINGER, fax (201) 348-4505, e-mail orders-ny@springer-sbm.com, or vi sit www.springeronline.com.

For information on translations, please e-mail rights@apress.com, or visit www.apress.com.

Apress and friends of ED book s may be purchased in bulk f or academic, corporate, or promo tional use. eBoo k versions and licenses are also available for most titles. For more information, reference our Special Bulk Sales–eBook Licensing web page at www.apress.com/bulk-sales.

Any source code or other supplementary materials referenced by the author i n this text is av ailable to re aders at www.apress.com. For detailed inf ormation about how to lo cate your book's source code, go to www.apress.com/source-code.

To Max, I am so proud of you.

–Dad

Contents at a Glance

Contents

About the Author

 **Robert Lair** has been working with .NET technologies since prior to its alpha when he built IBuySpy, the first-ever demo application used to show off .NET to the development community. He is a published author of many books and magazine articles, including previous versions of *Beginning Silverlight*. Robert has also been a speaker at a number of .NET technical conferences.

Technologies in which Robert specializes include Silverlight, mainframe modernization to .NET, ASP.NET custom application development, SharePoint development and integration, and many related technologies. Today Robert works as the development manager at T3 Technologies (www.t3t.com), a company that offers mainframe alternatives on the Windows platform. Follow Robert on twitter at www.twitter.com/robertlair and on the web at www.robertlair.com/blog.

About the Technical Reviewer

 Todd Meister has been working in the IT industry for over 15 years. He's been a technical editor on over 75 titles, ranging from SQL Server to the .NET Framework. Besides editing technical titles, he is the Senior IT Architect at Ball State University in Muncie, Indiana. He lives in central Indiana with his wife, Kimberly, and their five loving children.

Acknowledgments

I would like to thank the many people at Apress who made this book happen. I would especially like to thank Jennifer Blackwell, Ewan Buckingham, Dominic Shakeshaft, and Todd Meister. Without all of your hard work, this book would never have happened, thank you all.

I would also like to thank my family. To my wife, Debi, who has once again sacrificed much during the times when I was busy writing this book. And to my son, Max, who was very understanding when his father couldn't spend as much time with him.

–Robert Lair

Introduction

There are many ways you can learn a new technology such as Silverlight. For starters, Microsoft has gotten better and better with the documentation that is released with its programming technologies, and it has also supplemented that documentation with employee blogs and technology sites such as www.silverlight.net. There are widely used forums that are available where many experts participate. Training can also be purchased if you have the cash flow to justify it. While all of these are great options, many people still resort to purchasing a book on the technology. But with so many books on the market, how do you know what book is best?

My philosophy on learning a new technology is that there is no better way than to actually try it out for yourself. That is why I have written *Beginning Silverlight 5 in C#* focusing on a number of step-by-step, walk-through tutorials that will give you hands-on experience with the different topics and get you started developing Silverlight applications on your own.

Who Should Read This Book

This book is written for application developers who want to get started with Silverlight. It assumes that you have some experience developing applications using technologies related to Microsoft Visual Basic, ASP, or .NET and have worked with Microsoft Visual Studio. You should be familiar with the JavaScript, C#, and XML languages.

How This Book Is Organized

Each chapter focuses on a particular area of Silverlight and contains one or more "Try It Out" exercises that allow you to apply what you have learned. Here is a summary of what each chapter includes:

- Chapter 1, "Welcome to Silverlight 5," gives you an introduction to rich interactive (or Internet) applications (RIAs) and Silverlight. You will also learn about the tools used in developing Silverlight-enabled applications.

- Chapter 2, "Introduction to Visual Studio 2010," introduces Visual Studio 2010 and the important new features offered in this version. In this chapter, you will build your first Silverlight application.

- Chapter 3, "Layout Management in Silverlight," discusses Silverlight's flexible layout management system, which lets you specify how controls will appear in your applications. It describes Silverlight's layout management controls in depth.

- Chapter 4, "Silverlight Controls," introduces the common controls that are provided with Silverlight. You will continue to work with these controls throughout the book.

- Chapter 5, "Data Binding and Silverlight List Controls," looks at the Silverlight controls that display lists of data and how to bind data to these controls. You'll see that these controls are flexible and can show data in unique ways.

- Chapter 6, "Silverlight Toolkit," discusses the Silverlight Toolkit, an open-source project that extends the Silverlight control set to include a number a controls, themes, and frameworks that will help you be more productive as a Silverlight developer.

- Chapter 7, "Data Access and Networking," describes how data access in Silverlight applications works differently than it does in traditional applications. It then explores mechanisms for accessing data in Silverlight applications, focusing on the use of web services.

- Chapter 8, "Navigation Framework," looks at building Silverlight applications that allow the user to navigate through different pages, creating an experience similar to browsing through different pages of a web site.

- Chapter 9, "Isolated Storage in Silverlight," covers localized storage in Silverlight, which is handled by its isolated storage feature. You'll learn how to store user-specific data for your application and have that data persist over browser instances.

- Chapter 10, "System Integration and Device Support," covers how Silverlight applications can support notifications, integrate with legacy COM applications and libraries, access a user's web camera and microphone, and be enabled as a drop target.

- Chapter 11, "Introduction to Expression Blend," gets you started with Microsoft Expression Blend, which lets you edit XAML documents visually.

- Chapter 12, "Styling in Silverlight," describes how you can control the styles of your Silverlight application's user-interface elements. You'll learn about defining style properties inline using both Visual Studio and Expression Blend, as well as how to use Silverlight styles.

- Chapter 13, "Transformations and Animation," covers creating animations in Silverlight. You'll see how Expression Blend helps you create complex animations and transformations.

- Chapter 14, "Custom Controls," explains the basics of creating custom controls in Silverlight. First, it covers when it is appropriate to write custom controls in Silverlight, and then it describes how to build a custom control that has several different states.

- Chapter 15, "Printing in Silverlight," discusses how to add printing functionality to Silverlight applications.

- Chapter 16, "Deployment," covers the deployment and configuration of Silverlight applications as well as how to enable out-of-browser support.

By the time you finish this book, you will have a firm foundation in Silverlight, and you will be able to create your own Silverlight-enabled applications.

CHAPTER 1

Welcome to Silverlight 5

This chapter introduces Silverlight, a Microsoft cross-browser, cross-platform plug-in that allows you to create rich interactive (or Internet) applications (RIAs) for the Web. It begins with a brief look at the evolution of user interfaces, and then provides an overview of Silverlight. You'll learn how Silverlight fits into RIA solutions, the benefits it brings to developers, and the tools involved in developing Silverlight-enabled applications.

The Evolution of the User Interface

Software user interfaces are constantly evolving and improving. I remember back when I was still working with an early version of Windows and looking at Mac OS with envy. Then I remember seeing Linux systems with radical new desktop interfaces. More recently, I found myself looking again at the Mac OS X Dock (shown in Figure 1-1) and wanting that for my Windows XP machine—to the point where I purchased a product that mimicked it. I was dedicated to Windows through it all, but I was envious of some of the user experiences the different environments offered.

Figure 1-1. The Mac OS X Dock feature

The evolution of the user interface continues in the Windows operating system. Perhaps the most prominent difference between Windows 7 and previous versions of Windows is user-interface improvements. Microsoft was very intent on improving the richness of the operating system. One example is the new taskbar, where large icons replace the text descriptions and now when the user places the cursor over an icon Windows will display a window thumbnail, as shown in Figure 1-2.

Figure 1-2. Windows 7 taskbar

Another user-interface improvement in Windows 7 is the Aero Snap. This feature allows you to easily maximize your window by dragging it to the top of the screen, but it also allows you to drag the window to the left or right edge of the screen to tile the window to 50% of the left or right side of the screen as shown in Figure 1-3.

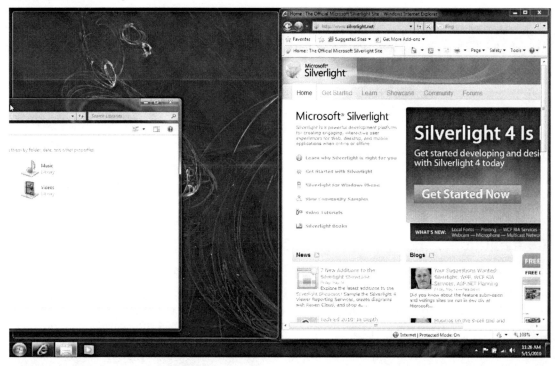

Figure 1-3. *Windows 7 Aero Snap feature*

These features reflect how operating systems have evolved over the years, but the same evolution pertains to all areas of development, and for just about all industries. It is now expected that applications not only contain necessary features, but that they also have slick user interfaces. However, while rich applications are now expected, it is not necessarily the priority for developers. Over the last decade, there has been a struggle to find the right balance of "rich" and "reach" in applications. If you consider standard desktop applications, the applications are installed on individual client machines. They allow for very rich and responsive user interfaces and additional features, such as offline support. The performance of the application depends on the machine on which it is installed. While desktop applications have a very rich experience, they have very small reach. The application needs to have a code base for each target platform, and every machine needs to have the application installed and maintained.

In contrast, we have web applications, which are HTML-focused programs designed to run within a browser and across platforms. For the Microsoft-based developer, this has recently meant developing with ASP.NET and building web services to offer services over the Internet. The focus of most of the logic and code has been placed on the server for the benefit of application performance. The price of this approach has been a poor user interface. These applications had excellent reach, but they were not very rich, as shown in Figure 1-4. Between these two extremes, there is a clear gap between the technologies.

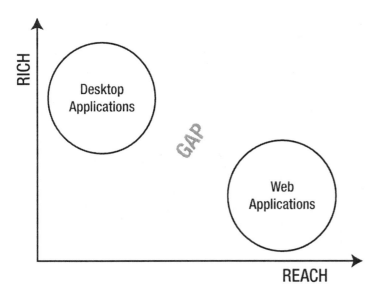

Figure 1-4. Rich and reach application comparison

To fill this gap, a new development approach has surfaced, as shown in Figure 1-5. This new approach is termed *RIA (Rich Internet Applications)*, which is defined as a web application that has the features and functionality found in traditional desktop applications. There are a number of RIA technologies, including Microsoft's Silverlight.

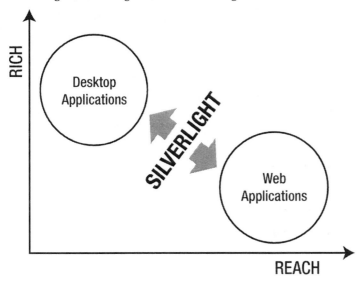

Figure 1-5. RIA fills the gap between rich and reach applications

Rich Internet Application Solutions

The concept of RIA has been around for quite some time, but the term "rich Internet application" was first used in 2002 in a Macromedia white paper. Before then, the terms "remote scripting" and "X Internet" were used to describe the concept.

Today, many different solutions fit the description of RIAs, but there is one consistent characteristic: all RIA solutions involve a runtime that runs on the client machine and, architecturally, sits between the user and the server.

In recent years, the technology most commonly used in RIAs has been Flash. When Flash was introduced, it brought to the Web rich user experiences never seen before. However, due to the lack of tools allowing Microsoft .NET developers to integrate Flash into their applications, to those developers Flash just seemed like a tool for adding some pretty effects to a web page, but nothing functional.

Then a wonderful thing happened when Adobe purchased Macromedia. All of the sudden, Flash was married to some of the development tools offered by Adobe. Microsoft retaliated by announcing Silverlight, formerly known as Windows Presentation Foundation Everywhere (WPF/E). Silverlight is the technology that many .NET developers have been waiting for.

What exactly is Silverlight? And what impact does Silverlight actually have on us as .NET developers? Well, I'm glad you asked.

What Is Silverlight?

As I explained in the previous section, all RIAs have one characteristic in common: a client runtime that sits between the user and the server. In the case of Microsoft's RIA solution, Silverlight is this client runtime. Specifically, Silverlight is a cross-platform, cross-browser plug-in that renders user interfaces and graphical assets on a canvas that can be inserted into an HTML page.

The markup used to define a Silverlight canvas is called *Extensible Application Markup Language* (XAML, pronounced "zammel"). XAML is an XML-based language that is similar to HTML in some ways. Like HTML, XAML defines which elements appear, as well as the layout of those elements. However, unlike HTML, XAML goes far beyond simple element definition and layout. Using XAML, you can also specify timelines, transformations, animations, and events.

The following is an example of a Silverlight canvas defined in XAML:

```
<UserControl
        xmlns="http://schemas.microsoft.com/winfx/2006/xaml/presentation"
        xmlns:x="http://schemas.microsoft.com/winfx/2006/xaml"
        x:Class="FirstLookXaml.MainPage"
        Width="640" Height="480">

        <Canvas x:Name="LayoutRoot" Background="White">
                <Rectangle Height="119" Canvas.Left="75" Stroke="Black"
                    Canvas.Top="92" Width="183"/>
                <Ellipse Height="119" Canvas.Left="347" Stroke="Black"
                  Canvas.Top="92" Width="189"/>
                <Button Content="XAML Rocks!" Height="43" Canvas.Left="233"
                  Canvas.Top="285" Width="161"/>
        </Canvas>
</UserControl>
```

Figure 1-6 shows this canvas in Microsoft Expression Blend, the design tool used to edit and create XAML for Silverlight applications. You can see that this XAML simply defines a rectangle on a canvas, as well as the properties associated with that rectangle, including its name, location, size, color, and border.

This simple example is just intended to give you an idea of what XAML looks like. You'll learn more about XAML in upcoming chapters. For now, let's continue by looking at the benefits of Silverlight.

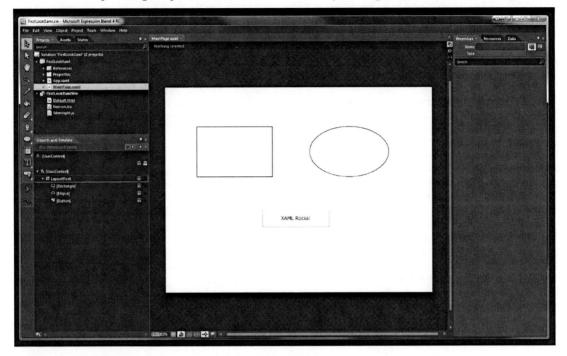

Figure 1-6. A basic XAML canvas in Microsoft Expression Blend

Benefits of Silverlight

Naturally, Silverlight offers all of the same benefits of RIAs, but there are a few features that set it apart from other RIA solutions, including the following:

- It offers cross-platform/cross-browser support.
- It provides a cross-platform version of the .NET Framework.
- XAML is a text-based markup language.
- Silverlight uses familiar technologies.
- Silverlight offers an Out of Browser and Full Trust option.
- Silverlight is the main development platform for Windows Phone 7.
- It's easy to deploy the Silverlight runtime to clients.

Let's take a closer look at each of these benefits.

Cross-Platform/Cross-Browser Support

When ASP.NET was released a number of years ago, one of the benefits touted was cross-browser support. Developers would need to have only one code base, and that code base would work in all modern browsers. For the most part, this is true. No matter which browser you are using, the application will function. However, to receive all of the bells and whistles offered by the ASP.NET controls, you must use the latest version of Internet Explorer. If you are using any other browser, you actually get a downgraded version of the web site, which contains fewer features.

Validation controls are a prime example. If you are using a browser that ASP.NET recognizes as an "upscale" browser, you can take advantage of client-side validation. If you are using any other browser, the validation controls still function, but they require a postback to the server to do the validation. So, although ASP.NET is cross-browser capable, users can get different experiences, depending on which browser they are using.

With Silverlight, this changes. Microsoft is once again pulling out the term "cross-browser," and also adding "cross-platform"—and this time they mean it. As a developer, you can create a Silverlight application and rest assured that it will run exactly the same on all supported platforms and browsers.

Currently, two platforms are supported. Naturally, the first is Windows-based platforms, and the second is Mac OS platforms. As for browser support, Internet Explorer, Firefox, Safari, and Google Chrome are currently covered.

This leaves one large platform unsupported: Linux. Although Microsoft does not have plans to support Linux, others do. Moonlight is an open-source implementation of Silverlight, targeted primarily at Linux-based operating systems. Moonlight is part of the Mono project, an open-source initiative to develop and run .NET client and server applications on Linux, Solaris, Mac OS X, Windows, and Unix. Although Moonlight brings Silverlight features to Linux, the project lags behind the aggressive Microsoft release cycles.

Cross-Platform Version of the .NET Framework

Silverlight 1.0 was released by Microsoft in the summer of 2007, but this version supported only Ecma languages that are interpreted in the client. Although Silverlight 1.0 works well for developers who are already familiar with client-side scripting, many developers have their eyes on the second release of Silverlight, version 2. Silverlight 1.0 is more or less in direct competition with Flash—some have called it Microsoft's "Flash killer." However, things really get exciting with Silverlight 2.

Silverlight 2 and beyond contains its own cross-platform version of the .NET Framework, which means it has its own version of the common language runtime (CLR), the full type system, and a .NET Framework programming library you can use in Visual Studio 2010 to build rich user experiences in the browser.

Use of Familiar Technologies

Microsoft is very good at creating tools that make application development easy. The Visual Studio integrated development environment (IDE) has been around for quite some time, and although new features are continually added to the tool, the environment itself has remained remarkably consistent.

Silverlight development is no different. At the core of developing Silverlight applications is Visual Studio 2010, the latest version in Visual Studio's long history. This gives Silverlight a distinct advantage, because developers do not need to learn how to use a new development environment.

In addition to Visual Studio, Microsoft has a suite of tools called Expression Studio. Included in this suite is Microsoft Expression Blend, which is used to edit and create XAML for Silverlight applications. While Expression Blend looks completely different, it still has many of the same elements as Visual Studio. In addition, Expression Blend works off of the same project as Visual Studio. This means that as you make changes in each of the editors—opening a project in Visual Studio, and then opening the same project in Expression Blend to edit the XAML—the edited files will request to be refreshed when opened again in the other tool.

Small Runtime and Simple Deployment

Because Silverlight requires that a client runtime be installed on the client machine, it is vital that this runtime has a small footprint and downloads quickly. Microsoft worked very hard to get the installation size as small as possible. The developers clearly succeeded with Silverlight 1.0, as the download size is a tiny 1 MB. For Silverlight 2, however, they had a harder chore ahead of them because Silverlight 2 contains its own .NET Framework and object library. Microsoft went to each .NET Framework team and allocated it a size to fit its portion. The result is astonishing—Silverlight 2 is approximately 4 MB in size. In Silverlight 5, even with the large amount of new features that have been added to the Silverlight runtime, the file size is still about 6 MB for the 32-bit version and just over 12 MB for the 64-bit version.

As for pushing the Silverlight runtime out to clients, Microsoft has provided a very easy detection mechanism. If the client does not have the proper Silverlight runtime installed, it will display a logo, similar to the one shown in Figure 1-7.

Figure 1-7. Silverlight runtime required logo

When users click the icon in the logo, the Silverlight runtime will start to download. Once the runtime is finished installing, the Silverlight application is immediately available to the user.

The Silverlight Development Environment

In the past, setting up an environment to work with Microsoft's latest and greatest has been relatively straightforward, typically involving only the setup of the latest version of Visual Studio and the appropriate software development kit (SDK). However, with Silverlight, the situation is quite a bit different due to the introduction of many new tools. Let's look at the tools involved in setting up a Silverlight development environment.

- *Visual Studio 2010:* As noted, this is the latest version of Microsoft's IDE (shown in Figure 1-8). For your Silverlight environment, you should install Visual Studio 2010, which automatically installs Microsoft .NET Framework 4. Chapter 2 covers Visual Studio 2010 in more depth.

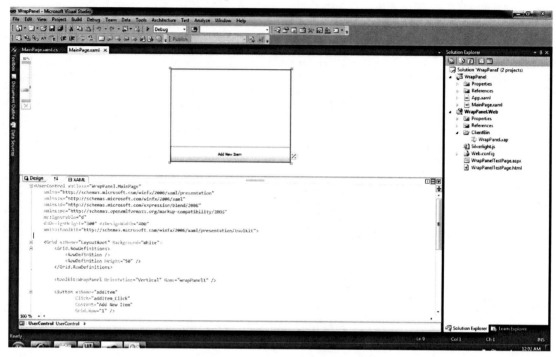

Figure 1-8. *Microsoft Visual Studio 2010*

- *Silverlight Tools for Visual Studio 2010:* This is a package that adds the necessary items to Visual Studio to teach it how to handle Silverlight projects. The package includes a number of items, some of which are listed here:

  - *Silverlight 5 Runtime:* Required on every computer that you want to be able to view a Silverlight-enabled web application.

  - *Silverlight 5 Software Development Kit:* This SDK is a collection of samples, Silverlight QuickStarts, documentation, and controls that are used to develop Silverlight applications.

  - *Silverlight Project Templates for Visual Studio 2010:* This adds the Silverlight templates in Visual Studio. As an example, it will add the template that enables you to create a Silverlight project from the Add New Project dialog box in Visual Studio.

- *Expression Blend 4 Preview for Silverlight 5*: The next thing to install for your Silverlight development environment is Expression Blend (shown in Figure 1-9). Expression Blend is a design tool for building XAML-based interfaces, including Windows Presentation Foundation (WPF) and Silverlight. Expression Blend is not required for creating Silverlight solutions, but it provides a richer designer than does Visual Studio 2010. Expression Blend is covered in detail in Chapter 11.

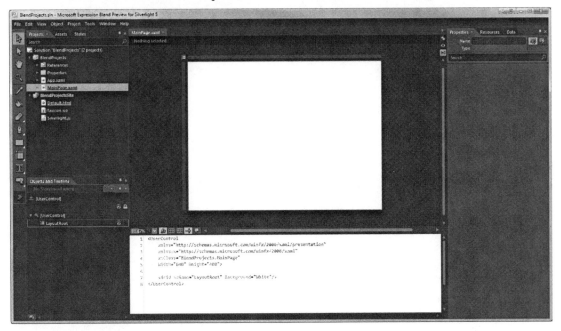

Figure 1-9. Microsoft Expression Blend preview for Silverlight 5

- *Silverlight 5 Toolkit.* The Silverlight Toolkit is an open-source CodePlex project whose goal is to develop additional controls for Silverlight applications. Controls within the toolkit are assigned a status that describes their maturity as controls, and the controls are supported by the open-source community. You can download the toolkit for Silverlight 5 at `http://silverlight/codeplex.com`. The Toolkit is discussed in Chapter 6.

Summary

In this chapter, you looked at the evolution of user interfaces in applications, as well as the history of RIAs. I then introduced Silverlight, talked about the benefits it brings to developers today and how it fits into RIA solutions. Finally, you learned about the tools involved in developing Silverlight-enabled applications.

Now it is time to get your hands dirty and start building some Silverlight applications! In the next chapter, I will provide an introduction to Microsoft Visual Studio 2010, one of the primary tools used to build Silverlight applications.

CHAPTER 2

Introduction to Visual Studio 2010

The previous chapter mentioned the tools required to develop Rich Internet Applications (RIAs) that utilize the Silverlight technology. At the core of all of these tools is Microsoft's flagship development product, Visual Studio. This chapter provides an introduction to Visual Studio 2010, the latest version. You will learn about some of the new features that are particularly helpful for developers building RIAs with Silverlight, and you will have an opportunity to create your first Silverlight application using Visual Studio 2010. Let's get started with a brief introduction to the Visual Studio IDE.

What Is Visual Studio?

Any developer who has developed applications using technologies related to Microsoft Visual Basic, ASP, or .NET has used some version of Visual Studio on a regular basis. This is because Visual Studio is Microsoft's primary development product. Whether you are developing desktop applications, web applications, mobile applications, web services, or just about any other .NET solution, Visual Studio is the environment you will be using.

Visual Studio is an IDE that allows .NET developers to implement a variety of .NET solutions within the confines of one editor. An IDE is a software application that contains comprehensive facilities to aid developers in building applications. Visual Studio fits this description for a number of reasons. First, Visual Studio offers a very rich code-editing solution. It includes features such as source code color-coding and code completion. Second, it offers an integrated debugger, which allows you to place breakpoints in your source code to stop execution at any given point, as well as step through the source line by line, analyzing the state of objects and fields at any given point in the execution. Add to these features rich support for application deployment, installation, and integration with database services, and you can understand how Visual Studio is an extremely valuable tool for developers.

Note This book assumes a basic understanding of Visual Studio. If you're new to Visual Studio, I recommend that you get started with a book devoted to the subject, such as *Introducing .NET 4.0: With Visual Studio 2010*, by Alex Mackey (Apress, 2009).

THE HISTORY OF VISUAL STUDIO

Visual Studio has quite a history. The first version was called "Visual Studio 97," which was most commonly known for Visual Basic 5.0. In 1998, Microsoft released Visual Studio 6.0. That version included Visual Basic 6.0, as well as Microsoft's first web-based development tool, Visual InterDev 1.0, which was used to develop ASP applications.

Next came the introduction of Microsoft .NET and ASP.NET 1.0, prompting Visual Studio.NET. As Microsoft was enhancing and releasing new versions of Microsoft .NET and ASP.NET, it also continued enhancing Visual Studio by releasing Visual Studio 2003 and then Visual Studio 2005. In addition, Microsoft has introduced a line of free development tools known as the Visual Studio Express tools, as well as the Visual Studio Team System, which can be used by large programming teams to build enterprise-level systems.

Microsoft released Visual Studio 2008 under the code name Orcas and added a number of features, such as some enhanced JavaScript debugging as well as some IDE improvements.

As for Visual Studio 2010, Microsoft started from the ground up and developed the IDE on top of WPF to make a number of new features possible.

What's New in Visual Studio 2010?

Microsoft has introduced a variety of new features in Visual Studio 2010, many of which are geared toward helping developers build RIAs with Silverlight and related Microsoft technologies, such as the Windows Communication Foundation (WCF), ADO.NET Data Services, and Ajax. Let's look at some of the new features in Visual Studio 2010 that are particularly helpful to Silverlight application developers.

Support for Multiple Monitors

Today it is common for developers to have multiple monitors attached to their development workstations and, unfortunately, previous versions of Visual Studio never took advantage of this extra real estate. Developers could use the extra screens for other applications, but often it would be nice to be able to view more than one source file at once. Visual Studio 2010 adds support for multiple monitors by allowing developers to pull source files, windows, and more out of the Visual Studio primary IDE and move them to other monitors. Take, for example, Figure 2-1. Visual Studio 2010 is open on the left monitor, and we are viewing the MainPage.xaml. However, I would like to inspect the class that my UI is bound to at the same time. To do so, I can simply drag the class out of the docked position in the IDE and move it to the second monitor. I could do the same thing for the toolbox, the properties window, or any window within Visual Studio 2010. A very nice new feature!

Figure 2-1. Multimonitor support

Zoom Support for Source Editor

Because Visual Studio 2010 has been almost completely rewritten in Windows Presentation Foundation (WPF), a number of user-interface enhancements have been added. One of these enhancements is the ability to zoom in and out of the source code editor. This feature allows you to simply use your mouse scroll wheel to zoom in to your source code. This is especially useful during presentations; however, there are times where developers could benefit from the ability to zoom in and out. For example, if you want to see a bigger portion of your source, you can zoom out and see your source from a greater distance, as shown in Figure 2-2.

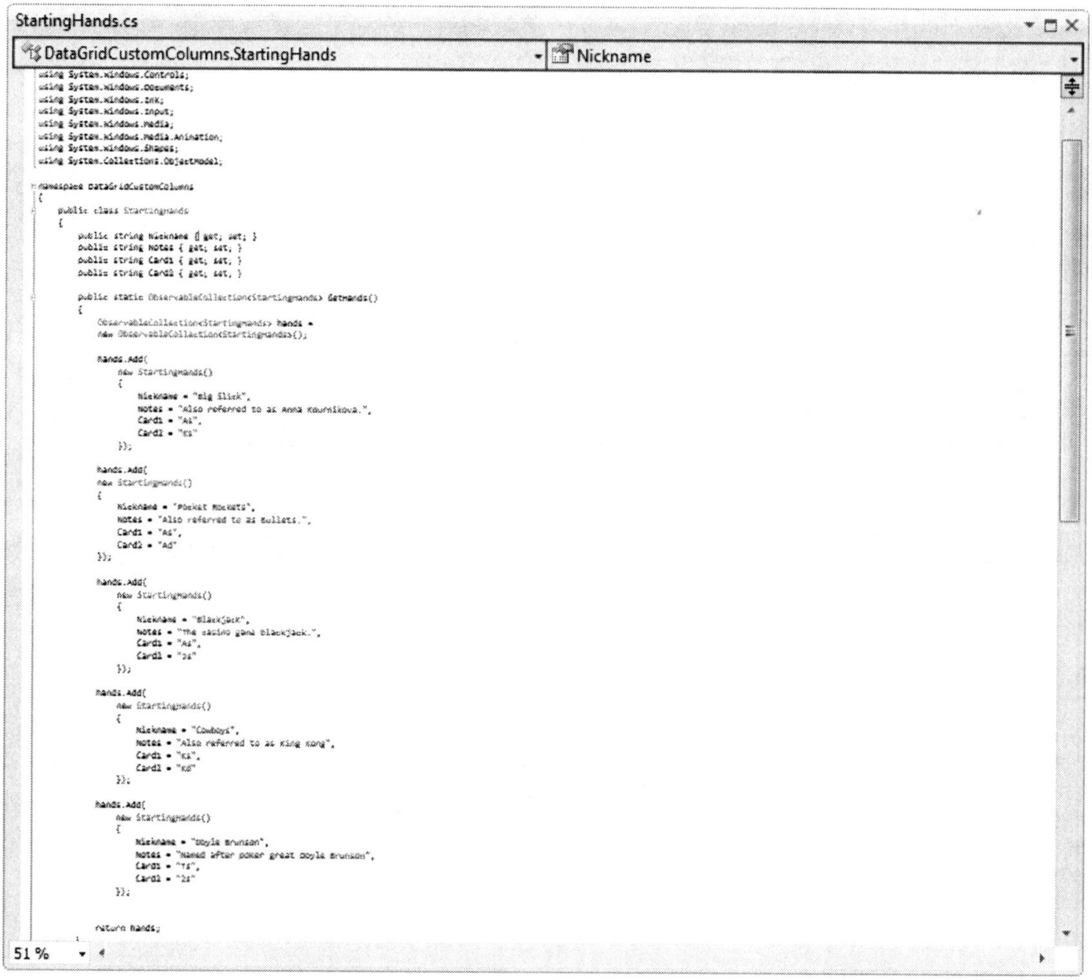

Figure 2-2. Zooming out in the Source Editor

Improved IntelliSense

Every developer who has used Visual Studio has become dependent on IntelliSense. When it is gone, you really notice how much you take it for granted and you find how dependent you really have become on it. Well, as great as IntelliSense is, in Visual Studio 2010 it just got better. The addition of partial string matching allows IntelliSense to more intelligently display entries based on what the developer has typed. For example, if the developer types *OC*, IntelliSense will display entries such as `ObservableCollection`, as shown in Figure 2-3, (notice that the letters OC are the capital letters of the Pascal-Cased object). In addition, if you type *collect*, `ObservableCollection` will also appear because the build is contained in the object name.

Figure 2-3. *Improved IntelliSense in Visual Studio 2010*

In addition to the partial string matching, the performance of IntelliSense has been dramatically improved. This allows developers to code without delays in IntelliSense and keep their rolls rolling.

Add References Performance

In Visual Studio 2008 and previous versions, developers noticed that when you open the Add Reference dialog (shown in Figure 2-4), it takes quite a bit of time for it to fully display the listing of components, especially for the COM components. In Visual Studio 2010, the Add Reference dialog has undergone many performance improvements, which will help prevent developers from having to wait on the Visual Studio IDE.

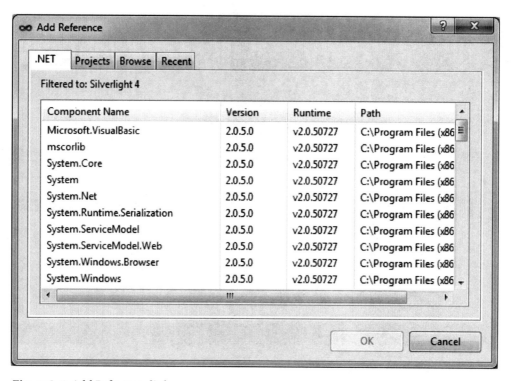

Figure 2-4. Add Reference dialog

Reference Highlighting

When you click anywhere within a symbol (class name, variable, object, field, and so on), all instances of that item are highlighted throughout the current document, as shown in Figure 2-5. This is not a simple text matching; the editor is smart enough to understand the scope of the different variables. So even if you have two items with identical names that belong to different objects, they are not both highlighted.

You can easily navigate between the different highlighted instances as well by pressing Ctrl+Shift+Up to move to the next instance, or Ctrl+Shift+Down to move to the previous instance.

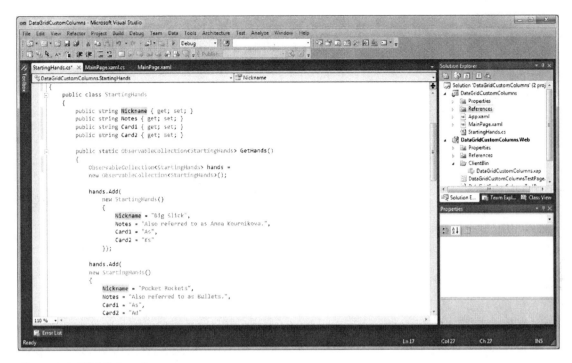

Figure 2-5. Highlight references

Box Selection

Another cool feature of Visual Studio 2010 is box selection. Consider the situation where you would have the following source:

```
public string Nickname { get; set; }
public string Notes { get; set; }
public string Card1 { get; set; }
public string Card2 { get; set; }
```

Let's say that you wanted to change all of these to be private properties instead of public. In Visual Studio 2010, you can hold down the Alt key and drag a box around just the public declarations, as shown in Figure 2-6.

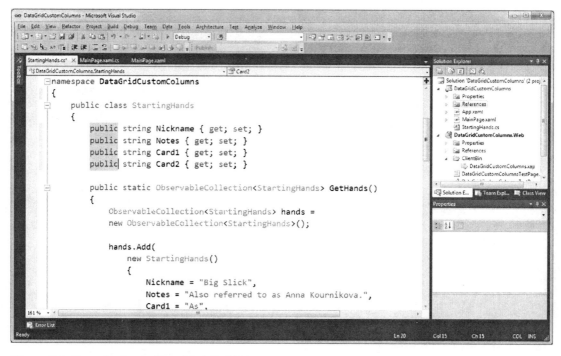

Figure 2-6. *Box selection in Visual Studio 2010*

Better yet, once you have this box selected you can edit all of the lines at once. With the selection made, simply type *private* and it will automatically replace *public* in each of the lines, as shown in Figure 2-7.

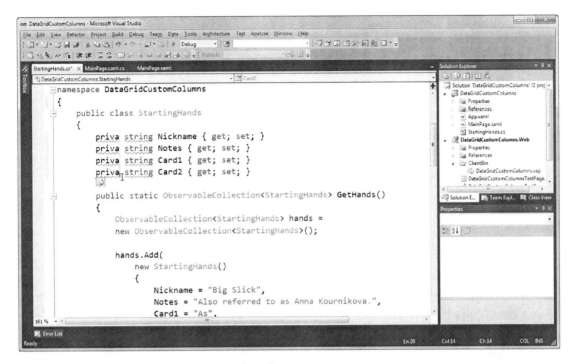

Figure 2-7. *Editing a box selection in Visual Studio 2010*

Call Hierarchy Window

The Call Hierarchy window displays two lists regarding a given member: first, all calls to the member (incoming) and then all calls from the member (outgoing). Within each of those lists, you can then drill into each member and see its incoming and outgoing calls, forming a very useful call hierarchy.

To open the Call Hierarchy window, simply right-click on any method, property, or constructor and select View Call Hierarchy. An example of the Call Hierarchy window is shown in Figure 2-8.

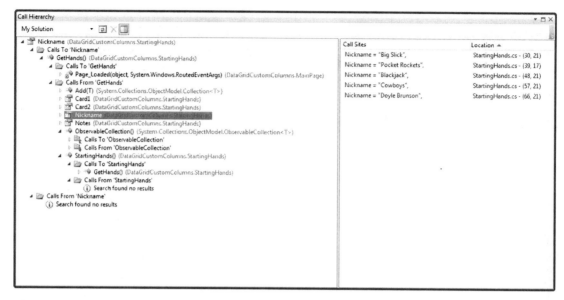

Figure 2-8. *Call Hierarchy window*

Code Generation

Visual Studio 2008 introduced the ability to generate a method stub from a given call in the source. Consider the following line of code calling the method NewMethod, which did not exist, and passing it an integer and a string:

```
Person.NewMethod(123, "Bob");
```

If you type this, Visual Studio will provide you with the option to Generate method stub for 'NewMethod'. By selecting this, Visual Studio will automatically create the following method stub in the Person class:

```
class Person
{
    internal static void NewMethod(int p, string p_2)
    {
        throw new NotImplementedException();
    }
}
```

Visual Studio 2010 expands on this code generation functionality by now allowing you to automatically generate classes, structs, and enumerations.

Extension Manager

Managing extensions and controls has always been a stressful point with Visual Studio 2008 and previous versions of Visual Studio. In Visual Studio 2010, the Extension Manager has been introduced. It allows you to easily browse an online library for different extensions as well as manage the extensions that are installed in your current development environment. You can view the Extensions Manager by selecting Extensions Manager from the Tools menu. The Extension Manager is shown in Figure 2-9.

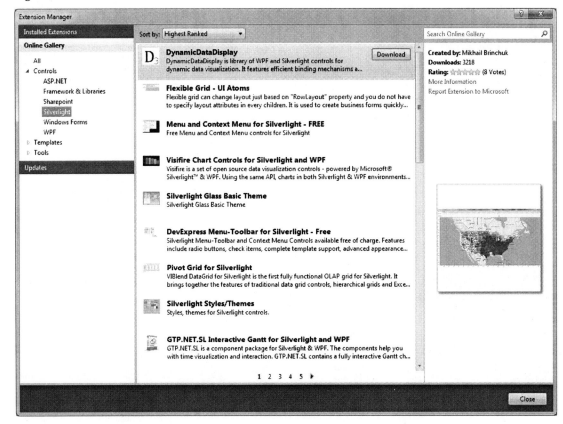

Figure 2-9. Extension Manager

Building Your First Silverlight Application in Visual Studio

The best way to explore the Visual Studio IDE is to get your hands dirty and play around with it. Let's build a Silverlight application.

Try It Out: Hello World in Silverlight 5

In this exercise, you'll build the Hello World Silverlight 5 application. I personally hate the Hello World sample, but it is used often because it is so simple and provides a good introduction. Who am I to break with tradition? Let's get started.

1. Start Visual Studio 2010, and select File ➤ New ➤ Project from the main menu.

2. In the New Project dialog box, select Visual C# as the project type, and in the list under that type, choose Silverlight. Select Silverlight Application as the template, and name the project HelloWorld, as shown in Figure 2-10. Then click OK.

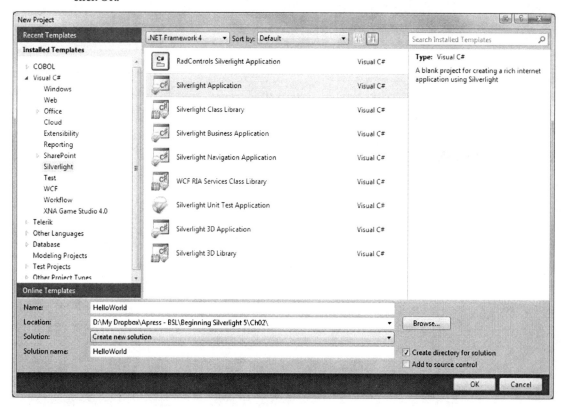

Figure 2-10. Creating a new Silverlight project

3. Visual Studio will display the New Silverlight Application dialog box, informing you that your Silverlight application needs to be hosted in an HTML web page. It offers the choices of hosting the Silverlight application in a web site or within a project. For this exercise, select Web Application Project and stick with the default name of HelloWorld.Web, as shown in Figure 2-11. Then click OK. See the next section for more information about choosing whether to use a web site or Web Application project for your own Silverlight applications.

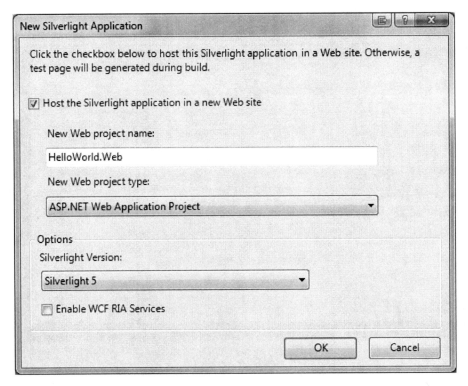

Figure 2-11. The New Silverlight Application dialog box

4. Visual Studio will now create the base project for you. Notice that there are two projects created within your solution: one called `HelloWorld.Web` and one called `HelloWorld`, as shown in Figure 2-12.

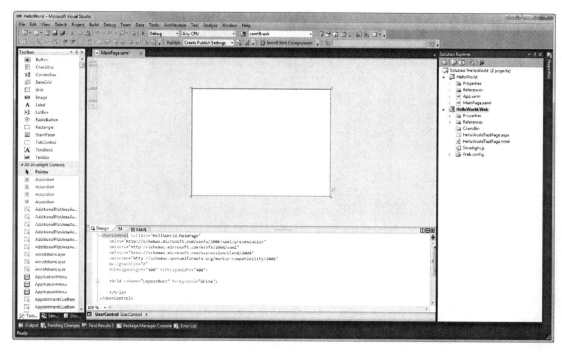

Figure 2-12. The default Silverlight project created in Visual Studio 2010

5. Visual Studio has already opened the MainPage.xaml file, which is where you
    will start working. Let's begin by adding a TextBlock control, which will display
    our "Hello World!" message. Add the TextBlock within your Canvas object, as
    follows:

```
<UserControl x:Class="HelloWorld.MainPage"
    xmlns="http://schemas.microsoft.com/winfx/2006/xaml/presentation"
    xmlns:x="http://schemas.microsoft.com/winfx/2006/xaml"
    xmlns:d="http://schemas.microsoft.com/expression/blend/2008"
    xmlns:mc="http://schemas.openxmlformats.org/markup-compatibility/2006"
    mc:Ignorable="d"
    d:DesignHeight="300" d:DesignWidth="400">

    <Grid x:Name="LayoutRoot" Background="White">

        <TextBlock x:Name="HelloMessage" Text="Hello World!" FontSize="30" />

    </Grid>
</UserControl>
```

6. Save the project and run it by pressing F5. If you see the Debugging Not
    Enabled dialog box, select "Modify the Web.config to enable debugging" and
    click OK. The result should be as shown in Figure 2-13.

Figure 2-13. Your first Silverlight application in Visual Studio 2010

7. I know this isn't very interesting, so let's change things up a bit by setting the display message in the MainPage.xaml.cs code behind. In the code behind, you will notice a constructor for your Page class, which contains one method called InitializeComponent(). Under that method, change the Text property of your TextBlock as follows (the line shown in bold):

```
namespace HelloWorld
{
    public partial class MainPage : UserControl
    {
        public MainPage()
        {
            InitializeComponent();

            this.HelloMessage.Text = "Hello Universe!";
        }
    }
}
```

8. Rebuild the application, and run it again. Your result should look like Figure 2-14.

Figure 2-14. *The final result from our first Silverlight application in Visual Studio 2010*

9. Close the application.

There you go! You have built your first Silverlight application. Of course, this application is extremely simple, but you did get an idea of how things work in Visual Studio 2010.

Hosting Your Silverlight Application: Web Site or Web Application?

In Visual Studio 2010, should you use a web site project or a Web Application project to host your Silverlight application? The main difference between a web site project and a Web Application project is how the files are compiled and deployed. Each has its advantages and disadvantages. In the end, the choice pretty much comes down to user preference. Let's take a quick look at each approach.

Using a Visual Studio Web Site

A Visual Studio web site is nothing more than a group of files and folders in a folder. There is no project file. Instead, the site simply contains all the files under the specific folder, including all text files, images, and other file types.

A Visual Studio web site is compiled dynamically at runtime. An assembly will not be created, and you won't have a bin directory.

The following are some advantages of using a Visual Studio web site:

- You don't need a project file or virtual directory for the site.

- The site can easily be deployed or shared by simply copying the folder containing the site.

The following are some disadvantages of this approach:

- There is no project file that you can double-click to open the site in Visual Studio. Rather, you must browse to the folder after opening Visual Studio.

- By default, all files within the site's directory are included in the web site project. If there are files within the site's directory that you do not want to be a part of the web site, you must rename the file, adding the extension .exclude.

Using a Visual Studio Web Application Project

A Visual Studio Web Application project is the more traditional type of web project used prior to Visual Studio 2005. When Microsoft developers introduced the "web site" concept, they did not take into account the many developers who were comfortable with the project-based solution approach. To accommodate those developers, Microsoft announced the Visual Studio 2005 Web Application project as an add-on to Visual Studio 2005. In Visual Studio 2008 and 2010, this project type is once again a part of Visual Studio.

The following are some of the advantages of using a Web Application project:

- All of the code files are compiled into a single assembly, placed in the bin directory.

- You can easily exclude files from a project, because all files within the project are defined within the project file.

- It's easier to migrate from older versions of Visual Studio.

A disadvantage is that it can be more difficult to share your solution with others, if that is your intent.

In the end, both approaches have their pros and cons. You need to determine which one is more suitable for your application, depending on your specific purpose and goals. For more information about these project types, refer to the MSDN documentation.

Summary

This chapter introduced Visual Studio 2010 and some of the new features offered in this version, including support for multiple monitors and managing extensions. In addition, you built your very first Silverlight application.

In the next chapter, you are going to start to dive into some of the Silverlight controls, beginning with the layout management controls. These controls enable you to lay out your Silverlight applications.

CHAPTER 3

Layout Management in Silverlight

The previous chapter provided an overview of Microsoft Visual Studio 2010, one of the primary tools used in developing Silverlight applications. In this chapter, you are going to start to dive into some Silverlight development by looking at the layout management controls.

As you learned, Silverlight applications consist of a number of Silverlight objects that are defined by XAML. Layout management involves describing the way that these objects are arranged in your application. Silverlight includes five layout management controls: Canvas, StackPanel, Grid, WrapPanel, and DockPanel. You will take a look at each of these in-depth. By the end of this chapter, you should have a good understanding of when to use which layout control.

Layout Management

Silverlight provides a very flexible layout management system that lets you specify how controls will appear in your Silverlight application. You can use a static layout as well as a liquid layout that allows your layout to automatically adjust as your Silverlight application is resized in the browser.

Each of the five layout controls provided in Silverlight has its advantages and disadvantages, as summarized in Table 3-1.

Let's begin by looking at the most basic layout control: the Canvas panel.

Table 3-1. Layout Control Pros and Cons

Control	Description	Pros	Cons
Canvas	Based on absolute position of controls.	Very simple layout.	Requires that every control have a Canvas.Top and Canvas.Left property attached to define its position on the canvas.
StackPanel	Based on horizontal or vertical "stacks" of controls.	Allows for a quick dynamic layout. Nesting StackPanel controls can provide some interesting layouts.	The layout is limited to stacks of items. Spacing is limited to adding margins to the individual controls and to adjusting the alignment (with the VerticalAlignment and HorizontalAlignment properties).

Continued

Control	Description	Pros	Cons
Grid	Mimics using table elements in HTML to lay out controls.	The most flexible and powerful layout control. You can define just about any type of layout using the Grid control.	Grid definitions can get somewhat complex at times. Nesting Grid components can be confusing.
WrapPanel	Based on horizontal or vertical "stacks" of controls wrapping to a second row or column when the width or height is reached.	Very similar to the StackPanel, except the WrapPanel automatically wraps items to a second row or column so that it is ideal for layouts containing an unknown number of items.	Limited control of layout because wrapping is automatic when items reach the maximum width or height.
DockPanel	Layout is based on "docked" horizontal or vertical panels.	Provides an easy way to create a basic layout, consuming the entire application space in vertical or horizontal panels.	Layout is limited to horizontal or vertical "fill" panels, often used in conjunction with other nested layout controls.

The Canvas Panel

The Canvas panel is a basic layout control that allows you to position Silverlight objects using explicit coordinates relative to the canvas location. You can position an object within the Canvas panel by using two XAML attached properties: Canvas.Left and Canvas.Top. Figure 3-1 shows how the object's position is affected by these properties.

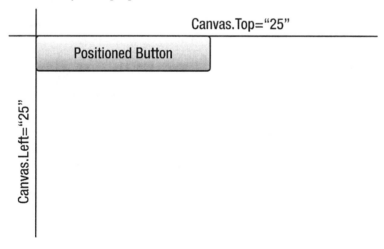

Figure 3-1. The XAML attached properties Canvas.Top and Canvas.Left allow you to position the Canvas.

The objects within a Canvas panel have no layout policies placed on them by the layout control and will not resize automatically when your application is resized within the browser.

Try It Out: Using the Canvas Panel

Let's try out a quick example of using the Canvas panel.

1. Open Visual Studio 2010, and create a new Silverlight application called CanvasPanel. Allow Visual Studio to create a Web Application project to host the application.

2. When the project is created, you should be looking at the MainPage.xaml file. If you do not see the XAML source, switch to that view so that you can edit the XAML. Within the main Grid element, add a Canvas element. Assign it a Width property of 300 and a Height property of 300. To see the Canvas panel in the application, also set the background color to green. The following XAML adds this Canvas:

```
<Grid x:Name="LayoutRoot" Background="White">
    <Canvas Background="Green" Width="300" Height="200">
    </Canvas>
</Grid>
```

3. At this point, your Silverlight application doesn't look that exciting. It contains only a single green rectangle positioned at the very center of your application, as shown in Figure 3-2.

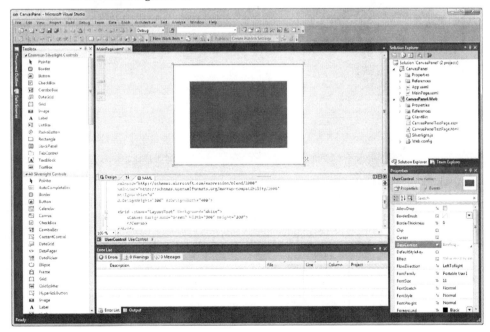

Figure 3-2. Default Canvas with a green background

4. Let's add a button to this `Canvas` panel. Add the following code to place the button, which has the label `Button1`, a `Width` property of 100, and a `Height` property of 30. (The `Button` control is covered in detail in Chapter 4.)

```
<Grid x:Name="LayoutRoot" Background="White">
    <Canvas Background="Green" Width="300" Height="200">
        <Button Width="100" Height="30" Content="Button 1" />
    </Canvas>
</Grid>
```

5. Figure 3-3 shows the button within the canvas.

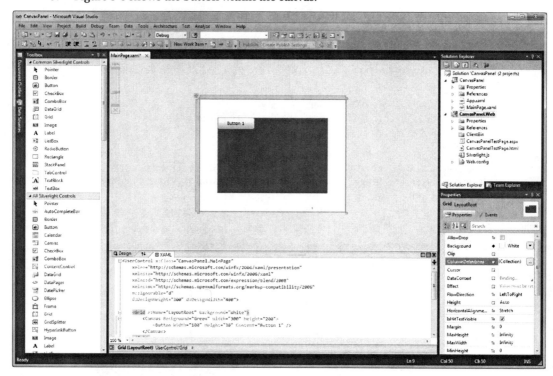

Figure 3-3. *Single button within the canvas*

6. Let's add another button to the `Canvas`, but this time position it below and a bit to the right of the first button by setting its `Canvas.Top` and `Canvas.Left` as attached properties. Give this button the label `Button 2`, as follows:

```
<Grid x:Name="LayoutRoot" Background="White">
    <Canvas Background="Green" Width="300" Height="200">
        <Button Width="100" Height="30" Content="Button 1" />
        <Button Width="100" Height="30" Content="Button 2"
                Canvas.Left="10" Canvas.Top="40" />
    </Canvas>
</Grid>
```

7. At this point, you now have two buttons within the canvas, but at different locations, as shown in Figure 3-4. This is still not very exciting, but this is about as cool as it gets with the Canvas.

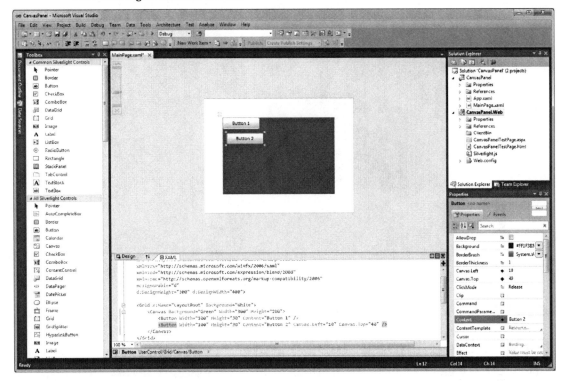

Figure 3-4. Two buttons positioned relative to the canvas

8. Go ahead and run the solution to see the end result as it will appear in the browser. The output is shown in Figure 3-5.

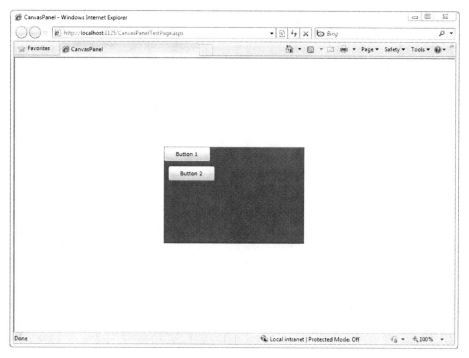

Figure 3-5. *The canvas and two buttons as seen in a browser*

Filling the Entire Browser Window with Your Application

By default, in a new Silverlight project, the root `UserControl` object is set to a width of 400 and a height of 300. In some cases, you might want to set the width and height of your Silverlight application within the browser. At other times, however, you will want your Silverlight application to take up the entire window of your browser, and to resize as the browser is resized. This is done very easily within Silverlight. When you want the width and height to be set to 100%, simply omit the element's `Height` and `Width` attributes.

As an example, the following source has been adjusted for the `Canvas` panel and the Silverlight application to take up the entire browser:

```
<UserControl x:Class="FillBrowser.MainPage"
    xmlns="http://schemas.microsoft.com/winfx/2006/xaml/presentation"
    xmlns:x="http://schemas.microsoft.com/winfx/2006/xaml"
    xmlns:d="http://schemas.microsoft.com/expression/blend/2008"
    xmlns:mc="http://schemas.openxmlformats.org/markup-compatibility/2006"
    mc:Ignorable="d">

    <Grid x:Name="LayoutRoot" Background="White">
        <Canvas Background="Green">
        </Canvas>
    </Grid>

</UserControl>
```

With the omission of the Height and Width declarations for UserControl and Canvas, when you run the Silverlight application, you will see that the canvas takes up 100% of the browser window, as shown in Figure 3-6. It will resize as the browser resizes.

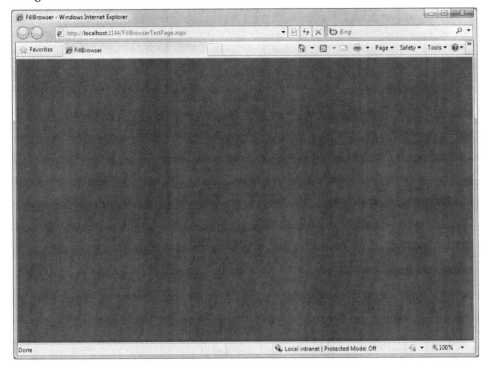

Figure 3-6. Silverlight application taking up the entire browser

As you've seen, the Canvas panel is a simple layout control. It can be used very effectively in a fixed layout. However, in most cases, you will want to use a static layout for your applications. The StackPanel control provides a more fluid layout control.

The StackPanel Control

The StackPanel provides developers with a quick layout option for positioning objects. The StackPanel control allows you to position Silverlight objects in more of a flow layout, stacking objects either horizontally or vertically. Figure 3-7 shows the basic concept of this layout control.

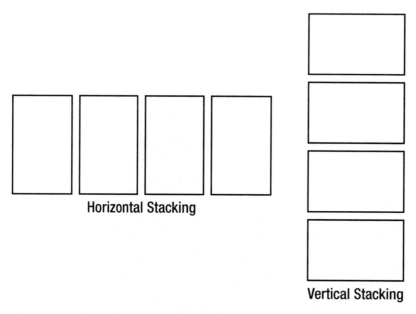

Horizontal Stacking

Vertical Stacking

Figure 3-7. The StackPanel control orientations

Try It Out: Using the StackPanel Control

To better understand the StackPanel control, let's run through an exercise.

1. In Visual Studio 2010, create a new Silverlight application named StackPanel and allow Visual Studio to create a web site project to host the application.

2. When the project is created, you should be looking at the MainPage.xaml file. If you do not see the XAML source, switch view so that you can edit the XAML. Within the main Grid element, add a StackPanel control and also three buttons with the labels Button 1, Button 2, and Button 3. Give all three buttons a width of 100 and a height of 30. The following XAML adds the StackPanel control and buttons (the new code is highlighted in bold in all the exercises):

```
<Grid x:Name="LayoutRoot" Background="White">
    <StackPanel>
        <Button Width="100" Height="30" Content="Button 1"></Button>
        <Button Width="100" Height="30" Content="Button 2"></Button>
        <Button Width="100" Height="30" Content="Button 3"></Button>
    </StackPanel>
</Grid>
```

3. At this point, your application should appear as shown in Figure 3-8. Notice that the buttons are stacked vertically. This is because the default stacking orientation for the StackPanel control is vertical.

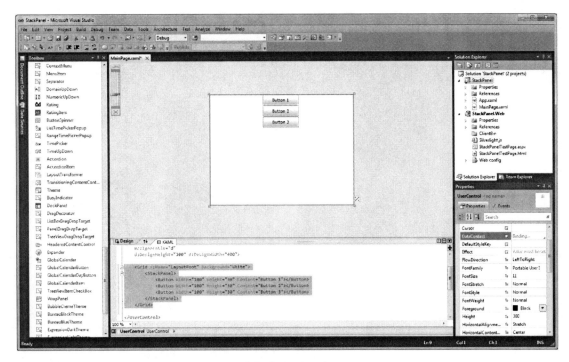

Figure 3-8. *The StackPanel control with its default orientation*

4. Change the orientation of the StackPanel control to be horizontal by setting the Orientation property to Horizontal, as follows:

```
<Grid x:Name="LayoutRoot" Background="White">
    <StackPanel Orientation="Horizontal">
        <Button Width="100" Height="30" Content="Button 1"></Button>
        <Button Width="100" Height="30" Content="Button 2"></Button>
        <Button Width="100" Height="30" Content="Button 3"></Button>
    </StackPanel>
</Grid>
```

5. With this simple change, the buttons are now stacked horizontally, as shown in Figure 3-9.

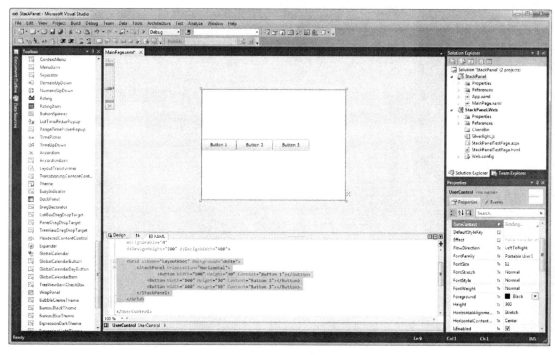

Figure 3-9. *The StackPanel control with horizontal orientation*

6. Notice that all the buttons are touching each other, which is unattractive. You can easily space them out by using their Margin property. In addition, you can center the buttons by setting the StackPanel control's HorizontalAlignment property to Center. Other options for HorizontalAlignment include Left, Right, and Stretch (which stretches the content to the left and right). Make the following changes to adjust the buttons:

```
<Grid x:Name="LayoutRoot" Background="White">
    <StackPanel Orientation="Horizontal" HorizontalAlignment="Center">
        <Button Width="100" Height="30" Content="Button 1"
                Margin="5"></Button>
        <Button Width="100" Height="30" Content="Button 2"
                Margin="5"></Button>
        <Button Width="100" Height="30" Content="Button 3"
                Margin="5"></Button>
    </StackPanel>
</Grid>
```

7. After you have made these changes, your buttons are spaced out nicely in the center of the application, as shown in Figure 3-10.

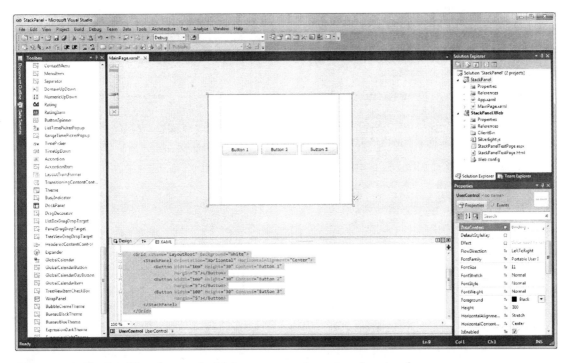

Figure 3-10. The StackPanel control with buttons spaced apart and centered

Try It Out: Nesting StackPanel Controls

Microsoft designed the control framework so that any object can be contained within another object. One way you can enhance your layout is by nesting a layout control within another layout control. In this example, you will nest a StackPanel control within another StackPanel control, but realize that you can nest any layout control within any other layout control to get the exact layout functionality you are seeking.

1. In Visual Studio 2010, create a new Silverlight application named *NestedStackPanel* and allow Visual Studio to create a Web Application project to host the application.

2. In the MainPage.xaml file, add the following items:

   • A StackPanel control to the root Grid with its Orientation property set to Horizontal and the HorizontalAlignment property set to Center.

   • Within that StackPanel, add two buttons, with the labels Button Left and Button Right.

   • In between the two buttons, add another StackPanel with Orientation set to Vertical and VerticalAlignment set to Center.

- Within that nested StackPanel, include three buttons with the labels Button Middle 1, Button Middle 2, and Button Middle 3.

- All buttons should have a Margin property set to 5, a Height set to 30, and a Width set to 100.

Here is what the updated source looks like:

```xml
<Grid x:Name="LayoutRoot" Background="White">
    <StackPanel Orientation="Horizontal" HorizontalAlignment="Center">
        <Button Width="100"
                Height="30"
                Content="Button Left"
                Margin="5" />
        <StackPanel VerticalAlignment="Center">
            <Button Width="100"
                    Height="30"
                    Content="Button Middle 1"
                    Margin="5"></Button>
            <Button Width="100"
                    Height="30"
                    Content="Button Middle 2"
                    Margin="5"></Button>
            <Button Width="100"
                    Height="30"
                    Content="Button Middle 3"
                    Margin="5"></Button>
        </StackPanel>
        <Button Width="100"
                Height="30"
                Content="Button Right"
                Margin="5"></Button>
    </StackPanel>
</Grid>
```

The cool result of this code is shown in Figure 3-11.

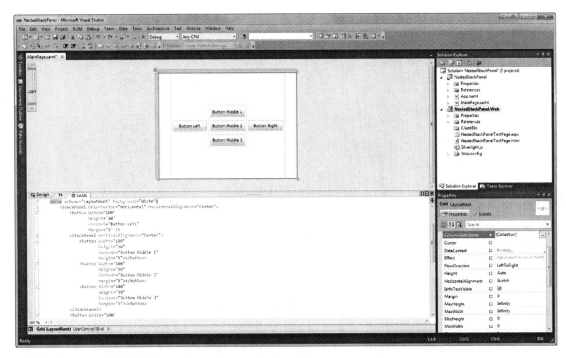

Figure 3-11. *Nested StackPanel controls*

3.　Run the application to see the results.

As you can see from these two exercises, the StackPanel control is a very useful layout option, and you will probably use it often in your Silverlight applications. By nesting Silverlight controls, you have a lot of flexibility when designing your applications. However, in the event that you want more control over the positioning of items in your application, without needing to resort to the absolute positioning used by the Canvas control, the Grid control might be just the layout option you need.

The Grid Control

The Grid control provides more fine-tuned layout in Silverlight applications. As a comparison, you can think of using the Grid layout control as similar to using table elements to position items in HTML, only more flexible. With the Grid control, you can define rows and columns, thus creating grid cells, and then add objects to individual cells in the grid or to multiple cells by using spanning.

To specify in which cell to place an object, you use the Grid.Column and Grid.Row attached properties. Note that these properties are *base zero*, so the top-left cell is row 0 and column 0. Figure 3-12 illustrates the row and column locations for the grid.

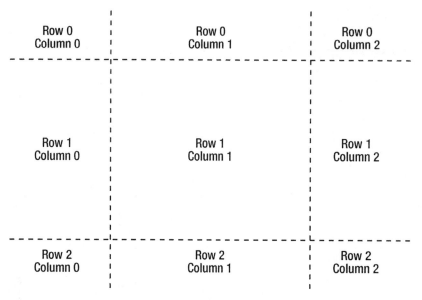

Figure 3-12. Row and column grid cell locations in the Grid control layout

For most developers, the Grid control most likely will be the layout option of choice because of its flexibility. At the same time, the Grid control is significantly more complex than the others, as you'll see in the following exercises.

Try It Out: Using the Grid Control

Let's try out a simple Grid panel with four buttons:

1. In Visual Studio 2010, create a new Silverlight application named GridPanel and allow Visual Studio to create a Web Application project to host the application.

2. For this example, you are going to need a bit more space in which to work. In the MainPage.xaml file, start out by changing the UserControl's DesignWidth to 600 and DesignHeight to 400, as follows:

```
<UserControl x:Class="GridPanel.MainPage"
    xmlns="http://schemas.microsoft.com/winfx/2006/xaml/presentation"
    xmlns:x="http://schemas.microsoft.com/winfx/2006/xaml"
    xmlns:d="http://schemas.microsoft.com/expression/blend/2008"
    xmlns:mc="http://schemas.openxmlformats.org/markup-compatibility/2006"
    mc:Ignorable="d"
    d:DesignHeight="400" d:DesignWidth="600">

    <Grid x:Name="LayoutRoot" Background="White">

    </Grid>
</UserControl>
```

3. Notice that, by default, a Grid control is already added to the page. To better see what is going on, turn on the display of grid lines by setting the ShowGridLines property to true. The following code shows these additions. Keep in mind that because you have not designated a size for the grid, it will automatically take up the entire size of the parent, and in this case, the entire Silverlight application.

```
<UserControl x:Class="GridPanel.MainPage"
    xmlns="http://schemas.microsoft.com/winfx/2006/xaml/presentation"
    xmlns:x="http://schemas.microsoft.com/winfx/2006/xaml"
    xmlns:d="http://schemas.microsoft.com/expression/blend/2008"
    xmlns:mc="http://schemas.openxmlformats.org/markup-compatibility/2006"
    mc:Ignorable="d"
    d:DesignHeight="400" d:DesignWidth="600">

    <Grid ShowGridLines="True" x:Name="LayoutRoot" Background="White">

    </Grid>
</UserControl>
```

4. Next, define the rows and columns in the Grid control. You do this using the XAML property elements Grid.RowDefinitions and Grid.ColumnDefinitions. Add the following XAML to your new grid:

```
<Grid ShowGridLines="True" x:Name="LayoutRoot" Background="White">
    <Grid.RowDefinitions>
        <RowDefinition Height="70" />
        <RowDefinition Height="*" />
        <RowDefinition Height="70" />
    </Grid.RowDefinitions>

    <Grid.ColumnDefinitions>
        <ColumnDefinition Width="150" />
        <ColumnDefinition Width="*" />
        <ColumnDefinition Width="150" />
    </Grid.ColumnDefinitions>
</Grid>
```

5. Notice that for the center row and column, you are setting the Height and Width properties to "*". The asterisk tells the row and column to take up all available space. As the Grid control is resized with the browser window, those columns will be resized to take up all the space not consumed by the fixed-sized columns. After you have added these row and column definitions, your canvas should appear as shown in Figure 3-13.

⬚ **Note** In the previous source, you are setting the height and width of the rows and columns to fixed pixel-based values. You can also set the height and width using star sizing, which indicates that the value will be expressed as a weighted proportion of the available space. As an example, if you had two rows, and the height of the first row was set to * and the height of the second row was set to 2*, the first row would take up a third of the available space, while the second row would take up two thirds of the available space.

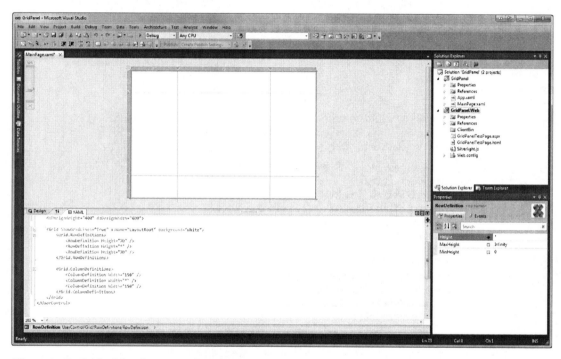

Figure 3-13. Grid with columns and rows

6. You can now add objects to the different grid cells. Place a button in each of the four corner cells, giving the buttons the corresponding labels Top Left, Top Right, Bottom Left, and Bottom Right. To place the buttons, add the following code:

```
<Grid ShowGridLines="True" x:Name="LayoutRoot" Background="White">
    <Grid.RowDefinitions>
        <RowDefinition Height="70" />
        <RowDefinition Height="*" />
        <RowDefinition Height="70" />
    </Grid.RowDefinitions>
```

```
<Grid.ColumnDefinitions>
    <ColumnDefinition Width="150" />
    <ColumnDefinition Width="*" />
    <ColumnDefinition Width="150" />
</Grid.ColumnDefinitions>

<Button Width="100"
        Height="30"
        Content="Top Left"
        Margin="5"
        Grid.Row="0"
        Grid.Column="0"></Button>
<Button Width="100"
        Height="30"
        Content="Top Right"
        Margin="5"
        Grid.Row="0"
        Grid.Column="2"></Button>
<Button Width="100"
        Height="30"
        Content="Bottom Left"
        Margin="5"
        Grid.Row="2"
        Grid.Column="0"></Button>
<Button Width="100"
        Height="30"
        Content="Bottom Right"
        Margin="5"
        Grid.Row="2"
        Grid.Column="2"></Button>

</Grid>
```

7. After the buttons are added, your application should look like Figure 3-14.

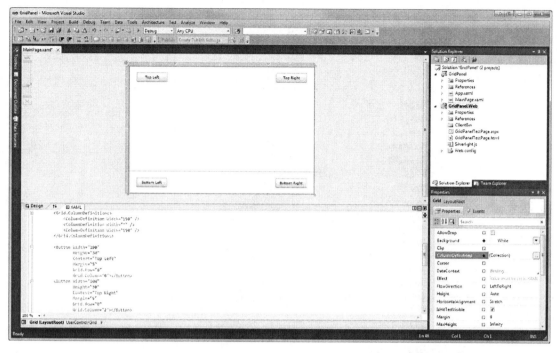

Figure 3-14. *The grid with buttons in the four corners*

Try It Out: Nesting a Grid and Spanning a Column

Next, you will nest another Grid control in the center cell of the Grid control you just added. This will make the application layout somewhat complex, but it will also serve to show how Grid panels are defined using XAML.

1. In the MainPage.xaml within the GridPanel project, add the following items:

   - A Grid control positioned at Grid.Column=1 and Grid.Row=1

   - Three RowDefinition and two ColumnDefinition elements

   - Buttons in the four corners of the new Grid control, as you just did in the outer Grid panel

2. The source code should look like the following:

```
<Grid ShowGridLines="True" x:Name="LayoutRoot" Background="White">
    <Grid.RowDefinitions>
        <RowDefinition Height="70" />
        <RowDefinition Height="*" />
        <RowDefinition Height="70" />
    </Grid.RowDefinitions>

    <Grid.ColumnDefinitions>
```

```
        <ColumnDefinition Width="150" />
        <ColumnDefinition Width="*" />
        <ColumnDefinition Width="150" />
</Grid.ColumnDefinitions>

<Button Width="100"
        Height="30"
        Content="Top Left"
        Margin="5"
        Grid.Row="0"
        Grid.Column="0"></Button>
<Button Width="100"
        Height="30"
        Content="Top Right"
        Margin="5"
        Grid.Row="0"
        Grid.Column="2"></Button>
<Button Width="100"
        Height="30"
        Content="Bottom Left"
        Margin="5"
        Grid.Row="2"
        Grid.Column="0"></Button>
<Button Width="100"
        Height="30"
        Content="Bottom Right"
        Margin="5"
        Grid.Row="2"
        Grid.Column="2"></Button>


<Grid Grid.Column="1" Grid.Row="1"  ShowGridLines="True">

    <Grid.RowDefinitions>
        <RowDefinition Height="*" />
        <RowDefinition Height="*" />
        <RowDefinition Height="*" />
    </Grid.RowDefinitions>

    <Grid.ColumnDefinitions>
        <ColumnDefinition Width="*" />
        <ColumnDefinition Width="*" />
    </Grid.ColumnDefinitions>

    <Button Width="100"
            Height="30"
            Content="Nested Top Left"
            Margin="5"
            Grid.Row="0"
            Grid.Column="0"></Button>
    <Button Width="100"
            Height="30"
```

```
                    Content="Nested Top Right"
                    Margin="5"
                    Grid.Row="0"
                    Grid.Column="2"></Button>
        <Button Width="100"
                Height="30"
                Content="Nested B. Left"
                Margin="5"
                Grid.Row="2"
                Grid.Column="0"></Button>
        <Button Width="100"
                Height="30"
                Content="Nested B. Right"
                Margin="5" Grid.Row="2"
                Grid.Column="2"></Button>

    </Grid>
```

```
</Grid>
```

At this point, your application should look like Figure 3-15. Now, this is a pretty cool layout.

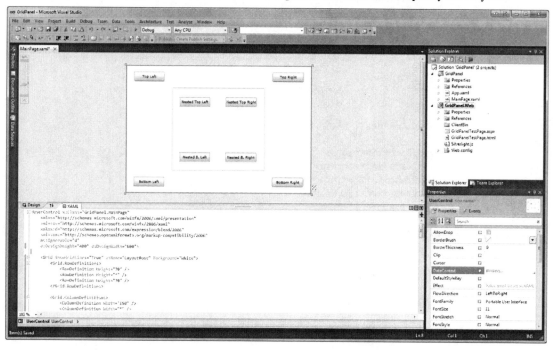

Figure 3-15. Nested grid with buttons

3. Notice that you have not placed anything in the two columns in the middle row of the new grid. Here, you're going to add a button that spans these two columns, so the button will appear in the center of the row. To do this, add the new button to the Grid control with the Grid.ColumnSpan attached property set to 2. The source changes to the innermost Grid control are as follows:

```
<Grid Grid.Column="1" Grid.Row="1"  ShowGridLines="True">

    <Grid.RowDefinitions>
        <RowDefinition Height="*" />
        <RowDefinition Height="*" />
        <RowDefinition Height="*" />
    </Grid.RowDefinitions>

    <Grid.ColumnDefinitions>
        <ColumnDefinition Width="*" />
        <ColumnDefinition Width="*" />
    </Grid.ColumnDefinitions>

    <Button Width="100"
            Height="30"
            Content="Nested Top Left"
            Margin="5"
            Grid.Row="0"
            Grid.Column="0"></Button>
    <Button Width="100"
            Height="30"
            Content="Nested Top Right"
            Margin="5"
            Grid.Row="0"
            Grid.Column="2"></Button>
    <Button Width="100"
            Height="30"
            Content="Nested B. Left"
            Margin="5"
            Grid.Row="2"
            Grid.Column="0"></Button>
    <Button Width="100"
            Height="30"
            Content="Nested B. Right"
            Margin="5" Grid.Row="2"
            Grid.Column="2"></Button>

    <Button Width="100"
            Height="30"
            Content="Nested Center"
            Margin="5"
            Grid.Row="1"
            Grid.Column="0"
            Grid.ColumnSpan="2"></Button>
</Grid>
```

4. Now that you have added the button to the center column, your application should look like Figure 3-16. Notice how the button spans the two columns and appears in the center. For experienced HTML developers who are used to laying out their forms with tables, this approach should be very comfortable because it closely mimics using the `colspan` attribute for a `<TD>` tag.

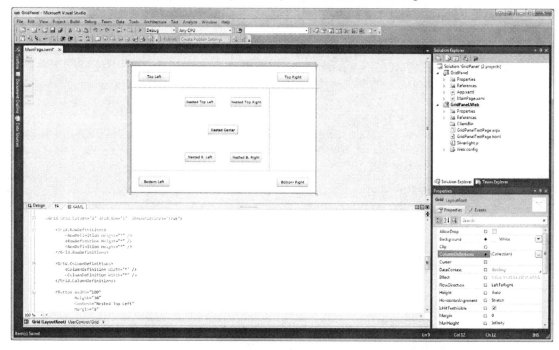

Figure 3-16. *Final application with a nested grid and buttons*

In this example, you saw how to create a relatively complex layout using the `Grid` control. As you can see, this is a very powerful and flexible layout tool for your Silverlight applications.

The WrapPanel Control

The `WrapPanel` control was first released in Silverlight 3 via the Silverlight Toolkit. It is very similar to the `StackPanel` control with one major difference: when items in a `WrapPanel` will not fit within the width or height of the control, they automatically wrap to a new row (if horizontal orientation) or column (if vertical orientation). This makes the `WrapPanel` ideal for laying out an unknown number of items as they will automatically wrap to take up the entire space of the control.

As an example, if you look at Figure 3-17 you will see how the `WrapPanel` handles placing six items when set to horizontal and vertical orientations. Horizontally, the `WrapPanel` places the items one after the other to the right, until no other items can fit within the width of the control. At that time, it starts to place the items in a new row directly below the first row. The same is true for vertical orientation except the items are stacked below the previous item until new items cannot fit within the height of the control, at which time they are placed directly to the right of the previous row.

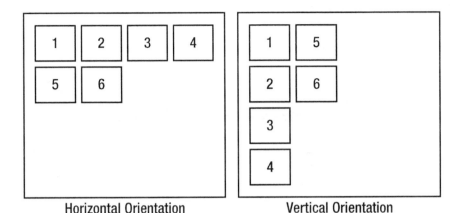

Figure 3-17. The WrapPanel control orientations

Try It Out: Using the WrapPanel Control

In this exercise, you will explore the WrapPanel control and how it can be used to display an unknown number of items in stacks vertically and horizontally. Let's get started.

1. Open Visual Studio 2010, and create a new Silverlight application called *WrapPanel*. Allow Visual Studio to create a Web Application to host the application.

2. When the project is created, the file MainPage.xaml is automatically created and opened in the XAML designer. You will add two rows to the root Grid control and then place a WrapPanel in the first row and a button with the label Add New Item in the second row.

3. The WrapPanel is not part of the core Silverlight control set, but rather it is part of the Silverlight Toolkit. Because of this, you need to make certain you have the Toolkit downloaded and installed. For more information on the Toolkit, please see Chapter 6. To get the proper XML namespace added for the WrapPanel, add it by double-clicking on the control from the Toolbox in Visual Studio. That way Visual Studio will automatically add the Xml namespace to the page.

4. When the WrapPanel is first added, you will notice that it has some properties set that you might not want set.

```
<toolkit:WrapPanel Height="100"
               HorizontalAlignment="Left"
               Margin="10,10,0,0"
               Name="wrapPanel1"
               VerticalAlignment="Top"
               Width="200" />
```

5. In this case, you want the WrapPanel to take up all the available space of the top row of your Grid. You do not need the HorizontalAlignment, Margin,

VerticalAlignment, or Width property set, so you can either delete these properties manually in the source or use a feature in Visual Studio 2010 to assist. In the designer, right-click on the WrapPanel and select Reset Layout ➤ All as shown in Figure 3-18.

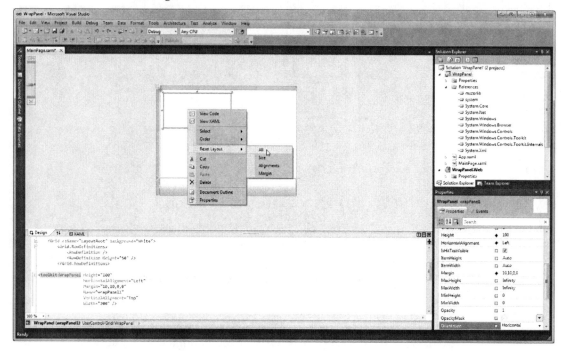

Figure 3-18. *Resetting elementlLayout with Visual Studio 2010*

6. You will then notice that the WrapPanel definition is reduced to the following source:

```
<toolkit:WrapPanel Name="wrapPanel1" />
```

7. Once the WrapPanel has been added, your XAML source should appear as follows:

```
<UserControl x:Class="WrapPanel.MainPage"
    xmlns="http://schemas.microsoft.com/winfx/2006/xaml/presentation"
    xmlns:x="http://schemas.microsoft.com/winfx/2006/xaml"
    xmlns:d="http://schemas.microsoft.com/expression/blend/2008"
    xmlns:mc="http://schemas.openxmlformats.org/markup-compatibility/2006"
    mc:Ignorable="d"
    d:DesignHeight="300" d:DesignWidth="400"
    xmlns:toolkit="http://schemas.microsoft.com/winfx/2006/xaml/presentation/toolkit">

    <Grid x:Name="LayoutRoot" Background="White">
        <Grid.RowDefinitions>
            <RowDefinition />
```

```xaml
        <RowDefinition Height="50" />
    </Grid.RowDefinitions>

    <toolkit:WrapPanel Name="wrapPanel1" />

    <Button x:Name="addItem"
            Click="addItem_Click"
            Content="Add New Item"
            Grid.Row="1" />

  </Grid>
</UserControl>
```

8. Now you need to add the code behind the button click event. Right-click on addItem_Click in the XAML and choose "Navigate to Event Handler." This takes you to the code behind of MainPage.xaml. Add the following code within the addItem_Click event handler:

```csharp
private void addItem_Click(object sender, RoutedEventArgs e)
{
    Rectangle newRect = new Rectangle();
    newRect.Width = 50;
    newRect.Height = 50;
    newRect.Margin = new Thickness(5);
    newRect.Fill = new SolidColorBrush(Color.FromArgb(255, 0, 0, 0));

    wrapPanel1.Children.Add(newRect);
}
```

9. You can now test the application. Once the application appears, start pressing the Add New Item button and watch the items appear horizontally as well as wrap to a new row when a new item cannot fit within the width of the control. (See Figure 3-19.)

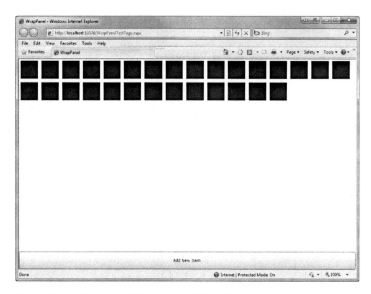

Figure 3-19. *Completed horizontal WrapPanel*

10. At this point, you can then go into the XAML designer for MainPage.xaml, add the property Orientation="Vertical" to the WrapPanel, and test the application once again. This time you will notice that the items appear vertically and wrap to new columns once they reach the maximum height, as shown in Figure 3-20.

Figure 3-20. *Completed vertical WrapPanel*

The DockPanel Control

The DockPanel control was first released in Silverlight 3 via the Silverlight Toolkit. It provides the ability to dock controls in all four directions: top, bottom, right, and left. Consider Figure 3-21, which is a possible layout with the DockPanel control involving five controls. The first two controls are docked in the left panel; the third control is docked in the top-center panel; the fourth control is docked in the bottom-center panel; and the fifth control is docked in the right panel.

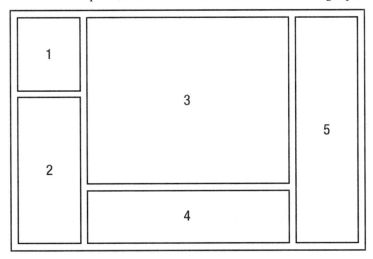

Figure 3-21. *Possible layout with the DockPanel*

To achieve this layout without the DockPanel would involve nested layout controls or a fairly complex Grid control. The point is that for certain situations the DockPanel can definitely be a very effective control.

Try It Out: Using the DockPanel Control

In this exercise, you will explore the DockPanel control and how it can be used to lay out controls docked in different directions.

1. Open Visual Studio 2010, and create a new Silverlight application called DockPanel. Allow Visual Studio to create a Web Application to host the application.

2. When the project is created, the file MainPage.xaml is automatically created and opened in the XAML designer. You will add a DockPanel to the root Grid and then add buttons that are docked in different positions.

3. Just like you did with the WrapPanel in the previous section, to get the proper XML namespace added for the DockPanel, add it by double-clicking on the control from the Toolbox in Visual Studio. That way, Visual Studio will automatically add the Xml namespace and assembly reference to the page.

Once the panel has been added, you can then modify the tag how you would like.

4. The default dock behavior is to dock the control left. However, if you want to change that, you can use the Dock extended property to change this behavior. As an example, to dock a control to the right, you would add the property controls:DockPanel.Dock="Right" to the control. (Note that the xmlns attribute is included, which is required.)

5. When you are finished adding the controls, your XAML should look like the following:

```
<Grid x:Name="LayoutRoot" Background="White">
    <toolkit:DockPanel Name="dockPanel1">
        <Button Content="Left Button" toolkit:DockPanel.Dock="Left" />
        <Button Content="Right Button" toolkit:DockPanel.Dock="Right" />
        <Button Content="Bottom Button" toolkit:DockPanel.Dock="Bottom" />
    </toolkit:DockPanel>
</Grid>
```

6. The result of this code should appear as shown in Figure 3-22.

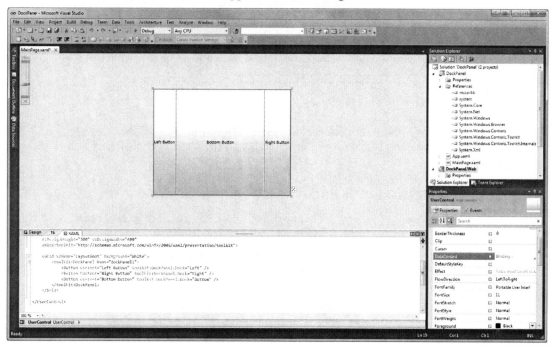

Figure 3-22. *Buttons placed in the DockPanel*

7. Notice that the last button placed in the DockPanel automatically fills the remaining space. This is the default behavior of the DockPanel. However, if you

do not want the DockPanel to do this, simply add the LastChildFill property set to False to the DockPanel.

```
<Grid x:Name="LayoutRoot" Background="White">
    <toolkit:DockPanel Name="dockPanel1" LastChildFill="False">
        <Button Content="Left Button" toolkit:DockPanel.Dock="Left" />
        <Button Content="Right Button" toolkit:DockPanel.Dock="Right" />
        <Button Content="Bottom Button" toolkit:DockPanel.Dock="Bottom" />
    </toolkit:DockPanel>
</Grid>
```

8. Once you have added this property, the result should appear as shown in Figure 3-23.

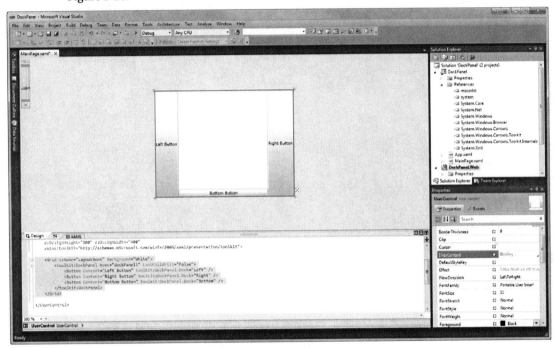

Figure 3-23. Buttons placed in the DockPanel without LastChildFill

9. The order in which you place the controls in the DockPanel determines how they are docked with the other controls. For example, notice that button labeled Bottom Button is docked around the left and right button, because they were added earlier in the DockPanel. However, if you add another button to the first button in the DockPanel and dock it to the top, it will occupy the entire width of the control.

57

```
<Grid x:Name="LayoutRoot" Background="White">
    <toolkit:DockPanel Name="dockPanel1" LastChildFill="False">

        <Button Content="Top Button" toolkit:DockPanel.Dock="Top" />

        <Button Content="Left Button" toolkit:DockPanel.Dock="Left" />
        <Button Content="Right Button" toolkit:DockPanel.Dock="Right" />
        <Button Content="Bottom Button" toolkit:DockPanel.Dock="Bottom" />
    </toolkit:DockPanel>
</Grid>
```

10. Once you have added this control, the result should appear as shown in Figure 3-24.

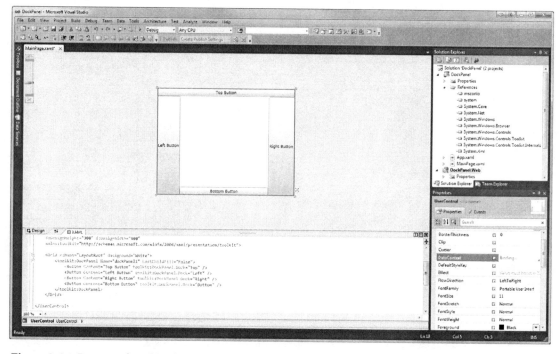

Figure 3-24. Buttons placed in the DockPanel with Top Dock

Summary

In this chapter, we explored the five layout controls that are available in Silverlight. We looked at the Canvas, StackPanel, Grid, WrapPanel, and DockPanel controls. In the next chapter, we will take an in-depth look at the form controls that come bundled with Silverlight.

CHAPTER 4

Silverlight Controls

For those who have worked with Silverlight 1.0, one of the first observations you most likely made was the lack of common controls such as the Button, TextBox, and ListBox. In fact, Silverlight 1.0 provided only two basic controls: Rectangle and TextBlock. From these, developers were expected to implement all of the rich controls they needed. As you can imagine, it was quite a bit of work to create all of the form controls using just these two base controls.

Since then, Microsoft's vision of Silverlight has gone beyond basic animations to spark up your applications and into the realm of feature-rich user interfaces (UIs). To this end, Silverlight includes a strong base of controls you can use within your Silverlight applications.

In this chapter, you will first look at the Silverlight controls in general by examining control properties and events. You will then take a brief tour of some of the more common form controls included in Silverlight. This chapter provides a high-level introduction to these common Silverlight controls. You will continue to work with the controls throughout the remainder of the book, so you will see more specific usage scenarios later.

Setting Control Properties

The most straightforward and simple way to set a property is by using attribute syntax. However, in some cases, you will use element syntax.

Attribute Syntax

Most properties that can be represented as a simple string can be set using attribute syntax. Setting an attribute in XAML is just like setting an attribute in XML. An XML element contains a node and attributes. Silverlight controls are defined in the same way, where the control name is the node and the properties are defined as attributes.

As an example, you can easily use attribute syntax to set the Width, Height, and Content properties of a Button control. The following control definition includes a Button element, and Width, Height, and Content attributes and 100, 30, and "Click Me" attribute values:

```
<Button Width="100" Height="30" Content="Click Me!"></Button>
```

Element Syntax

Element syntax is most commonly used when a property cannot be set using attribute syntax because the property value cannot be represented as a simple string. Again, this is very similar to using elements in XML. The following is an example of setting the background color of a button:

```
<Button Width="100" Height="30" Content="Click Me!">
    <Button.Background>
        <SolidColorBrush Color="Blue"/>
    </Button.Background>
    <Button.Foreground>
        <SolidColorBrush Color="Red"/>
    </Button.Foreground>
</Button>
```

Type-Converter-Enabled Attributes

Sometimes when defining a property via an attribute, the value cannot be represented as a simple string—rather, it is converted to a more complex type. A common usage of a type-converter-enabled attribute is Margin. The Margin property can be set as a simple string, such as in the following example:

```
<Button Width="100" Content="Click Me!" Margin="15"></Button>
```

When you set the Margin property in this fashion, the left, right, top, and bottom margins are all set to 15 pixels. What if you want to set the top margin to 15 pixels, but you want the other three margins to be 0? To do that, you set the Margin property as follows:

```
<Button Width="100" Content="Click Me!" Margin="0,15,0,0"></Button>
```

In this case, Silverlight takes the string "0,15,0,0" and converts it into a more complex type. The string is converted to four values: left margin = 0, top margin = 15, right margin = 0, and bottom margin = 0.

This type-conversion concept is not new to Silverlight. For those familiar with Cascading Style Sheets (CSS), the same sort of structure exists. As an example, when you are defining a border style, within the simple string value for a border, you are actually setting the thickness, color, and line style. The following border assignment in CSS sets the border thickness to 1 pixel, the line style to be solid, and the color to #333333 (dark gray):

```
border: 1px solid #333333;
```

Attached Properties

In Chapter 3, you learned how to set a control's position within a Canvas panel by using attached properties. An *attached property* is a property that is attached to a parent control. In the example in Chapter 3, you specified the Button control's position within the Canvas object by setting two attached properties: Canvas.Top and Canvas.Left. These two properties reference the Button control's parent, which is the Canvas.

```
<Canvas>
    <Button Width="100" Content="Click Me!"
            Canvas.Top="10" Canvas.Left="13" />
</Canvas>
```

Nesting Controls Within Controls

When you first look at the controls included in Silverlight, you will probably feel pretty comfortable, because they seem to be what would be expected. However, when you dig a bit deeper into the control features, you will find that the controls are much more flexible and powerful than they first appear.

One of the key features of controls in Silverlight is the ability to put just about anything within a control. A Button control can contain a StackPanel, which can contain an Ellipse control and a TextBlock control. There really are few limitations as to what the contents of a control can be. Figure 4-1 shows an example of a standard Silverlight Button control containing a StackPanel, a nested StackPanel, an Ellipse, a TextBlock, and a ListBox.

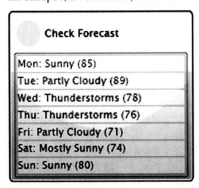

Figure 4-1. A Button control with nested controls

The following code was used to produce the control in Figure 4-1:

```
<Button Height="220" Width="200">
    <StackPanel Orientation="Vertical">
        <StackPanel
            Margin="5"
            Background="Transparent"
            VerticalAlignment="Center"
            Orientation="Horizontal">

            <Ellipse Fill="Yellow" Width="25" />

            <TextBlock
                VerticalAlignment="Center"
                Margin="5"
                Text="Check Forecast" />

        </StackPanel>
        <ListBox
            FontSize="11"
            Opacity="0.5"
            Background="Transparent"
            BorderThickness="0"
            Margin="2"
            x:Name="lstForecastGlance">
```

```
            <ListBoxItem>
                <TextBlock
                    VerticalAlignment="Center"
                    Text="Mon: Sunny (85)" />
            </ListBoxItem>
            <ListBoxItem>
                <TextBlock
                    VerticalAlignment="Center"
                    Text="Tue: Partly Cloudy (89)" />
            </ListBoxItem>
            <ListBoxItem>
                <TextBlock
                    VerticalAlignment="Center"
                    Text="Wed: Thunderstorms (78)" />
            </ListBoxItem>
            <ListBoxItem>
                <TextBlock
                    VerticalAlignment="Center"
                    Text="Thu: Thunderstorms (76)" />
            </ListBoxItem>
            <ListBoxItem>
                <TextBlock
                    VerticalAlignment="Center"
                    Text="Fri: Partly Cloudy (71)" />
            </ListBoxItem>
            <ListBoxItem>
                <TextBlock
                    VerticalAlignment="Center"
                    Text="Sat: Mostly Sunny (74)" />
            </ListBoxItem>
            <ListBoxItem>
                <TextBlock
                    VerticalAlignment="Center"
                    Text="Sun: Sunny (80)" />
            </ListBoxItem>
        </ListBox>
    </StackPanel>
</Button>
```

As the code shows, the example simply nests additional content within the Button control. As you can imagine, this can be a very powerful feature.

Handling Events in Silverlight

As with other Microsoft programming frameworks, Silverlight provides an event mechanism to track actions that take place within Silverlight applications. Two types of actions are tracked within Silverlight:

- Actions that are triggered based on some input from the user. Input actions are handled and "bubbled" up from the browser to the Silverlight object model.

- Actions that are triggered based on a change of state of a particular object, including the object's state in the application. These actions are handled directly from the Silverlight object model.

Event handlers are methods that are executed when a given event is triggered. You can define event handlers either in the XAML markup itself or in managed code. The following exercises demonstrate how to define event handlers in both ways.

Try It Out: Declaring an Event in XAML

Let's get started by defining event handlers within the XAML markup:

1. Open Visual Studio 2010, and create a new Silverlight project called *EventHandlers0000000000000000000000000000000000000000000000*. Allow Visual Studio to create a Web Application project to host the application.

2. When the project is created, you should be looking at the MainPage.xaml file. If you do not see the XAML source, switch to that view so that you can edit the XAML. Within the root Grid of the Silverlight page, add grid row and column definitions (as explained in Chapter 3) to define four rows and two columns, as follows:

```
<Grid x:Name="LayoutRoot" Background="White">
    <Grid.RowDefinitions>
        <RowDefinition Height="70" />
        <RowDefinition Height="70" />
        <RowDefinition Height="70" />
        <RowDefinition Height="*" />
    </Grid.RowDefinitions>

    <Grid.ColumnDefinitions>
        <ColumnDefinition Width="150" />
        <ColumnDefinition Width="*" />
    </Grid.ColumnDefinitions>
</Grid>
```

3. Next, add a Button control to the upper-left grid cell and a TextBlock control in the upper-right cell.

```
<Grid x:Name="LayoutRoot" Background="White">
    <Grid.RowDefinitions>
        <RowDefinition Height="70" />
        <RowDefinition Height="70" />
        <RowDefinition Height="70" />
        <RowDefinition Height="*" />
    </Grid.RowDefinitions>

    <Grid.ColumnDefinitions>
        <ColumnDefinition Width="150" />
        <ColumnDefinition Width="*" />
    </Grid.ColumnDefinitions>
```

```
<Button
    Width="125"
    Height="35"
    Content="XAML Event" />
<TextBlock
    Text="Click the XAML Event!"
    Grid.Column="1"
    VerticalAlignment="Center"
    HorizontalAlignment="Center" />
</Grid>
```

4. Add the Click property to the button. When you type Click=, Visual Studio prompts you with the option of automatically creating a new event handler, as shown in Figure 4-2. When the <New Event Handler> option is displayed, simply press Enter, and Visual Studio will complete the Click property, as follows:

```
<Button Width="125" Height="35"
    Content="XAML Event" Click="Button_Click" />
```

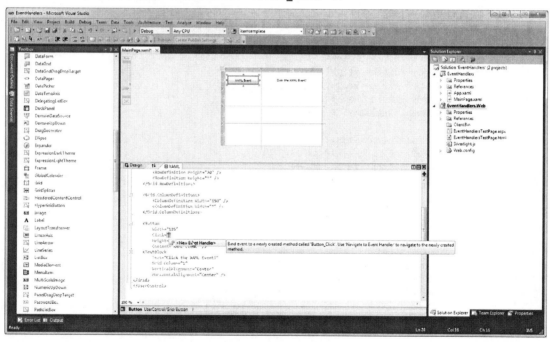

Figure 4-2. *Visual Studio's automatic creation of an event handler*

5. In addition, Visual Studio automatically adds an event handler called Button_Click to the code-behind class for the Silverlight application, as follows:

```
public partial class MainPage : UserControl
{
    public MainPage()
    {
        InitializeComponent();
    }

    private void Button_Click(object sender, RoutedEventArgs e)
    {

    }
}
```

6. For this example, you will change the Text property within the TextBlock. To do this, you first need to give the TextBlock a name so that you can access it from the code behind. Add the following code:

```
<TextBlock
    Name="txtXAMLEventText"
    Text="Click the XAML Event!"
    Grid.Column="1"
    VerticalAlignment="Center"
    HorizontalAlignment="Center" />
```

7. Now change the Text property of the TextBlock within the Button_Click event, as follows:

```
private void Button_Click(object sender, RoutedEventArgs e)
{
    txtXAMLEventText.Text = "Thank you for clicking!";
}
```

8. Run the application, and click the XAML Event button. The text to the right of the button changes to "Thank you for clicking!". Figures 4-3 and 4-4 show the application before and after clicking the XAML Event button.

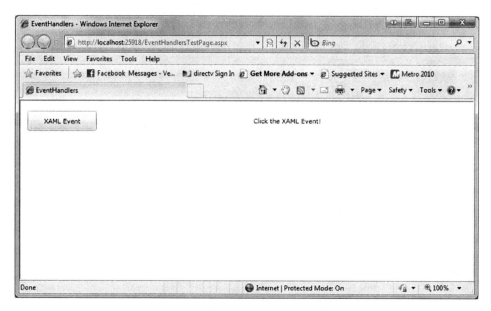

Figure 4-3. *The TextBlock before the button is clicked*

9. Now that you have seen how to define an event handler in the XAML markup, in the next exercise you will continue by adding another event handler using managed code.

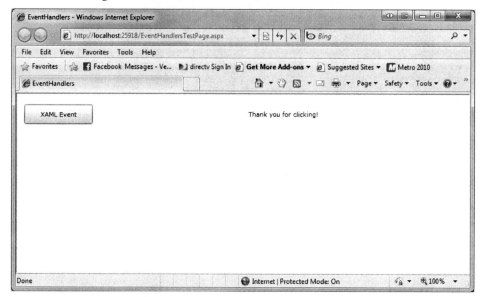

Figure 4-4. *The TextBlock after the button is clicked*

Try It Out: Declaring an Event Handler in Managed Code

Let's continue with the project named EventHandlers from the previous exercise. You'll add another button and wire up its event handler using managed code.

1. Add another Button and TextBlock in the second row of the Grid, as follows:

```
<Grid x:Name="LayoutRoot" Background="White">
    <Grid.RowDefinitions>
        <RowDefinition Height="70" />
        <RowDefinition Height="70" />
        <RowDefinition Height="70" />
        <RowDefinition Height="*" />
    </Grid.RowDefinitions>

    <Grid.ColumnDefinitions>
        <ColumnDefinition Width="150" />
        <ColumnDefinition Width="*" />
    </Grid.ColumnDefinitions>

    <Button
        Width="125"
        Click="Button_Click"
        Height="35"
        Content="XAML Event" />
    <TextBlock
        Name="txtXAMLEventText"
        Text="Click the XAML Event!"
        Grid.Column="1"
        VerticalAlignment="Center"
        HorizontalAlignment="Center" />

    <Button
        Width="125"
        Height="35"
        Content="Managed Event"
        Grid.Row="1" />
    <TextBlock
        Text="Click the Managed Event!"
        Grid.Column="1"
        VerticalAlignment="Center"
        HorizontalAlignment="Center"
        Grid.Row="1" />
</Grid>
```

2. To reference the new Button control in managed code, you must give it and the TextBlock control a name, as shown in the following snippet:

```
<Button
    Name="btnManaged"
    Width="125"
    Height="35"
    Content="Managed Event"
    Grid.Row="1" />
<TextBlock
    Name="txtManagedEventText"
    Text="Click the Managed Event!"
    Grid.Column="1"
    VerticalAlignment="Center"
    HorizontalAlignment="Center"
    Grid.Row="1" />
```

3. Your page should now appear as shown in Figure 4-5.

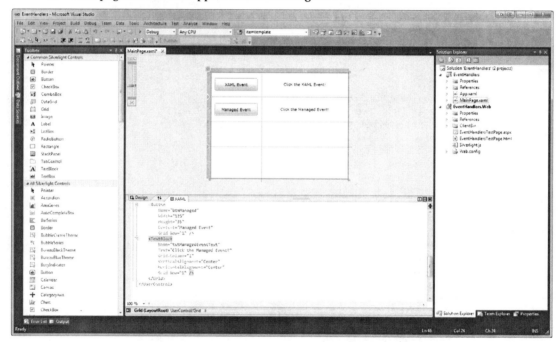

Figure 4-5. *The updated Silverlight page*

4. Next, you need to add the event handler for the Managed Event button Click
    event. Right-click the Silverlight page and select View Code. This switches to
    the code behind of the page.

5. From here, you will use the standard CLR language-specific syntax for adding
    event handlers. Because you are using C#, the syntax is to use the += operator
    and assign it to a new EventHandler. Visual Studio will help you with this.

6. After the InitializeComponent() method call in the Page constructor, start typing "this.btnManaged.Click +=". At this point, Visual Studio displays the message "new RoutedEventHandler(btnManaged_Click); (Press TAB to insert)," as shown in Figure 4-6. Press Tab to complete the event handler definition.

Figure 4-6. Visual Studio assisting with wiring up an event handler in managed code

7. Visual Studio once again prompts you for the name of the event handler. Go ahead and press Tab again to accept the default name. At this point, your source should look like this:

```
public partial class MainPage : UserControl
{
    public MainPage()
    {
        InitializeComponent();
        this.btnManaged.Click += new RoutedEventHandler(btnManaged_Click);
    }

    void btnManaged_Click(object sender, RoutedEventArgs e)
    {
        throw new NotImplementedException();
    }
```

```
        private void Button_Click(object sender, RoutedEventArgs e)
        {
            txtXAMLEventText.Text = "Thank you for clicking!";
        }
    }
```

8. Now the only thing left to do is add the code to the event handler. You will notice that, by default, Visual Studio added code to automatically throw a NotImplementedException. Remove that line, and replace it with the following line to change the TextBlock control's text.

```
void btnManaged_Click(object sender, RoutedEventArgs e)
{
    txtManagedEventText.Text = "Thank you for clicking";
}
```

9. Run the application, and click the Managed Event button. You will see the text for the second TextBlock is updated to say "Thank you for clicking", as shown in Figure 4-7.

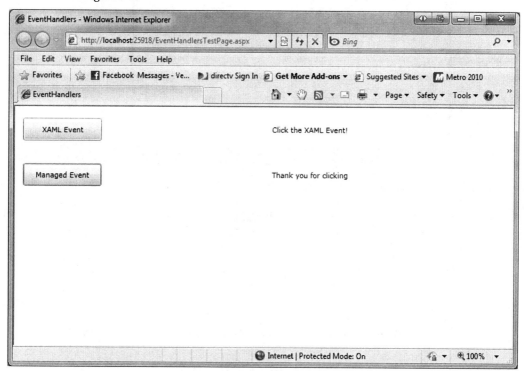

Figure 4-7. *The result of the managed code event handler*

This exercise demonstrated how to wire up an event handler using C# and managed code. In the remainder of the chapter, we will take a tour of additional form controls in Silverlight.

Multiple Mouse Click Support

One of the new features in Silverlight 5 is support for multiple clicks of the mouse, on both the right and left mouse buttons. You can use this feature to add support for double-clicking and triple-clicking (or however many clicks you would like to support). This is done with the addition of a new property on the MouseButtonEventArgs object called ClickCount. This property is now populated with the number of clicks that the user has made. Let's walk through a quick example to demonstrate this feature.

Try It Out: Multiple Click Support

Let's get started by defining event handlers within the XAML markup:

1. Create a new Silverlight application in Visual Studio called MultiClick. Allow Visual Studio to create a Web Application project to host the application.

2. In the MainPage.xaml file, add a Rectangle and a TextBlock to the LayoutRoot Grid as shown here:

```
<Grid x:Name="LayoutRoot" Background="White">
    <StackPanel VerticalAlignment="Center" HorizontalAlignment="Center">
        <Rectangle
            MouseLeftButtonDown="Rectangle_MouseLeftButtonDown"
            Stroke="Black"
            Fill="Red"
            Width="50"
            Height="50" />
        <TextBlock Name="ClickCount" />
    </StackPanel>
</Grid>
```

3. In the code behind for the MainPage.xaml file, add the following code to the event handler created for the MouseLeftButtonDown event. If the event wasn't automatically added, add it.

```
private void Rectangle_MouseLeftButtonDown(object sender, MouseButtonEventArgs e)
{
    this.ClickCount.Text = "You clicked " + e.ClickCount.ToString() + " times";
}
```

4. That's all there is to it. Now you can run the application. When the rectangle displays, double-click on it. You will see the message indicate that the mouse was clicked two times, as shown in Figure 4-8.

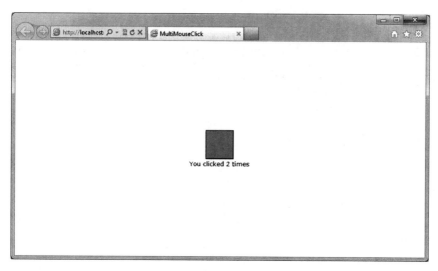

Figure 4-8. *Mutliclick support functionality*

The Border Control

The Border control provides a way to add a border and background to any one control in Silverlight. Even though a border is applied to only one control, you can always place a border around a StackPanel or Grid and, as a result, include many controls within a border.

The syntax to add a Border control to your Silverlight project is very simple, as you can see from the following example:

```
<Grid x:Name="LayoutRoot" Background="White">
    <Border BorderThickness="2" BorderBrush="Black" Margin="10">
        <StackPanel Margin="10">
            <Button Content="Sample Button" Margin="5" />
            <TextBlock Text="Sample TextBlock" Margin="5" />
            <ListBox Margin="5">
                <ListBoxItem>
                    <TextBlock Text="ListItem 1" />
                </ListBoxItem>
                <ListBoxItem>
                    <TextBlock Text="ListItem 2" />
                </ListBoxItem>
                <ListBoxItem>
                    <TextBlock Text="ListItem 3" />
                </ListBoxItem>
                <ListBoxItem>
                    <TextBlock Text="ListItem 4" />
                </ListBoxItem>
            </ListBox>
        </StackPanel>
    </Border>
</Grid>
```

Figure 4-9 shows the results.

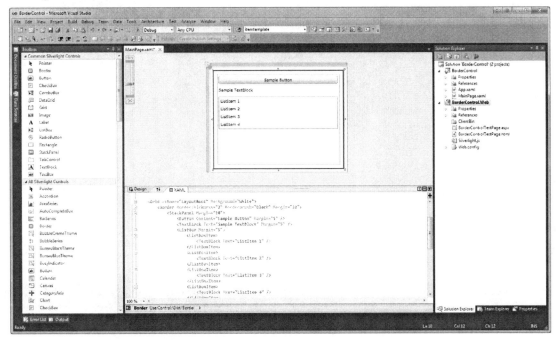

Figure 4-9. *Using the Border control*

Another feature of the Border control is the ability to round the corners of the border using the CornerRadius property. Here is how the preceding example could be modified to provide a Border control with a CornerRadius property of 10:

```
<Border
    BorderThickness="2"
    BorderBrush="Black"
    Margin="10"
    CornerRadius="10">
```

The border with rounded corners is shown in Figure 4-10.

You can declare a background color for your border using the Background property. Like the BorderBrush property, the Background property can be set to either a color or a brush type. Here is an example of setting a border with a background color of silver:

```
<Border
    BorderThickness="2"
    BorderBrush="Black"
    Margin="10"
    CornerRadius="10"
    Background="Silver">
```

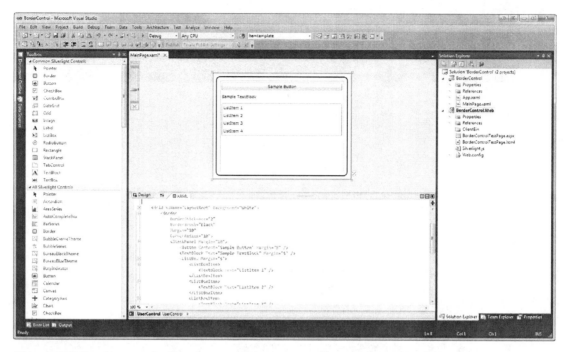

Figure 4-10. *Border control with a CornerRadius property of 10*

Figure 4-11 shows the result of adding the background color.

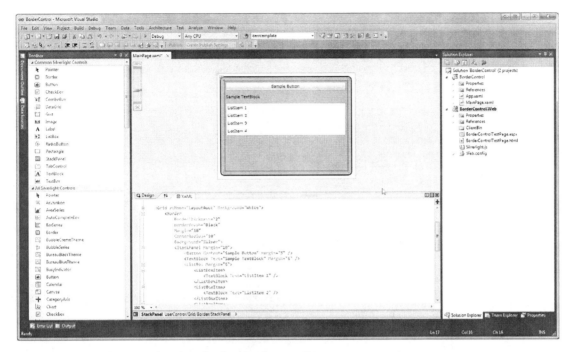

Figure 4-11. Border control with its background set to silver

The following is an example of a more complex Border control that contains a gradient for the border and background, which is accomplished by using a Brush object:

```
<Border BorderThickness="2" Margin="10" CornerRadius="10">
    <Border.Background>
        <LinearGradientBrush>
            <LinearGradientBrush.GradientStops>
                <GradientStop Color="Green" Offset="0" />
                <GradientStop Color="White" Offset="1" />
            </LinearGradientBrush.GradientStops>
        </LinearGradientBrush>
    </Border.Background>
    <Border.BorderBrush>
        <LinearGradientBrush>
            <LinearGradientBrush.GradientStops>
                <GradientStop Color="Black" Offset="0" />
                <GradientStop Color="White" Offset="1" />
            </LinearGradientBrush.GradientStops>
        </LinearGradientBrush>
    </Border.BorderBrush>

    <StackPanel Margin="10">
        <Button Content="Sample Button" Margin="5" />
        <TextBlock Text="Sample TextBlock" Margin="5" />
```

```
        <ListBox Margin="5">
            <ListBoxItem>
                <TextBlock Text="ListItem 1" />
            </ListBoxItem>
            <ListBoxItem>
                <TextBlock Text="ListItem 2" />
            </ListBoxItem>
            <ListBoxItem>
                <TextBlock Text="ListItem 3" />
            </ListBoxItem>
            <ListBoxItem>
                <TextBlock Text="ListItem 4" />
            </ListBoxItem>
        </ListBox>
    </StackPanel>
</Border>
```

Figure 4-12 shows the border with the gradient applied.

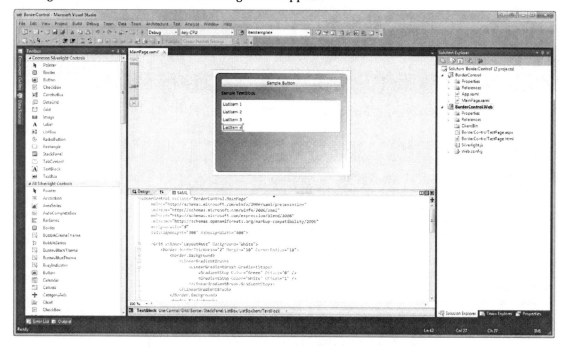

Figure 4-12. Border control with gradient brushes for the border and background

User Input Controls

One of the most common controls in applications is a text box, which is the standard control for collecting basic string input from the user. Also ubiquitous are check boxes and radio buttons, which allow users to select from a list of choices—more than one choice in the case of check boxes, and a single choice in the case of radio buttons. Silverlight provides the TextBox, CheckBox, and RadioButton for these standard controls. The following exercises also gives you a chance to work with the Ellipse and Rectangle controls.

Try It Out: Working with the TextBox Control

This exercise demonstrates the use of the TextBox control in Silverlight by creating a simple application that requests the red, green, and blue values to fill an ellipse with a given color. The resulting application appears as shown in Figure 4-13.

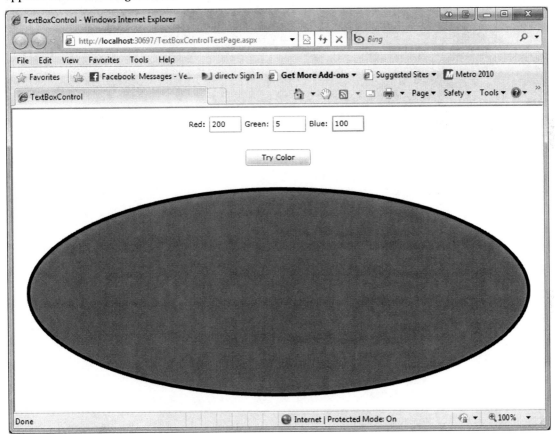

Figure 4-13. Sample application using TextBox controls

1. In Visual Studio, create a new Silverlight application named *TextBoxControl*. Allow Visual Studio to create a Web Application project to host your application.

2. In the MainPage.xaml file, within the root Grid element, add three RowDefinition items, as follows:

```
<Grid x:Name="LayoutRoot" Background="White">
    <Grid.RowDefinitions>
        <RowDefinition Height="50" />
        <RowDefinition Height="50" />
        <RowDefinition />
    </Grid.RowDefinitions>
</Grid>
```

3. Add three TextBox and TextArea controls contained in a horizontal-oriented StackPanel to the first row, a Button control to the second row, and an Ellipse control to the third row. In addition, place a TextBlock in the third row to stack on top of the Ellipse control for error-reporting purposes. Name each of the TextBox controls, as well as the Button control and the TextBlock. These additions are shown in the following code:

```
<Grid x:Name="LayoutRoot" Background="White">
    <Grid.RowDefinitions>
        <RowDefinition Height="50" />
        <RowDefinition Height="50" />
        <RowDefinition />
    </Grid.RowDefinitions>

    <StackPanel
        Orientation="Horizontal"
        HorizontalAlignment="Center">

        <TextBlock
            VerticalAlignment="Center"
            Text="Red:" />
        <TextBox
            Name="txtRed"
            Height="24"
            Width="50"
            Margin="5" />
        <TextBlock
            VerticalAlignment="Center"
            Text="Green:" />
        <TextBox
            Name="txtGreen"
            Height="24"
            Width="50"
            Margin="5" />
        <TextBlock
            VerticalAlignment="Center"
            Text="Blue:" />
        <TextBox
            Name="txtBlue"
            Height="24"
            Width="50"
            Margin="5" />
    </StackPanel>
```

```xml
<Button
    Name="btnTry"
    Content="Try Color"
    Grid.Row="1"
    Width="100"
    Height="24" />
<Ellipse
    Name="ellipse"
    Grid.Row="2"
    Stroke="Black"
    StrokeThickness="5"
    Margin="20" />
<TextBlock
    Name="lblColor"
    Grid.Row="2"
    HorizontalAlignment="Center"
    VerticalAlignment="Center"
    FontSize="20"
    FontFamily="Arial"
    FontWeight="Bold"  />
```

  </Grid>

4. Now add the Click event to the Button control. Do this in the code behind, as explained earlier in the section "Try It Out: Declaring an Event in XAML."

```csharp
public partial class MainPage : UserControl
{
    public MainPage()
    {
        InitializeComponent();
        this.btnTry.Click += new RoutedEventHandler(btnTry_Click);

    }

    void btnTry_Click(object sender, RoutedEventArgs e)
    {
        throw new NotImplementedException();
    }
}
```

5. When the button is clicked, the application changes the Fill property of the Ellipse control, which expects a SolidColorBrush. You can create the SolidColorBrush using the Colors.FromArgb() method, which accepts four arguments: one for opacity, and one byte each for the red, green, and blue values. You get the red, green, and blue values from the TextBox controls using the Text property.

```csharp
void btnTry_Click(object sender, RoutedEventArgs e)
{
    this.ellipse.Fill = new SolidColorBrush(
        Color.FromArgb(
            255,
```

```
        byte.Parse(this.txtRed.Text),
        byte.Parse(this.txtGreen.Text),
        byte.Parse(this.txtBlue.Text)
    ));

}
```

6. Because the values for red, green, and blue must be an integer from 0 to 255, you can either validate them using Silverlight validation or take the easy way out and just wrap your code in a try/catch block, and then report the error using the TextBlock. You'll go with the latter approach here. To keep things clean, you will make sure the error message is cleared if all works correctly. Here is the updated code:

```
void btnTry_Click(object sender, RoutedEventArgs e)
{
    try
    {
        this.ellipse.Fill = new SolidColorBrush(
        Color.FromArgb(
            255,
            byte.Parse(this.txtRed.Text),
            byte.Parse(this.txtGreen.Text),
            byte.Parse(this.txtBlue.Text)
        ));

        this.lblColor.Text = "";
    }
    catch
    {
        this.lblColor.Text = "Error with R,G,B Values";
    }
}
```

7. Build and run the application to see what you get. Type **255**, **0**, and **0** in the Red, Green, and Blue text boxes, respectively, and then click the Try Color button. You should see the ellipse turn red. Just for the fun of it, leave one of the values blank or enter a value other than 0 through 255 to see the error message.

Now that we have taken a quick look at the TextBox control, let's turn our attention to two other common controls: CheckBox and RadioButton.

Try It Out: Working with the RadioButton and CheckBox Controls

The following exercise gives you a first look at the RadioButton and CheckBox controls. You will build a simple survey, as shown in Figure 4-14.

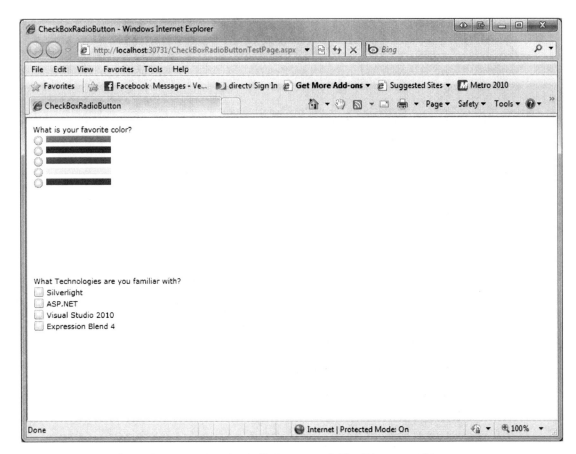

Figure 4-14. Sample application using the RadioButton and CheckBox controls

1. Create a new Silverlight application in Visual Studio, and call it
   CheckBoxRadioButton. Allow Visual Studio to create a Web Application project
   to host the application.

2. In the `MainPage.xaml` file, divide the root `Grid` into two rows. In each row, place
   a `StackPanel` with vertical orientation and a `Margin` property set to 10.

```
<Grid x:Name="LayoutRoot" Background="White">
    <Grid.RowDefinitions>
        <RowDefinition />
        <RowDefinition />
    </Grid.RowDefinitions>

    <StackPanel Orientation="Vertical" Grid.Row="0" Margin="10">
    </StackPanel>

    <StackPanel Orientation="Vertical" Grid.Row="1" Margin="10">
```

```
    </StackPanel>
  </Grid>
```

3. The top row will be used to demonstrate the use of the RadioButton control, and the bottom row will feature the CheckBox control. Let's begin with the RadioButton.

4. The RadioButton control allows users to select only one selection out of a number of RadioButton controls that share the same group name. This is set using the RadioButton's Grouping property.

5. Although you could simply type in each of the color choices for the radio buttons as text using the Content property, I thought it would be less boring to use colored rectangles instead. As we discussed earlier in the section "Nesting Controls Within Controls," one of the benefits of Silverlight controls is that you can nest just about anything within the different controls. This is just another example of that flexibility.

6. Place five RadioButton controls in the first StackPanel, each with a Rectangle control of a different color. For the group name, use FavoriteColor. To make the content of the RadioButton controls display as left-justified, set the HorizontalAlignment property to Left for each one. Here is the code:

```xml
<StackPanel Orientation="Vertical" Grid.Row="0" Margin="10">
    <TextBlock
        Text="What is your favorite color?" />
    <RadioButton HorizontalAlignment="Left" GroupName="FavoriteColor">
        <Rectangle Width="100" Height="10" Fill="Red" />
    </RadioButton>
    <RadioButton HorizontalAlignment="Left" GroupName="FavoriteColor">
        <Rectangle Width="100" Height="10" Fill="Blue" />
    </RadioButton>
    <RadioButton HorizontalAlignment="Left" GroupName="FavoriteColor">
        <Rectangle Width="100" Height="10" Fill="Green" />
    </RadioButton>
    <RadioButton HorizontalAlignment="Left" GroupName="FavoriteColor">
        <Rectangle Width="100" Height="10" Fill="Yellow" />
    </RadioButton>
    <RadioButton HorizontalAlignment="Left" GroupName="FavoriteColor">
        <Rectangle Width="100" Height="10" Fill="Purple" />
    </RadioButton>
</StackPanel>
```

7. Next, do the same for the CheckBox controls in the bottom row, except here, just go the boring route and supply the choices as text. In addition, CheckBox controls are left-justified by default, and they do not need to be grouped. Here is the code for the CheckBox portion:

```xml
<StackPanel Orientation="Vertical" Grid.Row="1" Margin="10">
    <TextBlock Text="What Technologies are you familiar with?" />
    <CheckBox Content="Silverlight" />
    <CheckBox Content="ASP.NET" />
    <CheckBox Content="Visual Studio 2010" />
```

```
<CheckBox Content="Expression Blend 4" />
</StackPanel>
```

8. Go ahead and run the solution to see the result as it will appear in the browser. The output is shown in Figure 4-14 Notice that, as you would expect, you are able to select only one radio button at a time, but you can click as many check boxes as you wish.

Extended Controls

When a Silverlight application is deployed, it goes into an .xap file. This file will need to be downloaded by every client that accesses the Silverlight application.

A big benefit of Silverlight is that the size of this .xap file is kept very small. One reason this file can be small is that the most commonly used controls are included in the Silverlight Runtime, which is already present on every machine with Silverlight installed.

However, Silverlight provides a number of controls beyond this commonly used set of controls. These controls are included in two separate assemblies: System.Windows.Controls.dll and System.Windows.Controls.Data.dll. These dynamic-link libraries (DLLs) will be included in the application .xap file only if the developer used a control from one of these extended control sets in that application.

Adding an Extended Control

When a developer uses a control from one of the other control libraries, an additional xmlns declaration is added in the UserControl definition. This xmlns has a prefix associated with it that will then be used to reference the individual controls.

For example, if you add a DataGrid to your Silverlight application in Visual Studio, your source appears as follows:

```
<UserControl
    xmlns:data=
     "clr-namespace:System.Windows.Controls;assembly=System.Windows.Controls.Data"
    x:Class="SilverlightApplication1.Page"
    xmlns="http://schemas.microsoft.com/winfx/2006/xaml/presentation"
    xmlns:x="http://schemas.microsoft.com/winfx/2006/xaml"
    Width="400" Height="300">
    <Grid x:Name="LayoutRoot" Background="White">
        <data:DataGrid></data:DataGrid>
    </Grid>
</UserControl>
```

Notice the additional xmlns declaration pointing to the System.Windows.Controls namespace within the System.Windows.Controls.Data assembly.

■ **Tip** To view which controls belong to which assemblies, first create a new Silverlight application and add a DataGrid and GridSplitter to the root Grid. Then select View ➤ Object Browser from the Visual Studio main menu. From the Object Browser's Browse drop-down list (in the top-left corner), select My Solution and browse the listing for three assemblies: System.Windows, System.Windows.Controls.Data, and System.Windows.Controls. Within each of those assemblies, drill down to the System.Windows.Controls namespace to see all of the controls that reside in that assembly.

Now you will work through an exercise using one of the controls in the System.Windows.Controls assembly.

Try It Out: Using the GridSplitter

One of the controls that resides in the System.Windows.Controls assembly is the GridSplitter. This control provides the ability for a user to change the width of a column or row in an application. If used properly, the GridSplitter can greatly improve the appearance of your application, as well as the user experience. In the following exercise, you implement a simple GridSplitter:

1. Create a new Silverlight application in Visual Studio called *GridSplitterControl*. Allow Visual Studio to create a Web Application project to host the application.

2. In the MainPage.xaml file, divide the root Grid into two columns. The first column should be 150 pixels in width, and the second should take up the remainder of the application. To be able to see what is going on in the grid, set ShowGridLines to True. Also, add two TextBlock controls to the application: one in the first column and one in the second column. Your source should appear as follows:

```
<Grid x:Name="LayoutRoot" Background="White">

    <Grid.ColumnDefinitions>
        <ColumnDefinition Width="150" />
        <ColumnDefinition />
    </Grid.ColumnDefinitions>

    <TextBlock
        Text="Apress, Inc." />
    <TextBlock
        Grid.Column="1"
        Text="Beginning Silverlight: From Novice to Professional" />

</Grid>
```

3. At this point, your Silverlight application should look like Figure 4-15.

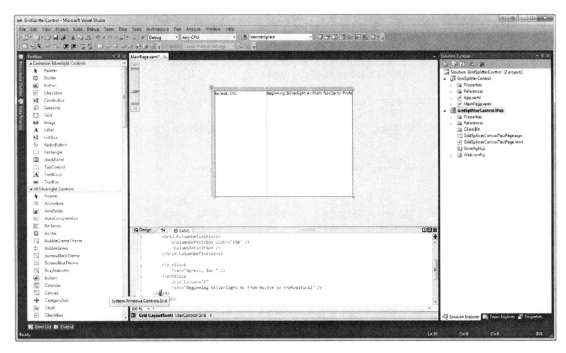

Figure 4-15. *The setup for the GridSplitter example*

4. Notice that you cannot see all of the text in the second column. Let's add a GridSplitter control to the application so that users can resize the two columns to be able to view all the text in both columns.

5. Within the XAML, place the cursor just below the TextBlock definitions you added. Then, in the Visual Studio Toolbox, double-click the GridSplitter control. This adds the xmlns to the System.Windows.Controls assembly, and it will also add the GridSplitter to the application. Remove all of the properties set by default except the Name property, and then set the Background property of the GridSplitter to LightGray. The source appears as follows:

```
<Grid x:Name="LayoutRoot" Background="White">
    <Grid.ColumnDefinitions>
        <ColumnDefinition Width="150" />
        <ColumnDefinition />
    </Grid.ColumnDefinitions>

    <TextBlock
        Text="Apress, Inc." />
    <TextBlock
        Grid.Column="1"
        Text="Beginning Silverlight: From Novice to Professional" />
    <sdk:GridSplitter Name="gridSplitter1" Background="LightGray" />
</Grid>
```

> ■ **Tip** As discussed earlier in this section, because the GridSplitter belongs in the Silverlight SDK control library instead of the standard controls library, you must add a references to the sdk control namespace and assembly. The entry in the UserControl definition is the following:
>
> xmlns:sdk="http://schemas.microsoft.com/winfx/2006/xaml/presentation/sdk">
>
> Because you named the reference "sdk," that is the prefix used in defining the GridSplitter
> (<sdk:GridSplitter>).

6. Run the application. It should look similar to Figure 4-16. Notice that you can now click and drag the GridSplitter to resize the two Grid columns.

Figure 4-16. The completed GridSplitter application

As you can see, it's quite easy to gain the rich functionality of a grid splitter in your application with the Silverlight `GridSplitter` control.

Summary

In this chapter, you took a brief look at some of the common form controls that are provided with Silverlight. The chapter was meant only as an introduction to the controls. You will be looking at the more advanced capacities of these controls in the upcoming chapters.

In the next chapter, you will look at the Silverlight list controls: `ListBox` and `DataGrid`.

CHAPTER 5

Data Binding and Silverlight List Controls

The previous chapter focused on a few of the form controls contained in Silverlight. In this chapter, you will look at two controls that are made to display lists of data: ListBox and DataGrid. These controls are typically bound to data through a technique known as *data binding*, which I'll explore first.

Data Binding

Through data binding, UI elements (called *targets*) are "bound" to data from a data source (called the *source*), as illustrated in Figure 5-1. When the data sources change, the UI elements bound to those data sources update automatically to reflect the changes. The data can come from different types of sources, and the target can be just about any UI element, including standard Silverlight controls.

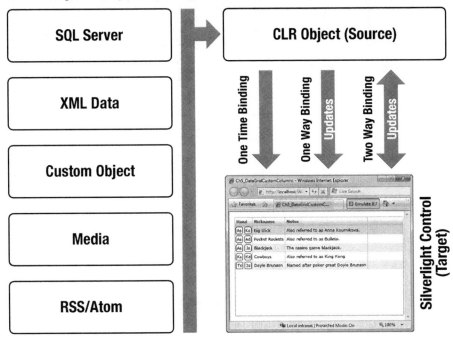

Figure 5-1. Data binding in Silverlight

Data binding simplifies application development. Because changes are reflected automatically, you do not need to manually update the UI elements. Also, by using data binding, you are able to separate the UI from the data in your application, which allows for a cleaner UI and easier maintenance.

The Binding Class

Data binding in Silverlight is accomplished by using the Binding class. The Binding class has two components—the source and target—and a property that defines the way the two are bound, called the *binding mode*. The source is the data that is to be bound, the target is a property of the control that the data is to be bound to, and the mode defines how the data is passed between the source and the target (one-way, one-time, or two-way). You'll see how this works in the upcoming exercise.

To define the binding of a control's property, you use XAML markup extensions, such as {Binding *<path>*}. For example, to bind the Text property of a TextBox to a data source's FirstName element, you use the following XAML:

```
<TextBox Text="{Binding FirstName }"  />
```

Try It Out: Simple Data Binding in Silverlight

To help explain data binding in Silverlight, let's build a very simple application. The application will include a Book object that contains two properties: Title and ISBN. These properties will be bound to two TextBox controls. Figure 5-2 shows the end result of the example.

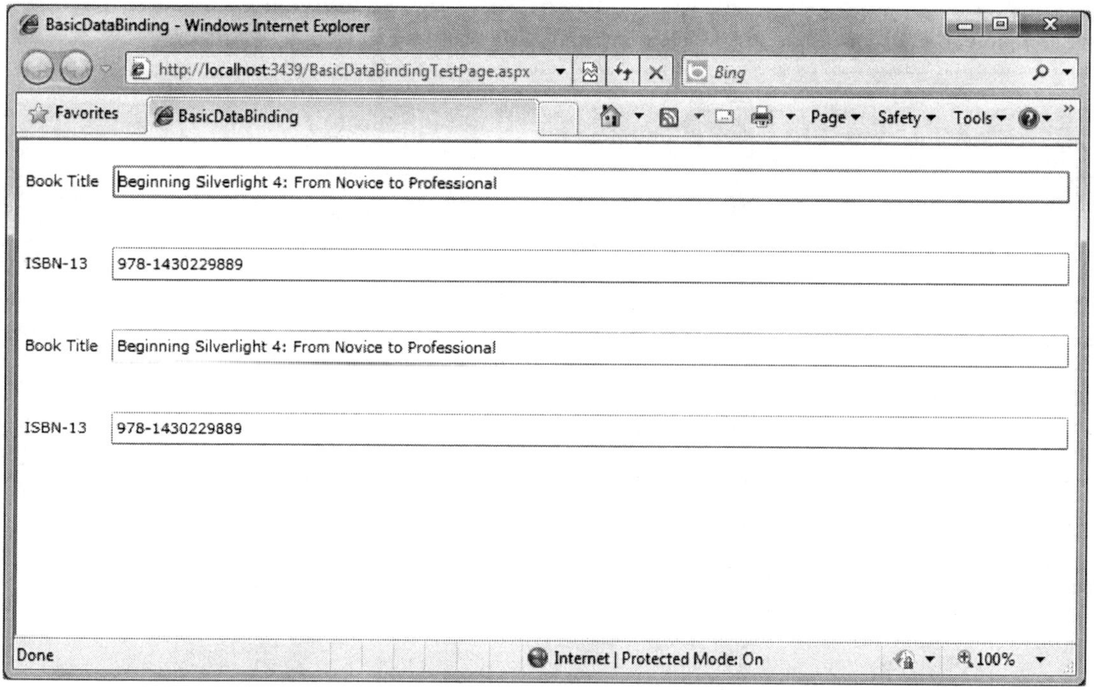

Figure 5-2. Simple data-binding example

1. Create a new Silverlight application in Visual Studio 2010. Name the project BasicDataBinding, and allow Visual Studio to create a Web Application project to host your application.

2. Edit the MainPage.xaml file to define two columns and six grid rows. Place a TextBlock in each row in column 1 and a TextBox in each row in column 2. Also, add some margins and some alignment assignments to improve the layout. The code for the page follows:

```
<Grid x:Name="LayoutRoot" Background="White">

    <Grid.ColumnDefinitions>
        <ColumnDefinition Width="Auto" />
        <ColumnDefinition />
    </Grid.ColumnDefinitions>
    <Grid.RowDefinitions>
        <RowDefinition />
        <RowDefinition />
        <RowDefinition />
        <RowDefinition />
        <RowDefinition />
        <RowDefinition />
    </Grid.RowDefinitions>

    <TextBlock Text="Book Title"
        VerticalAlignment="Center"
        Margin="5" />
    <TextBlock Text="ISBN-13"
        VerticalAlignment="Center"
        Margin="5"
        Grid.Row="1" />

    <TextBox Text="{Binding Title}"
        Height="24"
        Margin="5"
        Grid.Column="1" />
    <TextBox Text="{Binding ISBN}"
        Height="24"
        Margin="5"
        Grid.Column="1" Grid.Row="1" />

    <TextBlock Text="Book Title"
        VerticalAlignment="Center"
        Margin="5"
        Grid.Row="2" />
    <TextBlock Text="ISBN-13"
        VerticalAlignment="Center"
        Margin="5"
        Grid.Row="3" />
```

```xml
<TextBox Text="{Binding Title}"
    Height="24"
    Margin="5"
    Grid.Column="1" Grid.Row="2" />
<TextBox Text="{Binding ISBN}"
    Height="24"
    Margin="5"
    Grid.Column="1" Grid.Row="3" />

</Grid>
```

3. Next, edit the code behind, MainPage.xaml.cs. Add a Loaded event handler for the application, which will fire when the application is loaded by the client. This is accomplished with the following source code:

```csharp
public partial class MainPage : UserControl
{
    public MainPage()
    {
        InitializeComponent();
        this.Loaded += new RoutedEventHandler(Page_Loaded);
    }

    void Page_Loaded(object sender, RoutedEventArgs e)
    {

    }
}
```

4. Now you need to add a class to define a Book object. Below the MainPage class, add the following class definition:

```csharp
namespace BasicDataBinding
{
    public partial class MainPage : UserControl
    {
        public MainPage()
        {
            InitializeComponent();
            this.Loaded += new RoutedEventHandler(Page_Loaded);
        }

        void Page_Loaded(object sender, RoutedEventArgs e)
        {

        }
    }

    public class Book
    {
        public string Title { get; set; }
```

```
    public string ISBN { get; set; }
  }
}
```

5. Now that you have Book defined, you need to create an instance of Book and set it to the LayoutRoot's DataContext, as follows:

```
void Page_Loaded(object sender, RoutedEventArgs e)
{
    Book b = new Book()
    {
        Title = "Beginning Silverlight: From Novice to Professional",
        ISBN = "978-1430229889"
    };

    this.LayoutRoot.DataContext = b;
}
```

6. When you set up binding definitions for different controls, the controls do not know where they are going to get their data. The DataContext property sets the data context for a control that is participating in data binding. The DataContext property can be set directly on the control. If a given control does not have a DataContext property specified, it will look to its parent for its data context. The nice thing about this model is that if you look in the preceding XAML for the page, you will see little indication of where the controls are getting their data. This provides an extreme level of code separation, allowing designers to design XAML UIs and developers to work alongside the designers, defining the specifics of how the controls are bound to their data sources.

7. At this point, you can go ahead and start debugging the application. If all goes well, you will see the four text boxes populated with the data from the Book's instance. (See Figure 5-2.)

8. With the application running, change the book title in the first text box to just "Beginning Silverlight," by removing the "From Novice to Professional."

9. You might expect that, because the third text box is bound to the same data, it will automatically update to reflect this change. However, a couple of things need to be done to get this type of two-way binding to work.

10. One problem is that, currently, the Book class does not support notifying bound clients of changes to its properties. In other words, when a property changes in Book, the class will not notify the TextBox instances that are bound to the class of the change. You could take care of this by creating a change event for each property. This is far from ideal; fortunately, there is an interface that a class can implement that handles this for you. This interface is known as INotifyPropertyChanged. Let's use it.

11. Modify the Book class definition to inherit from INotifyPropertyChanged. Notice that when you inherit from INotifyPropertyChanged, you need to add using System.ComponentModel. Luckily, Visual Studio will help you with this, as shown in Figure 5-3.

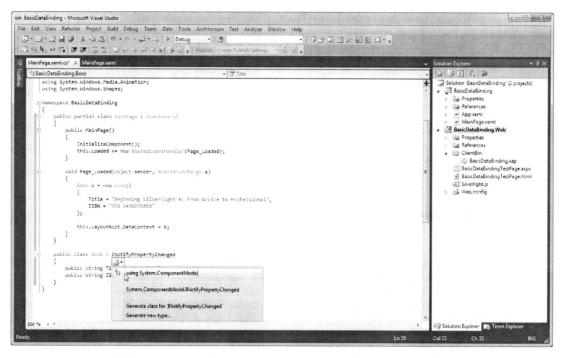

Figure 5-3. *Visual Studio assists when you need to add the System.ComponentModel namespace.*

12. Next, you can let Visual Studio do some more work for you. After adding the
`using System.ComponentModel` statement, right-click `INotifyPropertyChanged`
and select Implement Interface ➤ Implement Interface from the pop-up
menu, as shown in Figure 5-4.

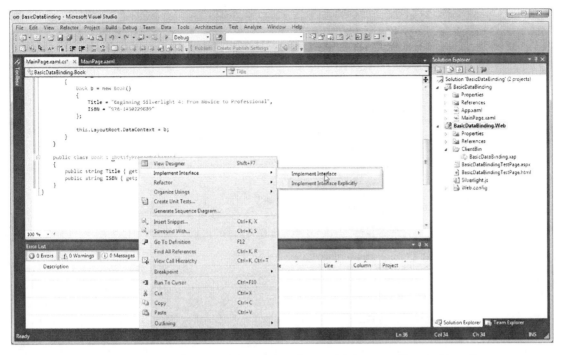

Figure 5-4. *Visual Studio also assists in implementing the INotifiyPropertyChanged interface.*

13. Now Visual Studio has added a new public event to your class:

```
public class Book : INotifyPropertyChanged
{
    public string Title { get; set; }
    public string ISBN { get; set; }

    public event PropertyChangedEventHandler PropertyChanged;
}
```

14. Next, you need to create a convenience method that will fire the
PropertyChanged event. Call it FirePropertyChanged, as shown in the following
code:

```
public class Book : INotifyPropertyChanged
{
    public string Title { get; set; }
    public string ISBN { get; set; }

    public event PropertyChangedEventHandler PropertyChanged;

    void FirePropertyChanged(string property)
    {
        if (PropertyChanged != null)
```

```
        {
            PropertyChanged(this,
                new PropertyChangedEventArgs(property));
        }
    }
}
```

15. Now you need to extend the simplified properties by adding private members and full get/set definitions to define the get and set operations, as shown in the following code. The get is just like a normal get operation, where you simply return the internal member value. For the set, you first set the internal member value, and then call the FirePropertyChanged method, passing it the name of the property.

```
public class Book : INotifyPropertyChanged
{
    private string _title;
    private string _isbn;

    public string Title
    {
        get
        {
            return _title;
        }
        set
        {
            _title = value;
            FirePropertyChanged("Title");
        }
    }

    public string ISBN
    {
        get
        {
            return _isbn;
        }
        set
        {
            _isbn = value;
            FirePropertyChanged("ISBN");
        }
    }

    public event PropertyChangedEventHandler PropertyChanged;
```

```
    void FirePropertyChanged(string property)
    {
        if (PropertyChanged != null)
        {
            PropertyChanged(this,
                new PropertyChangedEventArgs(property));
        }
    }
}
```

16. With this completed, your class is set up to notify bound clients of changes to the Title and ISBN properties. But you still need to take one more step. By default, when you bind a source to a target, the BindingMode is set to OneWay binding, which means that the source will send the data to the target, but the target will not send data changes back to the source. To get the target to update the source, you need to implement two-way (TwoWay) binding.

Note Earlier, I mentioned that there are three options for BindingMode. The third option is OneTime binding. In this mode, the values are sent to the target control property when the object is set to the DataContext. However, the values of the target property are not updated when the source value changes.

---

17. To change to two-way binding, add the Mode=TwoWay parameter when defining the {Binding} on a control, as follows:

```
<TextBlock Text="Book Title"
    VerticalAlignment="Center"
    Margin="5" />
<TextBlock Text="ISBN-13"
    VerticalAlignment="Center"
    Margin="5"
    Grid.Row="1" />

<TextBox Text="{Binding Title, Mode=TwoWay}"
    Height="24"
    Margin="5"
    Grid.Column="1" />
<TextBox Text="{Binding ISBN, Mode=TwoWay}"
    Height="24"
    Margin="5"
    Grid.Column="1" Grid.Row="1" />

<TextBlock Text="Book Title"
    VerticalAlignment="Center"
    Margin="5"
    Grid.Row="2" />
<TextBlock Text="ISBN-13"
    VerticalAlignment="Center"
```

```
                    Margin="5"
                    Grid.Row="3" />

            <TextBox Text="{Binding Title, Mode=TwoWay}"
                    Height="24"
                    Margin="5"
                    Grid.Column="1" Grid.Row="2" />
            <TextBox Text="{Binding ISBN, Mode=TwoWay}"
                    Height="24"
                    Margin="5"
                    Grid.Column="1" Grid.Row="3" />
```

18. Rebuild and run your application. Update any of the fields, and leave the focus on the control. You'll see that the two-way binding is triggered, and the corresponding field is also updated, as shown in Figure 5-5.

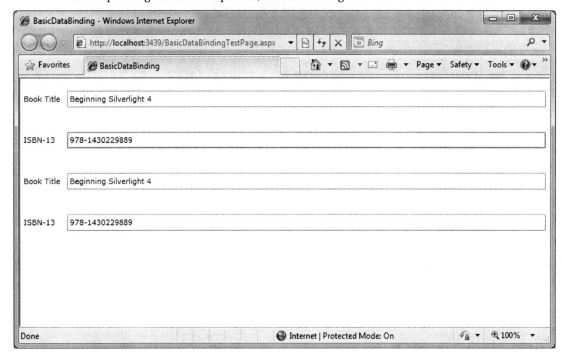

Figure 5-5. *Two-way binding in action*

Congratulations! You have just created a Silverlight application that allows for two-way data binding. We will now move on to look at data binding lists of data to the two list controls provided in Silverlight: DataGrid and ListBox.

Element-to-Element Binding

In addition to binding elements to data, you can bind them directly to other elements, which can significantly improve the readability and efficiency of your code. The syntax for binding to an element is very similar to binding to a data item—the only difference is that in the binding an ElementName is specified, which is very much like setting the ItemsSource to the Element. As an example, if you wanted to bind the IsEnabled property of a control to a check box's IsChecked property, assuming the check box is named EnableButton, the binding syntax would be the following:

```
IsEnabled="{Binding IsChecked, Mode=OneWay, ElementName=EnableButton}"
```

Notice that the binding is the same as it would be when binding to a data source, except that we have added the ElementName=EnableButton. Let's try this out in an exercise.

Try It Out: Element-to-Element Binding

To help explain element-to-element binding in Silverlight, let's build a simple application. The application will include a button and a check box. When the check box is selected, the button is enabled, when the check box is deselected, the button is disabled. Let's get started.

1. Create a new Silverlight application in Visual Studio 2010. Name the project *ElementBinding*, and allow Visual Studio to create a Web Application project to host your application.

2. Edit the MainPage.xaml file to add a StackPanel to the root Grid. Place a ToggleButton and CheckBox named EnableButton within that StackPanel so that the ToggleButton appears above the CheckBox. Add a margin of 20 on the StackPanel and 5 on the ToggleButton and CheckBox to add some spacing between the controls. The code for the page follows:

```
<Grid x:Name="LayoutRoot" Background="White">
    <StackPanel Margin="20">

        <ToggleButton Margin="5" Content="Click to Toggle" />

        <CheckBox
            x:Name="EnableButton" IsChecked="true"
            Margin="5" Content="Enable Button" />

    </StackPanel>
</Grid>
```

3. Next, you need to bind the ToggleButton's IsEnabled property to the CheckBox's IsChecked property. You do this with one-way binding as described earlier in this chapter. Set the ElementName to EnableButton, which is the name you gave to your CheckBox. The updated source code should now look like the following:

```
<Grid x:Name="LayoutRoot" Background="White">
    <StackPanel Margin="20">

        <ToggleButton
            Margin="5" Content="Click to Toggle"
```

```
        IsEnabled="{Binding IsChecked, Mode=OneWay,

        ElementName=EnableButton}" />

    <CheckBox
        x:Name="EnableButton" IsChecked="true"
        Margin="5" Content="Enable Button" />

    </StackPanel>
</Grid>
```

4. That is it! No coding is required for this demo. Run the sample, and you will see that the ToggleButton is enabled, as shown in Figure 5-6.

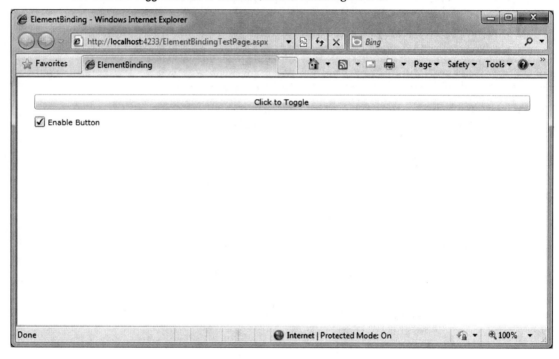

Figure 5-6. *Element binding example with ToggleButton enabled*

5. Now deselect the Enable Button check box, and you will see that the ToggleButton is no longer enabled, as shown in Figure 5-7.

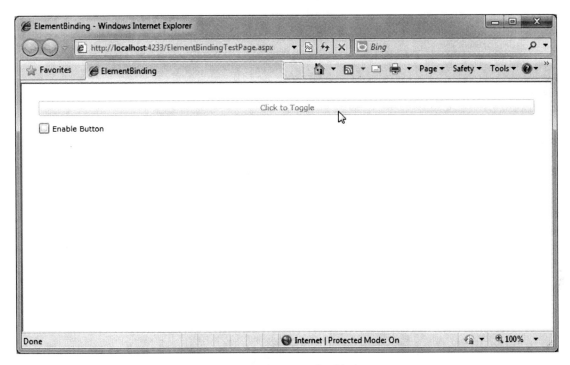

***Figure 5-7.** Element binding example with ToggleButton disabled*

The DataGrid Control

The data grid type of control has been around for ages and has been the primary choice for developers who need to display large amounts of data. The DataGrid control provided by Silverlight is not just a standard data grid, however. It contains a great deal of rich user functionality that, in the past, has been present only in third-party data grid components. For example, the Silverlight DataGrid handles resizing and reordering of grid columns.

Figure 5-8 shows an example of a simple DataGrid, where the columns were automatically generated. Notice how the column titled Male is a check box. The DataGrid control has built-in intelligence to automatically show Boolean data types as check-box cells.

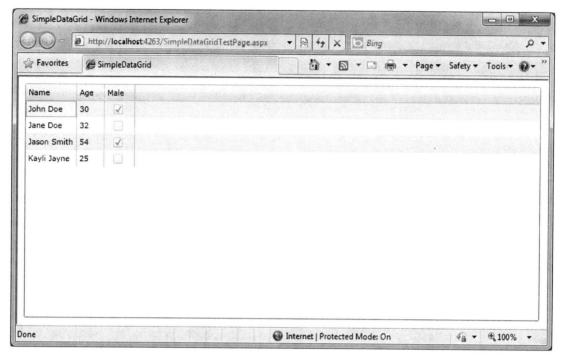

Figure 5-8. *A simple DataGrid example*

Try It Out: Building a Simple DataGrid

Let's run through a simple DataGrid example:

1.   Create a new Silverlight application in Visual Studio 2010. Name the project *SimpleDataGrid*, and have Visual Studio create a hosting web application for you.

2.   Add the DataGrid to your application. To do this, simply add the DataGrid to the root Grid in your XAML, and set the Margin property to 10 to get some spacing around the grid. In addition, give the DataGrid the name grid. Note that, by default, the Grid's AutoGenerateColumns property is set to true. If you were going to define the columns manually, you would want to set this property to false. However, because you want the grid to create the columns automatically, you can simply omit the property. The DataGrid definition follows:

```
<Grid x:Name="LayoutRoot" Background="White">
    <sdk:DataGrid Name="grid" Margin="10" />
</Grid>
```

> **Note** Why use `<sdk:DataGrid>`? As discussed in Chapter 4, the `DataGrid` is contained in an assembly called `System.Windows.Controls.Data`, which is not added to Silverlight applications by default. This way, if your application does not need any of the extended controls, the file size of your Silverlight application can be smaller. However, to add a `DataGrid` to your application, you need to reference the new assembly and add an `xmlns` reference to the assembly in the `UserControl` definition:
>
> `xmlns:sdk=http://schemas.microsoft.com/winfx/2006/xaml/presentation/sdk`
>
> As you might expect by now, Visual Studio can do all the work for you. To use this functionality in Visual Studio, drag the `DataGrid` control from the Toolbox to add it to your application (or simply double-click on the `DataGrid` in the Toolbox). Visual Studio will add a new `xmlns` reference in the `UserControl` at the top of the `.xaml` page called data.

3. Next, build the class that will be bound to the `DataGrid`. Call the class `GridData` for simplicity, and give it three properties: `Name` (`string`), `Age` (`int`), and `Male` (Boolean). Also for simplicity, create a static method that will return an `ObservableCollection` (which requires adding a `using` clause for `System.Collections.ObjectModel`) containing some sample data that will be bound to the grid. In addition, define the class directly in the `MainPage.xaml.cs` file. This is not really a good idea in the real world, but for the sake of an example, it will work just fine. Ideally, you want to define your classes in separate files or even in completely separate projects and assemblies. The code for the `GridData` class follows:

```
namespace SimpleDataGrid
{
    public partial class MainPage : UserControl
    {
        public MainPage()
        {
            InitializeComponent();
        }
    }

    public class GridData
    {
        public string Name { get; set; }
        public int Age { get; set; }
        public bool Male { get; set; }

        public static ObservableCollection<GridData> GetData()
        {
            ObservableCollection<GridData> data =
                new ObservableCollection<GridData>();
```

```
            data.Add(new GridData()
            {
                Name = "John Doe",
                Age = 30,
                Male = true
            });

            data.Add(new GridData()
            {
                Name = "Jane Doe",
                Age = 32,
                Male = false
            });

            data.Add(new GridData()
            {
                Name = "Jason Smith",
                Age = 54,
                Male = true
            });

            data.Add(new GridData()
            {
                Name = "Kayli Jayne",
                Age = 25,
                Male = false
            });

            return data;
        }
    }
}
```

■ **Note** When you are binding a collection of data to a DataGrid or ListBox, you might be tempted to use the List generic class. The problem with using the List class is that it does not have built-in change notifications for the collection. To bind a DataGrid and ListBox to dynamic data that will be updated, you should use the ObservableCollection generic class. The ObservableCollection class represents a collection of dynamic data that provides built-in notification when items in the collection are added, removed, or refreshed.

---

4. Now that you have the XAML and the class defined, you can wire them up. To do this, first create an event handler for the Loaded event of the page, as follows:

```
public partial class MainPage : UserControl
{
    public MainPage()
```

```
    {
        InitializeComponent();
        this.Loaded += new RoutedEventHandler(Page_Loaded);
    }

    void Page_Loaded(object sender, RoutedEventArgs e)
    {

    }
}
```

5. When the page is loaded, you want to call GetData() from the GridData class and bind that to the DataGrid's ItemsSource property, as follows:

```
public partial class MainPage : UserControl
{
    public MainPage()
    {
        InitializeComponent();
        this.Loaded += new RoutedEventHandler(Page_Loaded);
    }

    void Page_Loaded(object sender, RoutedEventArgs e)
    {
        this.grid.ItemsSource = GridData.GetData();
    }
}
```

6. Build and run the application. If all is well, you should see the DataGrid displayed. (See Figure 5-8.)

Let's take a few moments and play around with this DataGrid to explore some of its features. First of all, if you click any of the column headers, you will notice that sorting is automatically available, as shown in Figure 5-9.

Next, if you place your cursor at the edge of one of the columns, you can use the mouse to click and drag the column's edge to resize the column, as shown in Figure 5-10. Again, this functionality is provided for free with the DataGrid's rich client-side functionality.

Finally, if you click and hold the mouse on one of the column headers, and then drag it left or right to another column header's edge, you will see the column header move and a dark gray border appear between the columns. For instance, click and drag the Male column to the left of the Age column, as shown in Figure 5-11. When a dark-gray border shows up between the two columns, release the mouse, and you will see that the Male column now appears to the left of the Age column in the DataGrid.

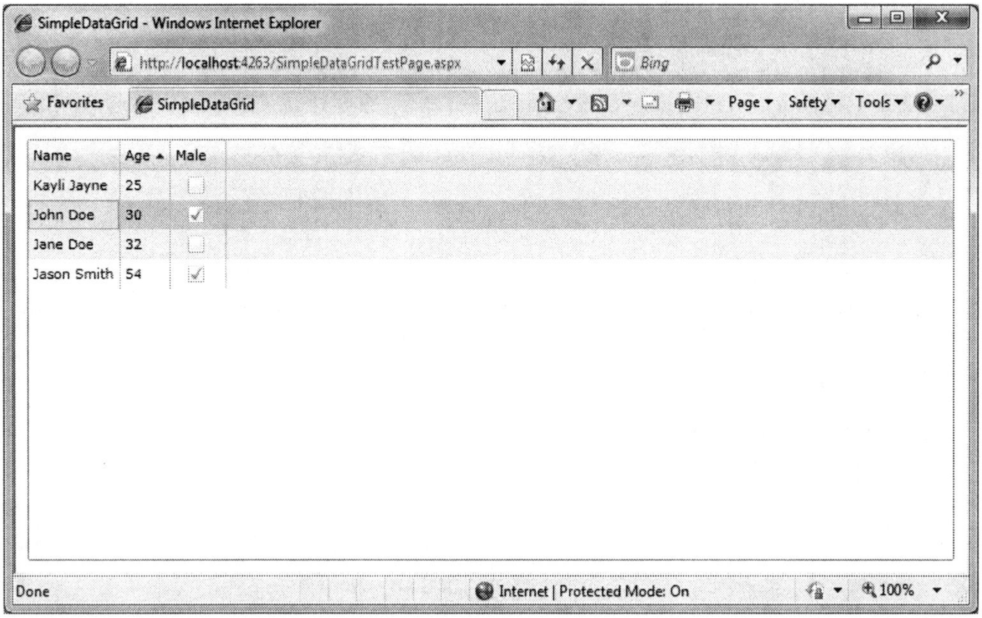

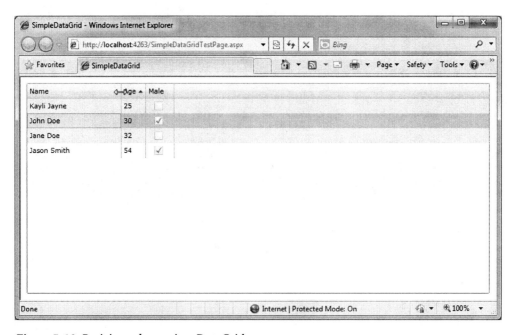

Figure 5-9. Sorting in the DataGrid

Figure 5-10. Resizing columns in a DataGrid

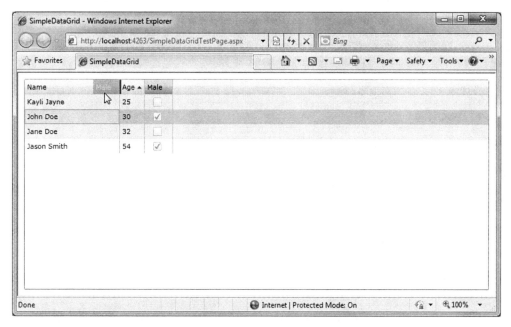

Figure 5-11. Column reordering in action

You'll agree that this is pretty nice out-of-the-box functionality for simply defining a DataGrid with this code:

```
<sdk:DataGrid x:Name="grid" Margin="10" />
```

Now that you have implemented a simple DataGrid example, let's explore some of the additional options available.

The Columns Collection

In the previous example, you allowed the DataGrid to automatically generate columns based on the data to which it was bound. This is not a new concept—it has been around in data grid components since the initial release of ASP.NET. But what if you want to have some additional control over the columns that are created in your DataGrid? What if you want to add a column that contains some more complex information, such as an image? You can do this by first setting the AutoGenerateColumns property on the grid to false. Then you need to generate the columns manually.

Columns are defined in a DataGrid using the Columns collection. The following is an example of setting the Columns collection in XAML. Notice that it sets the AutogenerateColumns property to False. If you neglect to do this, you will get all of the autogenerated columns in addition to the columns you define within the Columns collection.

```
<sdk:DataGrid x:Name="grid" Margin="10" AutoGenerateColumns="False">
    <sdk:DataGrid.Columns>

    </sdk:DataGrid.Columns>
</sdk:DataGrid>
```

You can place three types of columns within a Columns collection: a text column (DataGridTextColumn), a check-box column (DataGridCheckBoxColumn), and a template column (DataGridTemplateColumn). All of the column types inherit from type DataGridColumn. A number of notable properties apply to all three column types, as shown in Table 5-1.

Table 5-1. DataGridColumn Properties

Property	Description
CanUserReorder	Turns on and off the ability for the user to drag columns to reorder them
CanUserResize	Turns on or off the ability for the user to resize the column's width with the mouse
DisplayIndex	Determines the order in which the column appears in the DataGrid
Header	Defines the content of the column's header
IsReadOnly	Determines if the column can be edited by the user
MaxWidth	Sets the maximum column width in pixels
MinWidth	Sets the minimum column width in pixels
Visibility	Determines whether or not the column will be visible to the user
Width	Sets the width of the column, or can be set to automatic sizing mode

DataGridTextColumn

The DataGridTextColumn defines a column in your grid for plain text. This is the equivalent to BoundColumn in the ASP.NET DataGrid. The primary properties that can be set for a DataGridTextColumn are the Header, which defines the text that will be displayed in the columns header, and the DisplayMemberBinding property, which defines the property in the data source bound to the column.

The following example defines a text column with the header Name and is bound to the data source's Name property:

```
<sdk:DataGrid x:Name="grid" Margin="10" AutoGenerateColumns="False">
    <sdk:DataGrid.Columns>
        <sdk:DataGridTextColumn
                Header="Name"
                Binding="{Binding Name}" />
        </sdk:DataGrid.Columns>
</sdk:DataGrid>
```

DataGridCheckBoxColumn

As you would expect, the `DataGridCheckBoxColumn` contains a check box. If you have data that you want to display as a check box in your grid, this is the control to use. Here is an example of the `DataGridCheckBoxColumn` that contains the header `Male?` and is bound to the data source's `Male` property:

```
<sdk:DataGrid x:Name="grid" Margin="10" AutoGenerateColumns="False">
    <sdk:DataGrid.Columns>
        <sdk:DataGridCheckBoxColumn
                Header="Male?"
                Binding="{Binding Male}" />
        </sdk:DataGrid.Columns>
</sdk:DataGrid>
```

DataGridTemplateColumn

If you want data in your grid column that is not plain text and is not a check box, the `DataGridTemplateColumn` provides a way for you to define the content for your column. The `DataGridTemplateColumn` contains a `CellTemplate` and `CellEditingTemplate`, which determine what content is displayed, depending on whether the grid is in normal view mode or in editing mode.

Note that while you get features such as automatic sorting in the other types of `DataGrid` columns, that is not true of the `DataGridTemplateColumn`. These columns will need to have additional logic in place to allow for sorting.

Let's consider an example that has two fields: `FirstName` and `LastName`. Suppose that when you are in normal view mode, you want the data to be displayed side by side in `TextBlock` controls. However, when the user is editing the column, you want to display two `TextBox` controls that allow the user to edit the `FirstName` and `LastName` columns independently.

```
<sdk:DataGridTemplateColumn Header="Name">
    <sdk:DataGridTemplateColumn.CellTemplate>
        <DataTemplate>
            <StackPanel Orientation="Horizontal">
                <TextBlock Padding="5,0,5,0"
                    Text="{Binding FirstName}"/>
                <TextBlock Text="{Binding LastName}"/>
            </StackPanel>
        </DataTemplate>
    </sdk:DataGridTemplateColumn.CellTemplate>
    <sdk:DataGridTemplateColumn.CellEditingTemplate>
        <DataTemplate>
            <StackPanel Orientation="Horizontal">
                <TextBox Padding="5,0,5,0"
                    Text="{Binding FirstName}"/>
                <TextBox Text="{Binding LastName}"/>
            </StackPanel>
        </DataTemplate>
    </sdk:DataGridTemplateColumn.CellEditingTemplate>
</sdk:DataGridTemplateColumn>
```

Now that we have covered the basics of manually defining the grids in a `DataGrid`, let's try it out.

Try It Out: Building a DataGrid with Custom Columns

I thought it would be fun to build a DataGrid that contains a list of starting hands in poker. If you have ever watched poker on TV, you most likely heard the players refer to things like "pocket rockets" and "cowboys." These are simply nicknames they have given to starting hands. The DataGrid you are going to build in this example will look like Figure 5-12.

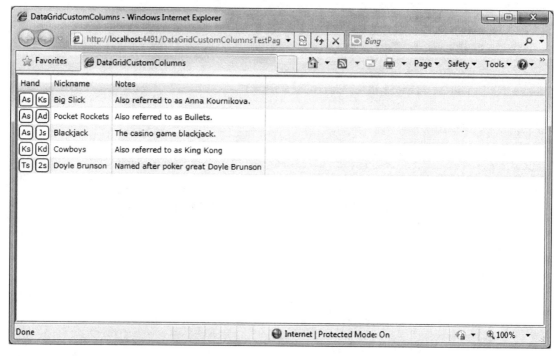

Figure 5-12. DataGrid with custom columns

1. Create a new Silverlight application called *DataGridCustomColumns*. Allow Visual Studio to create a web site project to host the application.

2. After the project is loaded, right-click the DataGridCustomColumns project and select Add New Item. In the Add New Item dialog box, select Code File for the template, and name the class StartingHands.cs, as shown in Figure 5-13. Click the Add button to add the class to the project.

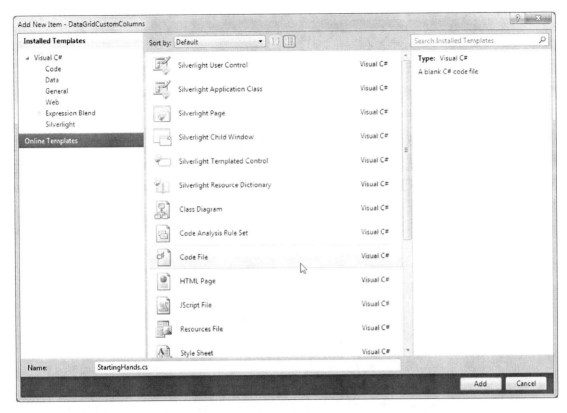

Figure 5-13. Adding a new class to the Silverlight project

3. Now define the StartingHands class. The class will contain four properties: Nickname (string), Notes (string), Card1 (string), and Card2 (string). Also, create a static method in the class called GetHands(), which returns an ObservableCollection of StartingHands instances. The code follows:

```csharp
using System;
using System.Net;
using System.Windows;
using System.Windows.Controls;
using System.Windows.Documents;
using System.Windows.Ink;
using System.Windows.Input;
using System.Windows.Media;
using System.Windows.Media.Animation;
using System.Windows.Shapes;
using System.Collections.ObjectModel;

namespace DataGridCustomColumns
{
    public class StartingHands
```

```
{
    public string Nickname { get; set; }
    public string Notes { get; set; }
    public string Card1 { get; set; }
    public string Card2 { get; set; }

    public static ObservableCollection<StartingHands> GetHands()
    {
        ObservableCollection<StartingHands> hands =
        new ObservableCollection<StartingHands>();

        hands.Add(
            new StartingHands()
            {
                Nickname = "Big Slick",
                Notes = "Also referred to as Anna Kournikova.",
                Card1 = "As",
                Card2 = "Ks"
            });

        hands.Add(
        new StartingHands()
        {
            Nickname = "Pocket Rockets",
            Notes = "Also referred to as Bullets.",
            Card1 = "As",
            Card2 = "Ad"
        });

        hands.Add(
            new StartingHands()
            {
                Nickname = "Blackjack",
                Notes = "The casino game blackjack.",
                Card1 = "As",
                Card2 = "Js"
            });

        hands.Add(
            new StartingHands()
            {
                Nickname = "Cowboys",
                Notes = "Also referred to as King Kong",
                Card1 = "Ks",
                Card2 = "Kd"
            });

        hands.Add(
            new StartingHands()
            {
                Nickname = "Doyle Brunson",
```

```
                    Notes = "Named after poker great Doyle Brunson",
                    Card1 = "Ts",
                    Card2 = "2s"
              });


          return hands;
        }
    }
}
```

4. Now that the class is built, in the MainPage.xaml file, add a DataGrid named grdData to the root Grid by double-clicking the DataGrid control in the Toolbox. Add a 15-pixel margin around the DataGrid for some spacing, and set the AutoGenerateColumns property to False. The code follows:

```
<Grid x:Name="LayoutRoot" Background="White">
    <sdk:DataGrid AutoGenerateColumns="False" Name="grdData" />
</Grid>
```

5. Next, define the columns in the DataGrid. To do this, add the DataGrid.Columns collection, as follows:

```
<Grid x:Name="LayoutRoot" Background="White">
    <sdk:DataGrid AutoGenerateColumns="False" Name="grdData">
        <sdk:DataGrid.Columns>

        </sdk:DataGrid.Columns>
    </sdk:DataGrid>
</Grid>
```

6. Referring back to Figure 5-12, the first column in the Grid contains the two cards in the hand. To build this, you use a DataGridTemplateColumn. Within the DataGridTemplateColumn, add a CellTemplate containing a Grid with two columns, each containing a Border, Rectangle, and TextBlock, which will overlap each other. Bind the two TextBlock controls to the Card1 and Card2 properties from the data source. Enter the following code:

```
<sdk:DataGrid AutoGenerateColumns="False" Name="grdData">
    <sdk:DataGrid.Columns>
        <sdk:DataGridTemplateColumn Header="Hand">
            <sdk:DataGridTemplateColumn.CellTemplate>
                <DataTemplate>
                    <Grid>
                        <Grid.ColumnDefinitions>
                            <ColumnDefinition />
                            <ColumnDefinition />
                        </Grid.ColumnDefinitions>
                        <Border
                            Margin="2" CornerRadius="4"
                            BorderBrush="Black" BorderThickness="1" />
                        <Rectangle
```

```
                        Margin="4" Fill="White" Grid.Column="0" />
                    <Border
                        Margin="2" CornerRadius="4" BorderBrush="Black"
                        BorderThickness="1" Grid.Column="1" />
                    <Rectangle
                        Margin="4" Fill="White" Grid.Column="1" />
                    <TextBlock
                        Text="{Binding Card1}" HorizontalAlignment="Center"
                        VerticalAlignment="Center" Grid.Column="0" />
                    <TextBlock
                        Text="{Binding Card2}" HorizontalAlignment="Center"
                        VerticalAlignment="Center" Grid.Column="1" />
                </Grid>
            </DataTemplate>
        </sdk:DataGridTemplateColumn.CellTemplate>
    </sdk:DataGridTemplateColumn>
    </sdk:DataGrid.Columns>
</sdk:DataGrid>
```

7. Again, referring back to Figure 5-12, the next two columns contain the
   nickname of the starting hand and notes about the starting hand. To
   implement this, use two DataGridTextColumn columns. Set the Headers of the
   columns to Nickname and Notes accordingly:

```
<sdk:DataGrid AutoGenerateColumns="False" Name="grdData">
    <sdk:DataGrid.Columns>
        <sdk:DataGridTemplateColumn Header="Hand">
            <sdk:DataGridTemplateColumn.CellTemplate>
                <DataTemplate>
                    <Grid>
                        <Grid.ColumnDefinitions>
                            <ColumnDefinition />
                            <ColumnDefinition />
                        </Grid.ColumnDefinitions>
                        <Border
                            Margin="2" CornerRadius="4"
                            BorderBrush="Black" BorderThickness="1" />
                        <Rectangle
                            Margin="4" Fill="White" Grid.Column="0" />
                        <Border
                            Margin="2" CornerRadius="4" BorderBrush="Black"
                            BorderThickness="1" Grid.Column="1" />
                        <Rectangle
                            Margin="4" Fill="White" Grid.Column="1" />
                        <TextBlock
                            Text="{Binding Card1}" HorizontalAlignment="Center"
                            VerticalAlignment="Center" Grid.Column="0" />
                        <TextBlock
                            Text="{Binding Card2}" HorizontalAlignment="Center"
                            VerticalAlignment="Center" Grid.Column="1" />
                    </Grid>
                </DataTemplate>
```

```
                </sdk:DataGridTemplateColumn.CellTemplate>
            </sdk:DataGridTemplateColumn>
            <sdk:DataGridTextColumn
                Header="Nickname"
                Binding="{Binding Nickname}" />
            <sdk:DataGridTextColumn
                Header="Notes"
                Binding="{Binding Notes}" />
        </sdk:DataGrid.Columns>
    </sdk:DataGrid>
```

8. Finally, wire up the controls to the data source. To do this, navigate to the MainPage.xaml.cs file and add an event handler to the Page Loaded event. Within that Loaded event, simply set the DataGrid's ItemsSource property equal to the return value of the StartingHands.GetHands() static method. Here's the code:

```
public partial class MainPage : UserControl
{
    public MainPage()
    {
        InitializeComponent();
        this.Loaded += new RoutedEventHandler(Page_Loaded);
    }

    void Page_Loaded(object sender, RoutedEventArgs e)
    {
        this.grdData.ItemsSource = StartingHands.GetHands();
    }
}
```

9. Compile and run your application. If all goes well, your application should appear, as shown earlier in Figure 5-12.

This completes our DataGrid with custom columns example. Naturally, in a real-world application, you would be getting the data for these hands from an external data source, such as a web service or an XML file. We will be looking at that in Chapter 6. Now, let's take a look at the ListBox control.

The ListBox Control

In the past, the list-box type of control has been considered one of the common controls in programming—no more special than a drop-down list. However, in Silverlight, this has all changed. The ListBox is perhaps one of the most flexible controls used to display lists of data. In fact, referring back to ASP.NET controls, the Silverlight ListBox is more a cousin to the DataList control than the ASP.NET ListBox control. Let's take a peek at this powerful control.

Default and Custom ListBox Items

If you wire up the ListBox to your Person data from the earlier DataGrid example, you will see that, by default, the ListBox really is just a standard ListBox:

```
<ListBox Margin="10" x:Name="list" DisplayMemberPath="Name" />
```

One additional property you might have noticed in this `ListBox` definition is `DisplayMemberPath`. If you are defining a simple text-based `ListBox`, the `ListBox` needs to know which data member to display. Because the `Person` class contains three properties (`Name`, `Age`, and `Male`), you need to tell it that you want the `Name` to be displayed. Figure 5-14 shows the results.

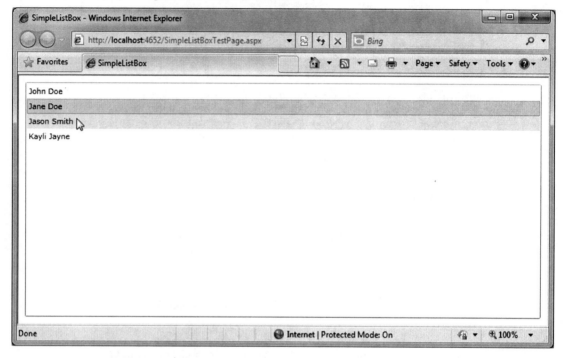

Figure 5-14. *A simple default ListBox*

However, the `ListBox` control can contain much more than plain text. In fact, if you define a custom `ItemTemplate` for the `ListBox`, you can present the items in a more interesting way. Here's an example using the same `Person` data:

```
<ListBox Margin="10" x:Name="list">
    <ListBox.ItemTemplate>
        <DataTemplate>
            <StackPanel Margin="5" Orientation="Vertical">
                <TextBlock
                    FontSize="17"
                    FontWeight="Bold"
                    Text="{Binding Name}" />
                <StackPanel Margin="5,0,0,0" Orientation="Horizontal">
                    <TextBlock Text="Age: " />
                    <TextBlock Text="{Binding Age}" />
                    <TextBlock Text=", Male: " />
                    <TextBlock Text="{Binding Male}" />
                </StackPanel>
```

```
            </StackPanel>
          </DataTemplate>
        </ListBox.ItemTemplate>
</ListBox>
```

Figure 5-15 shows how this custom ListBox appears in a browser.

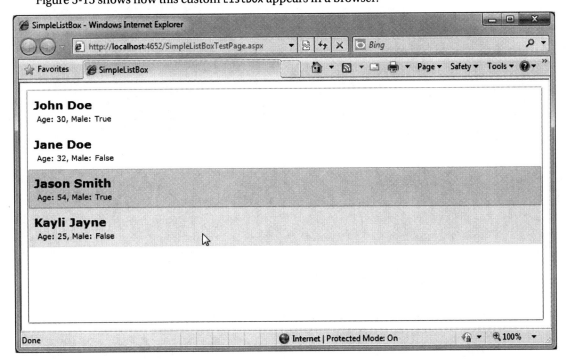

Figure 5-15. *A customized ListBox example*

Try It Out: Building a ListBox with Custom Content

Let's take the same data that displayed poker starting hands from the previous exercise and see what type of cool ListBox you can build with it. Figure 5-16 shows the custom ListBox you'll create in this exercise.

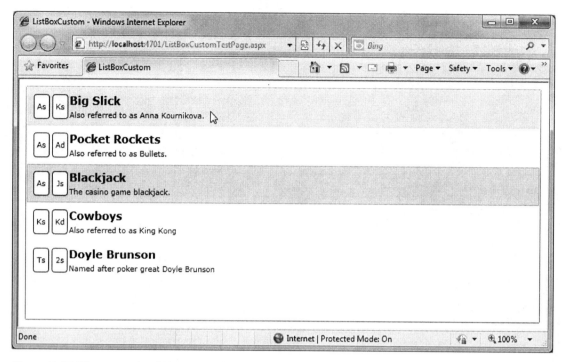

Figure 5-16. The customized ListBox application

1. Start out by creating a new Silverlight application called `ListBoxCustom,` and allow Visual Studio to create a hosting web site.

2. You will use the same class that you built in the earlier `DataGrid` exercise. Right-click the Silverlight project, choose Add Existing Item, and browse to `StartingHands.cs` to add that class to the project.

3. When you add the existing `StartingHands.cs` class, it is in a different namespace than your current project. You can reference that namespace by adding a using statement at the top of your Silverlight application, or you can just change the namespace, as follows:

```
namespace ListBoxCustom
{
    public class StartingHands
    {
        public string Nickname { get; set; }
        public string Notes { get; set; }
        public string Card1 { get; set; }
        public string Card2 { get; set; }

        ...
    }
}
```

4. Next, you need to define the ListBox's ItemTemplate. The ItemTemplate will contain a horizontal-oriented StackPanel including the grid to display the two cards. It will also include a nested vertical-oriented StackPanel that will contain two TextBlock controls to display the Nickname and Notes data. Here is the code:

```
<Grid x:Name="LayoutRoot" Background="White">
    <ListBox Margin="10" x:Name="list">
        <ListBox.ItemTemplate>
            <DataTemplate>
                <StackPanel Margin="5" Orientation="Horizontal">
                    <Grid>
                        <Grid.ColumnDefinitions>
                            <ColumnDefinition />
                            <ColumnDefinition />
                        </Grid.ColumnDefinitions>

                        <Border
                            Margin="2" CornerRadius="4"
                            BorderBrush="Black" BorderThickness="1" />
                        <Rectangle Margin="4" Fill="White"
                            Grid.Column="0" Width="20" />
                        <Border
                            Margin="2" CornerRadius="4" BorderBrush="Black"
                            BorderThickness="1" Grid.Column="1" />
                        <Rectangle Margin="4" Fill="White"
                            Grid.Column="1" Width="20" />
                        <TextBlock
                            Text="{Binding Card1}" HorizontalAlignment="Center"
                            VerticalAlignment="Center" Grid.Column="0" />
                        <TextBlock
                            Text="{Binding Card2}" HorizontalAlignment="Center"
                            VerticalAlignment="Center" Grid.Column="1" />
                    </Grid>

                    <StackPanel Orientation="Vertical">
                        <TextBlock
                            Text="{Binding Nickname}"
                            FontSize="16"
                            FontWeight="Bold" />
                        <TextBlock
                            Text="{Binding Notes}" />
                    </StackPanel>
                </StackPanel>
            </DataTemplate>
        </ListBox.ItemTemplate>
    </ListBox>
</Grid>
```

5. The only thing left to do is to wire up the ListBox to the data source. To do this, navigate to the MainPage.xaml.cs code behind, and add an event handler for

the Page Loaded event. Then, within that Loaded event handler, add the following code to set the ListBox's ItemsSource to the return value from the StartingHands.GetHands() method, as you did earlier in the DataGrid example:

```
public partial class MainPage : UserControl
{
    public MainPage()
    {
        InitializeComponent();
        this.Loaded += new RoutedEventHandler(Page_Loaded);
    }

    void Page_Loaded(object sender, RoutedEventArgs e)
    {
        list.ItemsSource = StartingHands.GetHands();
    }
}
```

6. Run the application. If all goes well, you will see the ListBox shown in Figure 5-16.

As you can see, the ListBox control's flexibility lets developers display lists of data in some very cool ways.

Data Binding and String Formatting

To simplify the process of creating bindings that require formatting, Silverlight allows you to format data directly in XAML. Adding string formatting is as simple as adding a StringFormat extension in the XAML markup of the data binding. The StringFormat extension supports the same formatting options as the String's Format method.

Consider the following XAML. There are four text boxes displayed, all bound to the same property in code behind. The difference, however, is that each TextBox change displays the data differently based on the binding's StringFormat extension. The first TextBox shows the raw data, the second TextBox formats the data to three decimal places, the third TextBox shows the value in scientific notation, and the fourth TextBox shows the data as currency. The result is shown in Figure 5-17.

```
<Grid x:Name="LayoutRoot" Background="White">
    <Grid.RowDefinitions>
        <RowDefinition Height="*" />
        <RowDefinition Height="*" />
        <RowDefinition Height="*" />
        <RowDefinition Height="*" />
    </Grid.RowDefinitions>
    <TextBox
        Margin="5"
        Grid.Row="0"
        Text="{Binding DecimalValue}" />
    <TextBox
        Margin="5"
        Grid.Row="1"
        Text="{Binding DecimalValue, StringFormat='##.###'}" />
    <TextBox
```

```
            Margin="5"
            Grid.Row="2"
            Text="{Binding DateValue, StringFormat='MMM dd, yyyy'}" />
        <TextBox
            Margin="5"
            Grid.Row="3"
            Text="{Binding DecimalValue, StringFormat='c'}" />
</Grid>
```

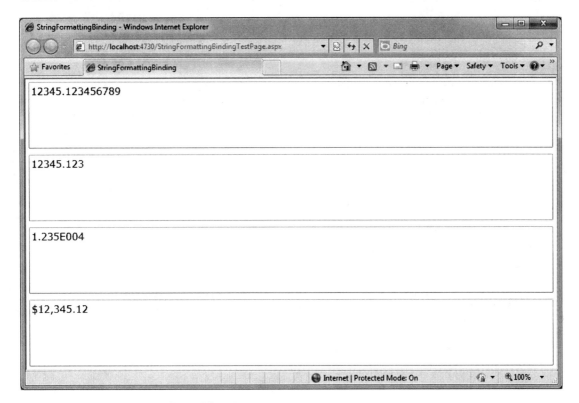

Figure 5-17. Using DataBinding with StringFormat

As you can see from this example, you can easily change the format of data directly through the XAML.

Implicit Data Templates

In the earlier ListBox example, you created a DataTemplate to format poker starting hands. This was pretty straightforward because all of the objects contained in the ListBox were the same object. What if you had an instance where you had a collection of different objects, each requiring a different DataTemplate. This would become quite a bit of additional work. Implicit templates are data templates that are associated with a specific data type. When the template is within the scope of a control that is trying to display the template's data type, it will be rendered according to the implicit template.

To see implicit templates in action, let's take a look at an example.

Try It Out: Working with Implicit Data Templates

In this example, you will create a Silverlight application that will utilize implicit data templates. The application will contain a ListBox that displays different types of contacts, each of which will be displayed slightly differently.

1. Open Visual Studio 2010, and create a new Silverlight project called ImplicitTemplates. Allow Visual Studio to create a Web Application project to host the application.

2. When the project is created, you should be looking at the MainPage.xaml file. If you do not see the XAML source, switch to that view so that you can edit the XAML. Within the root Grid of the Silverlight page, add a ListBox named ContactList.

```
<UserControl x:Class="ImplicitTemplates.MainPage"
    … >

    <Grid x:Name="LayoutRoot" Background="White">
        <ListBox Name="ContactList" />
    </Grid>
</UserControl>
```

3. Next you need to add the classes that will contain the data you will bind to your ListBox. To demonstrate the implicit data templates, you will display contact information for a company or for a person. To store this data, you will have a Company class and a Person class, both of which will inherit from the base Contact class. To add this class to the project, right-click on the Silverlight application project and select Add →Class. When the Add New Item dialog appears, be sure that Class is selected and type in Contact.cs for the name of the class. Click Add to add the class to the project.

4. Add the following class definitions to the class:

```
using System;
using System.Net;
using System.Windows;
using System.Windows.Controls;
using System.Windows.Documents;
using System.Windows.Ink;
using System.Windows.Input;
using System.Windows.Media;
using System.Windows.Media.Animation;
using System.Windows.Shapes;
using System.Collections.Generic;

namespace ImplicitTemplates
{
    public class Contact
```

```
    {
        public string PhoneNumber { get; set; }
    }

    public class Person : Contact
    {
        public string FirstName { get; set; }
        public string LastName { get; set; }
    }

    public class Company : Contact
    {
        public string Name { get; set; }
    }
}
```

5. Next you need to create some sample data. To do this, you will add a new class called Contacts that will contain a single static method called GetContacts() that will return a List of contacts. Add the Contacts class to the Contact.cs file:

```
using System;
using System.Net;
using System.Windows;
using System.Windows.Controls;
using System.Windows.Documents;
using System.Windows.Ink;
using System.Windows.Input;
using System.Windows.Media;
using System.Windows.Media.Animation;
using System.Windows.Shapes;
using System.Collections.Generic;

namespace ImplicitTemplates
{
    public class Contact
    {
        public string PhoneNumber { get; set; }
    }

    public class Person : Contact
    {
        public string FirstName { get; set; }
        public string LastName { get; set; }
    }

    public class Company : Contact
    {
        public string Name { get; set; }
    }

    public class Contacts
    {
```

```
public static List<Contact> GetContacts()
{
    var contactList = new List<Contact>()
    {
        new Company() {
            PhoneNumber = "123-456-7890",
            Name = "Company One" },
        new Person() {
            PhoneNumber = "111-111-1111",
            FirstName="John",
            LastName="Doe" },
        new Person() {
            PhoneNumber = "222-222-2222",
            FirstName="Jane",
            LastName="Doe" },
        new Company() {
            PhoneNumber = "333-333-3333",
            Name = "Company Two" }
    };

    return contactList;
}
}
}
```

6. Next you need to bind the contact data to the ListBox. In the code behind of
   the MainPage user control, add the following code that will set the ItemsSource
   of the ListBox to your GetContacts() method:

```
namespace ImplicitTemplates
{
    public partial class MainPage : UserControl
    {
        public MainPage()
        {
            InitializeComponent();
            Loaded += new RoutedEventHandler(MainPage_Loaded);
        }

        void MainPage_Loaded(object sender, RoutedEventArgs e)
        {
            this.ContactList.ItemsSource = Contacts.GetContacts();
        }
    }
}
```

7. You can now press F5 to test the application. You will see the ListBox displays
   the type names of your different objects as shown in Figure 5-18.

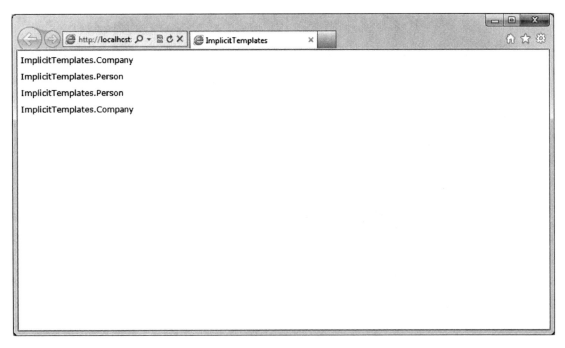

Figure 5-18. ListBox with multiple object types

8. Now let's implement the implicit data templates. In the MainPage.xaml file, you
    will first add a reference to your ImplicitTemplates namespace. You will give
    the reference the name model:

```
<UserControl x:Class="ImplicitTemplates.MainPage"
    xmlns="http://schemas.microsoft.com/winfx/2006/xaml/presentation"
    xmlns:x="http://schemas.microsoft.com/winfx/2006/xaml"
    xmlns:d="http://schemas.microsoft.com/expression/blend/2008"
    xmlns:mc="http://schemas.openxmlformats.org/markup-compatibility/2006"
    xmlns:model="clr-namespace:ImplicitTemplates"
    mc:Ignorable="d"
    d:DesignHeight="300" d:DesignWidth="400">

    <Grid x:Name="LayoutRoot" Background="White">
        <ListBox Name="ContactList" />
    </Grid>
</UserControl>
```

9. Now that you have the namespace referenced, you can add your implicit data
    templates. There are a number of places that you can define these templates,
    and as long as the control that needs them is in the scope of the templates,
    they will be used. In this case, you will define the templates at the UserControl
    level. To do this, add the UserContol.Resources tag above the root grid in the
    MainPage.xaml file. Then add the following template definitions. The result
    should be as shown next. Notice that you are using the namespace name

model as you define it in your namespace reference in
step 8.

```xaml
<UserControl x:Class="ImplicitTemplates.MainPage"
    xmlns="http://schemas.microsoft.com/winfx/2006/xaml/presentation"
    xmlns:x="http://schemas.microsoft.com/winfx/2006/xaml"
    xmlns:d="http://schemas.microsoft.com/expression/blend/2008"
    xmlns:mc="http://schemas.openxmlformats.org/markup-compatibility/2006"
    xmlns:model="clr-namespace:ImplicitTemplates"
    mc:Ignorable="d"
    d:DesignHeight="300" d:DesignWidth="400">

    <UserControl.Resources>
        <DataTemplate DataType="model:Company">
            <TextBlock Text="Company Contact" />
        </DataTemplate>
        <DataTemplate DataType="model:Person">
            <TextBlock Text="Person Contact" />
        </DataTemplate>
    </UserControl.Resources>

    <Grid x:Name="LayoutRoot" Background="White">
        <ListBox Name="ContactList" />
    </Grid>
</UserControl>
```

10. If you run the application again, you will see that the ListBox now uses the
implicit templates to display the different items as shown in Figure 5-19.

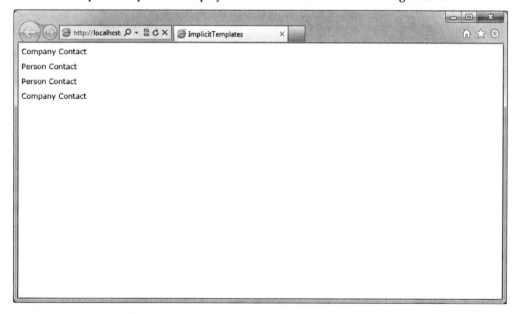

Figure 5-19. *ListBox with implicit templates*

11. Now that you have the implicit templates working, let's modify them to make the display more practical. Update the templates as shown here:

```
<UserControl.Resources>
    <DataTemplate DataType="model:Company">
        <StackPanel Orientation="Horizontal">
            <Border Width="30" Height="30" Background="Red" CornerRadius="5" >
                <Viewbox  Stretch="Uniform">
                    <TextBlock Foreground="White" Text="C" />
                </Viewbox>
            </Border>
            <StackPanel Margin="5" Orientation="Vertical">
                <TextBlock Text="{Binding Name}" />
                <TextBlock Text="{Binding PhoneNumber}" />
            </StackPanel>
        </StackPanel>
    </DataTemplate>
    <DataTemplate DataType="model:Person">
        <StackPanel Orientation="Horizontal">
            <Border Width="30" Height="30" Background="Blue" CornerRadius="5" >
                <Viewbox  Stretch="Uniform">
                    <TextBlock Foreground="White" Text="P" />
                </Viewbox>
            </Border>
            <StackPanel Margin="5" Orientation="Vertical">
                <StackPanel Orientation="Horizontal">
                    <TextBlock Text="{Binding LastName}" />

                    <TextBlock Text=", " />
                    <TextBlock Text="{Binding FirstName}" />
                </StackPanel>
                <TextBlock Text="{Binding PhoneNumber}" />
            </StackPanel>
        </StackPanel>
    </DataTemplate>
</UserControl.Resources>
```

12. You are finished! If you run the application, you will see the finished application as shown in Figure 5-20.

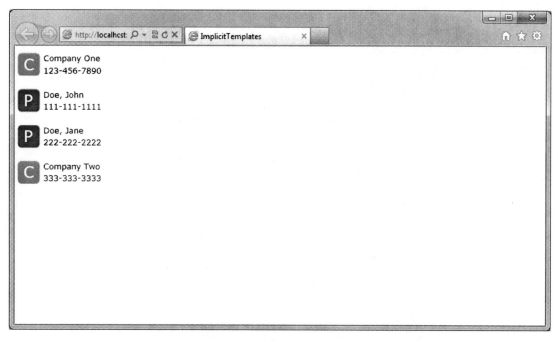

Figure 5-20. ListBox with finished implicit templates

Summary

In this chapter, you looked at how to bind lists of data to Silverlight controls. Then you focused on two controls typically bound to data: the DataGrid control and the ListBox control. You saw how these controls are flexible and can show data in unique ways. However, in all of these examples, the classes contained static data. In real-world examples, the data that you will normally list in a DataGrid or ListBox will come from some external data source, such as an XML file or a web service. In the next chapter, you will look at how to get data from these external data sources and how to use that data to bind to your Silverlight applications.

CHAPTER 6

Silverlight Toolkit

When the first version of Silverlight was released, it contained a whopping two controls: the `TextBlock` and the `Rectangle`. Silverlight developers had to build all other controls from these two. Luckily, each new version of Silverlight added a number of controls, to the point that the control set included out of the box in Silverlight is now quite impressive. However, a number of commonly used controls are still not included in Silverlight.

One example of a control missing from the base Silverlight set is a tree-view control. Developers who want to create an application using a tree view are faced with a choice. They can build a tree-view control themselves, purchase a third-party control, or find a free or open-source tree-view control. Although all three options are completely valid, in this chapter we'll focus on the last one—and the place we'll find those controls is the Silverlight Toolkit.

The Silverlight Toolkit is an open-source project containing a collection of Silverlight controls, components, and utilities. The toolkit contains full open-source code, unit tests, samples, and documentation. The latest toolkit, released at the time of the Silverlight 5 release, contains more than 30 Silverlight controls, including a number of themes and charting controls.

In this chapter, we'll look at a few of the different components of the Silverlight Toolkit in detail. Let's get started!

Overview of the Silverlight Toolkit

Because the components in the Silverlight Toolkit are released at different times, they are at different levels of maturity. The components are divided into a number of quality bands that define the maturity levels of the different components.

Mature/SDK Quality Band

Controls that have reached a mature quality level are included in the Mature quality band. These controls are not only considered extremely stable, they are shipped in the Silverlight software development kit (SDK). As controls reach this quality level, they are added to the Silverlight SDK. At that point, they are still considered part of the Silverlight Toolkit, but they will be installed on workstations when developers install the Silverlight SDK. At the time of the Silverlight 5 release, the following ten controls were included in the mature quality band:

- `AutoCompleteBox`
- `Calendar`
- `ChildWindow`

- DataGrid
- DataPager
- DatePicker
- GridSplitter
- HeaderedItemsControl
- TabControl
- TreeView

Stable Quality Band

Stable controls that have not yet reached the Mature quality level are placed in the Stable quality band. This band includes the following controls:

- DockPanel
- Expander
- HeaderedContentControl
- Label
- NumericUpDown
- Viewbox
- WrapPanel

Preview Quality Band

Controls that have not yet had enough testing to reach a stable quality belong to the Preview quality band. The following controls (as well as 11 themes) belong in this band:

- Accordion
- Charting
- ContextMenu
- DataForm
- DomainUpDown
- ImplicitStyleManager
- LayoutTransformer
- Rating
- TimePicker
- TimeUpDown

- 11 Silverlight Themes

Experimental Quality Band

New additions to the Silverlight Toolkit get placed in the Experimental quality band. These are components that should be used with caution because they are still under development and have not been tested to the point to reach even a Preview quality level. Controls and components in this band include the following:

- GlobalCalendar

- TransitioningContentControl

- TreeMap

- Drag-and-drop support for items controls

- BusyIndicator

Installing the Toolkit

You'll find the toolkit on CodePlex at http://silverlight.codeplex.com. (See Figure 6-1.)

Figure 6-1. *The Silverlight 5 Toolkit web site*

You can get the latest toolkit by clicking on the Downloads tab and selecting either the MSI install or a zip containing the source code. For the purpose of this book, just download and install the MSI; the content in this book is based on the December 2011 release of the Silverlight 5 toolkit as shown in Figure 6-2.

Figure 6-2. The MSI install for the Silverlight 5 Toolkit

Toolkit Controls

The Silverlight Toolkit contains a number of controls. We've discussed some of these earlier in the book—DataGrid (Chapter 5), GridSplitter (Chapter 4), and WrapPanel (Chapter 3). In this section, we'll look at a few others.

Accordion

The Accordion control lets you include a collection of expandable and collapsible panels that allow you to show groups of content. Each accordion contains a header item and a content item. When the user clicks on the header item, it either expands or collapses the section, showing or hiding its content items. Accordion-like controls are used in many common applications, but probably the one that's most familiar to developers is Visual Studio's Toolbox, as shown in Figure 6-3. Each tab in the toolbox can be considered a header item, and the controls contained under each header can be considered the content items.

Figure 6-3. The Visual Studio Toolbox

Try It Out: Working with the Accordion Control

In this example, you will use the Accordion control to display a list of books, grouped by category. Figure 6-4 shows the result you'll be working toward.

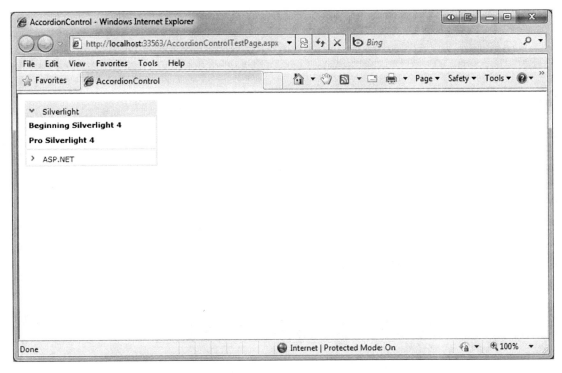

Figure 6-4. The finished Accordion example

1. Create a new Silverlight application in Visual Studio 2010 called AccordionControl. Allow Visual Studio to create a Web Application project to host the application.

2. With the MainPage.xaml file selected, position the cursor in the source in the Layout Grid. Find and double-click on the Accordion control in the Toolbox. This will add the control to the page, as well as the proper namespace reference:

   xmlns:toolkit="http://schemas.microsoft.com/winfx/2006/xaml/presentation/toolkit"

3. After you've added the Accordion, right-click on the control in the design view and select Reset Layout ➤ All, as shown in Figure 6-5. Then Name the Accordion BookList, set its Width to 200, and specify a Margin of 10.

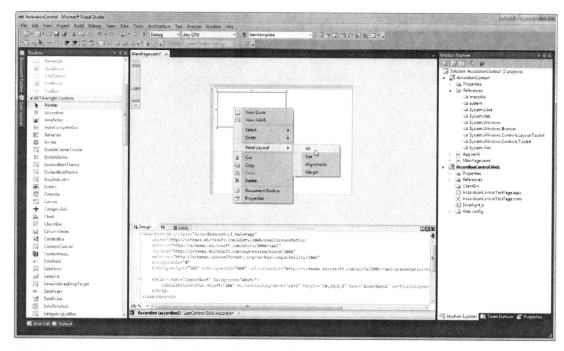

Figure 6-5. *Resetting the layout of the Accordion control*

```
<Grid x:Name="LayoutRoot" Background="White">
    <toolkit:Accordion Name="BookList" Width="200" Margin="10" />
</Grid>
```

4. Switch to the code behind in the file MainPage.xaml.cs. You need to define the data you'll be binding to the Accordion. For simplicity, define the data right in the code-behind file. Add two classes, one for Categories and one for Books.

```
namespace AccordionControl
{
    public partial class MainPage : UserControl
    {
        public MainPage()
        {
            InitializeComponent();
        }
    }

    public class BookCategory
    {
        public string CategoryName { get; set; }
        public List<Book> Books { get; set; }
    }
```

```
public class Book
{
    public string Title { get; set; }
}
}
```

5. Next you need to populate the classes with some data. To do this, first wire up
    the Loaded event and insert the following code:

```
public partial class MainPage : UserControl
{
    public MainPage()
    {
        InitializeComponent();
        this.Loaded += new RoutedEventHandler(MainPage_Loaded);
    }

    void MainPage_Loaded(object sender, RoutedEventArgs e)
    {
        List<BookCategory> Library = new List<BookCategory>();

        BookCategory cat1 = new BookCategory() {
            CategoryName = "Silverlight",
            Books = new List<Book>() };
        cat1.Books.Add(new Book() { Title = "Beginning Silverlight 5" });
        cat1.Books.Add(new Book() { Title = "Pro Silverlight 5" });
        Library.Add(cat1);

        BookCategory cat2 = new BookCategory() {
            CategoryName = "ASP.NET",
            Books = new List<Book>() };
        cat2.Books.Add(new Book() { Title = "Pro ASP.NET 5" }) ;
        Library.Add(cat2);
    }
}

public class BookCategory
{
    public string CategoryName { get; set; }
    public List<Book> Books { get; set; }
}

public class Book
{
    public string Title { get; set; }
}
```

6. Now you need to define the header and content items, using the ItemTemplate
    for the header and the ContentTemplate for the content. For the ItemTemplate,
    you'll simply define a TextBlock that will display the BookCategory. For the
    ContentTemplate, define a ListBox control that will contain a list of TextBlocks,

each displaying a book Title. Switch back to the XAML view in Visual Studio, and add the following code:

```
<toolkit:Accordion
    Name="BookList"
    Margin="10"
    Width="200">
    <toolkit:Accordion.ContentTemplate>
        <DataTemplate>
            <ListBox ItemsSource="{Binding Books}" BorderThickness="0">
                <ListBox.ItemTemplate>
                    <DataTemplate>
                        <TextBlock FontWeight="Bold" Text="{Binding Title}" />
                    </DataTemplate>
                </ListBox.ItemTemplate>
            </ListBox>
        </DataTemplate>
    </toolkit:Accordion.ContentTemplate>
    <toolkit:Accordion.ItemTemplate>
        <DataTemplate>
            <TextBlock Text="{Binding CategoryName}" />
        </DataTemplate>
    </toolkit:Accordion.ItemTemplate>
</toolkit:Accordion>
```

7. Next you need to bind the Library data source to the Accordion control:

```
void MainPage_Loaded(object sender, RoutedEventArgs e)
{
    List<BookCategory> Library = new List<BookCategory>();

    BookCategory cat1 = new BookCategory() {
        CategoryName = "Silverlight",
        Books = new List<Book>() };
    cat1.Books.Add(new Book() { Title = "Beginning Silverlight 4" });
    cat1.Books.Add(new Book() { Title = "Pro Silverlight 4" });
    Library.Add(cat1);

    BookCategory cat2 = new BookCategory() {
        CategoryName = "ASP.NET",
        Books = new List<Book>() };
    cat2.Books.Add(new Book() { Title = "Pro ASP.NET 4" }) ;
    Library.Add(cat2);

    this.BookList.ItemsSource = Library;
}
```

8. Press F5 to run the solution. If things go as planned, you should see the Accordion displayed. If you click on ASP.NET, the Silverlight section will collapse and hide those books, while the ASP.NET section will expand and display its books, as shown in Figure 6-6.

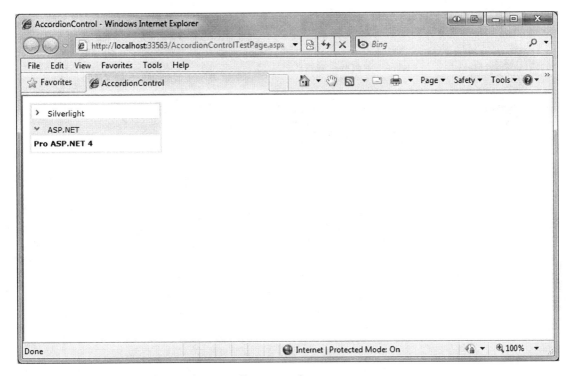

Figure 6-6. Changing headers in the Accordion example

AutoCompleteBox

The `AutoCompleteBox` is another mature-band toolkit control that is now available through the Silverlight SDK. Its functionality is nothing new to users, because autocomplete text boxes have been around for many years. As you start typing in a text box, items that match what you are typing are displayed below. You can pick an item from the list instead of having to finish typing it yourself. Because the `AutoCompleteBox` is contained in the SDK, a reference to the SDK namespace is required to access the control:

```
xmlns:sdk="http://schemas.microsoft.com/winfx/2006/xaml/presentation/sdk"
```

To define an `AutoCompleteBox` in XAML is no different from defining other controls, such as `Buttons`:

```
<sdk:AutoCompleteBox Name="FavoriteColor" Width="200" Height="25" />
```

In the code behind, you can then easily add the items that are displayed when the user types by binding a collection to the `ItemsSource` property. For example, you can bind to a simple string array containing colors.

```
public MainPage()
{
    InitializeComponent();
    this.FavoriteColor.ItemsSource = new string[]
    {
        "aqua", "azure", "beige", "black", "blue", "brown", "cyan",
        "gold", "gray", "ivory", "lime", "magenta", "maroon", "navy",
        "olive", "orange", "pink", "purple", "red", "tan", "teal",
        "violet", "wheat", "white", "yellow"
    };
}
```

When this control is displayed and a user starts to type in the text box, the colors matching the typed text are displayed below in a list, as shown in Figure 6-7.

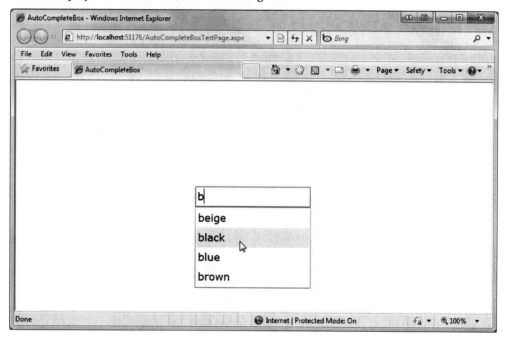

Figure 6-7. *An AutoCompleteBox*

You might have also noticed that many autocomplete text boxes automatically complete the text for you as you type. You need to enable this functionality because it is not set by default. This is done by setting the property IsTextCompletionEnabled to True:

```
<sdk:AutoCompleteBox
    Name="FavoriteColor"
    Width="200" Height="35"
    FontSize="18"
    IsTextCompletionEnabled="True"    />
```

Once this property has been set, you will see that the text automatically completes as you type, as shown in Figure 6-8.

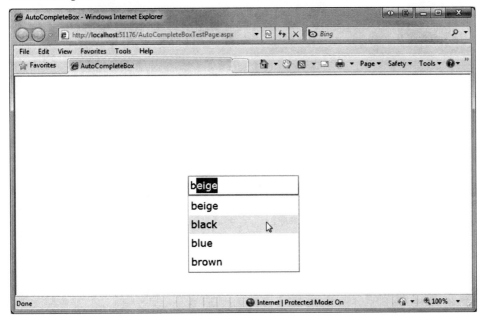

Figure 6-8. *The AutoCompleteBox with IsTextCompletionEnabled set to True*

TabControl

The TabControl provides a way to separate your application's user interface into different tabs. Using the control is very straightforward—you simply create a different TabItem for each tab, and define the content of the tab within the TabItem tags. That's all there is to it. Consider the following example:

```
<Grid x:Name="LayoutRoot" Background="White">
    <sdk:TabControl Height="100" Width="200">
        <sdk:TabItem Header="Tab #1">
            <TextBlock Text="Content for Tab #1" />
        </sdk:TabItem>
        <sdk:TabItem Header="Tab #2">
            <TextBlock Text="Content for Tab #2" />
        </sdk:TabItem>
    </sdk:TabControl>
</Grid>
```

This code creates two tabs and displays a TextBlock for each, as shown in Figure 6-9.

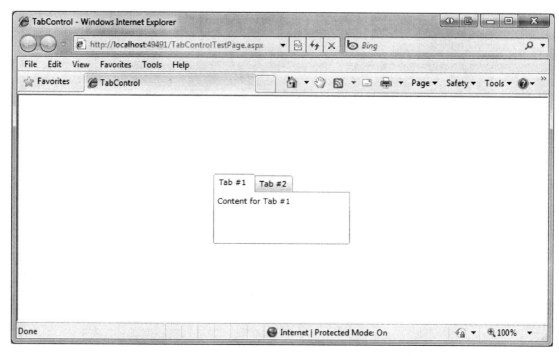

Figure 6-9. *The TabControl example*

ViewBox

The ViewBox is a control that was first offered through the toolkit and is now part of the standard Silverlight control library. As a result, you don't need to define any additional namespace references. Any content placed within the ViewBox is automatically sized to fill the entire ViewBox. This can be ideal if you want to automatically position elements the way you want within the ViewBox. When you need items to change size, instead of changing each one individually, you can simply change the size of the ViewBox and all items are automatically resized to fit. As a quick example, let's create an icon with some text underneath it, as shown in Figure 6-10.

```
<StackPanel>
    <Image Width="175" Source="cherry.jpg" />
    <TextBlock Text="Cherry" FontSize="30"
        HorizontalAlignment="Center" />
</StackPanel>
```

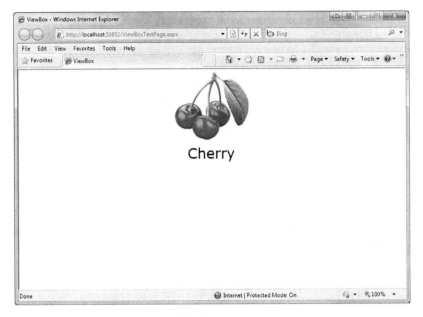

Figure 6-10. *An icon with a text label*

If you want to resize these two items without a ViewBox, you need to change the size of each item. However, by placing both items within a ViewBox, all you need to do is resize the ViewBox. To demonstrate this, place the same source for the icon and text in three different-sized ViewBox controls:

```
<StackPanel Orientation="Horizontal" HorizontalAlignment="Center">
    <Viewbox Width="40" Margin="5">
        <StackPanel>
            <Image Width="175" Source="cherry.jpg" />
            <TextBlock Text="Cherry" FontSize="30"
                HorizontalAlignment="Center" />
        </StackPanel>
    </Viewbox>
    <Viewbox Width="100" Margin="5">
        <StackPanel>
            <Image Width="175" Source="cherry.jpg" />
            <TextBlock Text="Cherry" FontSize="30"
                HorizontalAlignment="Center" />
        </StackPanel>
    </Viewbox>
    <Viewbox Width="200" Margin="5">
        <StackPanel>
            <Image Width="175" Source="cherry.jpg" />
            <TextBlock Text="Cherry" FontSize="30"
                HorizontalAlignment="Center" />
        </StackPanel>
    </Viewbox>
</StackPanel>
```

The result is shown in Figure 6-11. As you can see, the icon and text are resized to fit each ViewBox and the proportion and positioning is maintained.

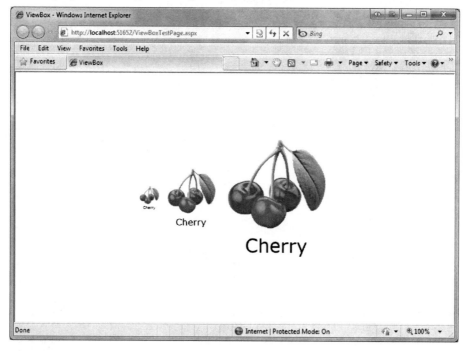

Figure 6-11. Icon and text label in three ViewBox controls

Modal Windows

Another feature in the Silverlight Toolkit is the Modal Child Window. This provides functionality to pop up a window that disables the rest of the application until the window is closed, something that is very common in Windows desktop development. The Silverlight modal window's visual appearance and content is defined by XAML, just like everything else in Silverlight, which gives you a lot of control.

REFACTORING THE CHILD WINDOW

Out of the box, the Child Window can operate only as a modal dialog, which means that it has to disable the content of the application while it is open. However, at times you might prefer to have the child window behave more like a standard window. Good news! The Child Window was developed out of the Silverlight Toolkit project on CodePlex, and as a result, you have access to the entire source code under the Ms-PL license. You can download the source from http://silverlight.codeplex.com and make any modifications you'd like, including refactoring the Child Window to operate not only as a modal dialog, but also as a standard floating and draggable window.

To show a modal dialog, let's create an instance of the window and call its Show() method. The Show() method is an asynchronous call and it returns immediately, so you won't be able to get the result from the dialog using this method. Instead, you'll need to handle the Closed event from the window and check the DialogResult there:

```
Confirm confirmDlg = new Confirm();
confirmDlg.Closed += new EventHandler(confirmDlg_Closed);
confirmDlg.Show();
void confirmDlg_Closed(object sender, EventArgs e)
{
    Confirm confirmDlg = (Confirm)sender;
    if (confirmDlg.DialogResult == true)
    {
        // User Clicked OK
    }
    else if (confirmDlg.DialogResult = false)
    {
        // User Clicked Cancel
    }
}
```

Note that the DialogResult is not a standard Boolean type; it is a nullable Boolean. Therefore, there are three possible values: true, false, and null. In C#, a nullable Boolean is specified with the syntax bool?.

```
void confirmDlg_Closed(object sender, EventArgs e)
{
    Confirm confirmDlg = (Confirm)sender;
    bool? Result = confirmDlg.DialogResult;
}
```

In addition to simply getting a true/false/null response from the Child Window, you can implement your own properties that can be passed from the dialog. To retrieve these property values, in the Closed()event handler, you cast the sender object to your child window's type and simply access the property:

```
void confirmDlg_Closed(object sender, EventArgs e)
{
    Confirm confirmDlg = (Confirm)sender;
    string myPropValue = confirmDlg.MyProperty;
}
```

Let's run through a quick exercise to see how to create a modal pop-up window in Silverlight.

Try It Out: Using the Modal Child Window

In this exercise, you'll create a simple registration form that accepts a first name and last name. When someone presses the button to register, a modal window will appear with a terms-and-conditions notice that users must agree to before proceeding. You won't fully code the registration form; you'll just send a result to a TextBlock so that you can see what's going on. Let's get started.

1. Create a new Silverlight application in Visual Studio 2010 called ModalWindow. Allow Visual Studio to create a Web Application project to host the application.

2. In the `MainPage.xaml` file, divide the root Grid into five rows and two columns. The height of the first four rows should be 40 pixels, and the fifth row should take up the remainder of the application. The width of the first column should be 150 pixels, and the second column should take up the remainder of the application. In addition, change the `d:DesignWidth` of the UserControl to 600.

```
<UserControl x:Class="ModalWindow.MainPage"
    xmlns="http://schemas.microsoft.com/winfx/2006/xaml/presentation"
    xmlns:x="http://schemas.microsoft.com/winfx/2006/xaml"
    xmlns:d="http://schemas.microsoft.com/expression/blend/2008"
    xmlns:mc="http://schemas.openxmlformats.org/markup-compatibility/2006"
    mc:Ignorable="d"
    d:DesignHeight="300" d:DesignWidth="600">

<Grid x:Name="LayoutRoot" Background="White">
    <Grid.ColumnDefinitions>
        <ColumnDefinition Width="150" />
        <ColumnDefinition Width="*" />
    </Grid.ColumnDefinitions>
    <Grid.RowDefinitions>
        <RowDefinition Height="40" />
        <RowDefinition Height="40" />
        <RowDefinition Height="40" />
        <RowDefinition Height="40" />
        <RowDefinition Height="40" />
    </Grid.RowDefinitions>
</Grid>

</UserControl>
```

3. In the first row, add a TextBlock for a header with the Text "Register for a new Account" that spans both columns. In the second row, add a TextBlock in the first column with the Text "First Name", and add a TextBox in the second column. Add some Margin and Padding to improve the appearance.

```
<Grid x:Name="LayoutRoot" Background="White">
    <Grid.ColumnDefinitions>
        <ColumnDefinition Width="150" />
        <ColumnDefinition Width="*" />
    </Grid.ColumnDefinitions>
    <Grid.RowDefinitions>
        <RowDefinition Height="40" />
        <RowDefinition Height="40" />
        <RowDefinition Height="40" />
        <RowDefinition Height="40" />
        <RowDefinition Height="40" />
    </Grid.RowDefinitions>

    <TextBlock Text="Register for a New Account"
        FontSize="20"
        FontWeight="Bold"
        Margin="5"
```

```
            Grid.ColumnSpan="2" />

    <TextBlock Padding="5"
        Margin="5"
        Text="First Name"
        FontSize="12"
        Grid.Row="1" />

    <TextBox Padding="5"
        Margin="5"
        FontSize="12"
        Grid.Column="1"
        Grid.Row="1" />

</Grid>
```

4. In the third row, add another TextBlock in the first column with the Text "Last Name", and add a TextBox in the second column. Add some Margin and Padding to improve the appearance. In the fourth row, add a Button to the second column with the Text "Register. Finally, in the fifth row, add a TextBlock to the second column with the Text blank. Name the TextBlock "Result". Your XAML should look like the following code, with the result as shown in Figure 6-12:

```
<Grid x:Name="LayoutRoot" Background="White">
    <Grid.ColumnDefinitions>
        <ColumnDefinition Width="150" />
        <ColumnDefinition Width="*" />
    </Grid.ColumnDefinitions>
    <Grid.RowDefinitions>
        <RowDefinition Height="40" />
        <RowDefinition Height="40" />
        <RowDefinition Height="40" />
        <RowDefinition Height="40" />
        <RowDefinition Height="40" />
    </Grid.RowDefinitions>

    <TextBlock Text="Register for a New Account"
        FontSize="20"
        FontWeight="Bold"
        Margin="5"
        Grid.ColumnSpan="2" />

    <TextBlock Padding="5"
        Margin="5"
        Text="First Name"
        FontSize="12"
        Grid.Row="1" />

    <TextBox Padding="5"
        Margin="5"
        FontSize="12"
```

```xml
                Grid.Column="1"
                Grid.Row="1" />

        <TextBlock Padding="5"
            Margin="5"
            Text="Last Name"
            FontSize="12"
            Grid.Row="2" />

        <TextBox Padding="5"
            Margin="5"
            FontSize="12"
            Grid.Column="1"
            Grid.Row="2" />

        <Button Content="Register"
            Padding="5"
            Margin="5"
            FontSize="12"
            Grid.Column="1"
            Grid.Row="3"
            Click="Button_Click" />

        <TextBlock Text=""
            FontSize="14"
            FontWeight="Bold"
            Grid.Column="1"
            Grid.Row="4"
            Margin="5"
            Name="Result" />

    </Grid>
```

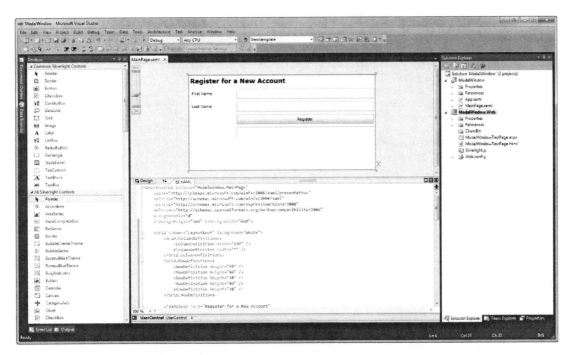

Figure 6-12. Modal window example with finished XAML layout

5. Now that you have the main form laid out, turn your attention to the child window. To add a child window to the project, right-click on the Silverlight project (`ModalWindow`) and select Add ➤ New Item. From the Add New Item dialog, select Silverlight Child Window and name the window `Confirm.xaml`, as shown in Figure 6-13.

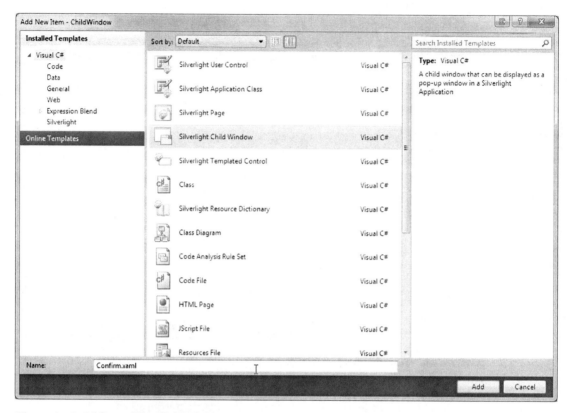

Figure 6-13. *Adding a Silverlight Child Window*

6. When the Child Window has been added to the project, it will contain the following XAML by default:

```
<controls:ChildWindow x:Class="ChildWindow.Confirm"
    xmlns="http://schemas.microsoft.com/winfx/2006/xaml/presentation"
    xmlns:x="http://schemas.microsoft.com/winfx/2006/xaml"
    xmlns:controls="clr-namespace:System.Windows.Controls;
assembly=System.Windows.Controls"
    Width="400" Height="300"
    Title="Confirm">

<Grid x:Name="LayoutRoot" Margin="2">
    <Grid.RowDefinitions>
        <RowDefinition />
        <RowDefinition Height="Auto" />
    </Grid.RowDefinitions>

    <Button
        x:Name="CancelButton"
        Content="Cancel"
```

```
            Click="CancelButton_Click"
            Width="75"
            Height="23"
            HorizontalAlignment="Right"
            Margin="0,12,0,0"
            Grid.Row="1" />

        <Button
            x:Name="OKButton"
            Content="OK"
            Click="OKButton_Click"
            Width="75"
            Height="23"
            HorizontalAlignment="Right"
            Margin="0,12,79,0"
            Grid.Row="1" />
    </Grid>
</controls:ChildWindow>
```

7. Notice that two buttons have been added for you already: one for Cancel and
    one for OK. If you look at the code behind for the window, you'll also see that
    some code is already present:

```
namespace ModalWindow
{
    public partial class Confirm : ChildWindow
    {
        public Confirm()
        {
            InitializeComponent();
        }

        private void OKButton_Click(object sender, RoutedEventArgs e)
        {
            this.DialogResult = true;
        }

        private void CancelButton_Click(object sender, RoutedEventArgs e)
        {
            this.DialogResult = false;
        }
    }
}
```

8. Two event handlers, one for each button, have been wired up, but notice that
    the code is simply setting the DialogResult property on the window. In the
    property setter, it will automatically set the response and execute the dialog's
    Close() method, so that's all the code you need.

9. For now, just leave the Child Window as is, but you do need to call it from the
    Silverlight application. Open the MainPage.xaml.cs code-behind file. Add the
    Button_Click event as well as the code to create an instance of the Child
    Window and execute the Show() method:

```
private void Button_Click(object sender, RoutedEventArgs e)
{
    Confirm confirmDlg = new Confirm();
    confirmDlg.Show();
}
```

10. Now run the application, and click the Register button. You will see that the Child Window appears, as shown in Figure 6-14. You can drag the window, but notice that the main user interface for your application is inaccessible. Click OK or Cancel, and you'll find that the Child Window closes and the application's user interface is once again functioning.

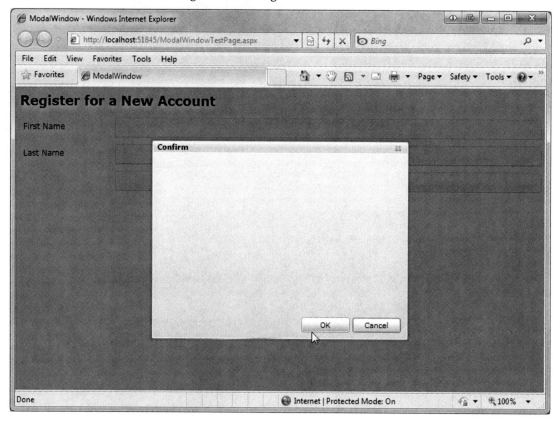

Figure 6-14. The default Child Window

11. Very cool, but let's not stop there. Let's modify the Child Window to show that its content can be customized any way you like by editing the window's XAML. To do this, open the Confirm.xaml file in XAML design mode. Change the Title of the window to "Terms and Conditions." Let's also change the height of the Window to 200 pixels and make the Text of the two buttons read "I Accept" and "I Do Not Accept." Because you are changing the text, you must also adjust the

width of the buttons and the margins. (Note that you can just as easily put these two buttons in a horizontal StackPanel instead of spacing them using margins.) Finally, add two TextBlock controls to the first row of the root Grid for the header, and add one below it for the terms and conditions text. Your updated XAML should now be similar to the following:

```xaml
<Grid x:Name="LayoutRoot" Margin="2">
    <Grid.RowDefinitions>
        <RowDefinition />
        <RowDefinition Height="Auto" />
    </Grid.RowDefinitions>

    <StackPanel>

        <TextBlock
            Text="Please Accept the Terms and Conditions to Continue"
            FontWeight="Bold"
            FontSize="12" />

        <TextBlock
            Text="These are the terms and conditions..." />

    </StackPanel>

    <Button
        x:Name="CancelButton"
        Content="I Do Not Accept" Click="CancelButton_Click"
        Width="125"
        Height="23" HorizontalAlignment="Right"
        Margin="0,12,0,0" Grid.Row="1" />

    <Button
        x:Name="OKButton"
        Content="I Accept" Click="OKButton_Click"
        Width="100"
        Height="23" HorizontalAlignment="Right"
        Margin="0,12,134,0" Grid.Row="1" />

</Grid>
```

12. Go ahead and run the application again, and then click the Register button to open the Child Window. Notice that the content changes are reflected, as shown in Figure 6-15. Keep in mind that the content of these window controls is completely customizable with XAML. You can add any controls you want with any layout you want.

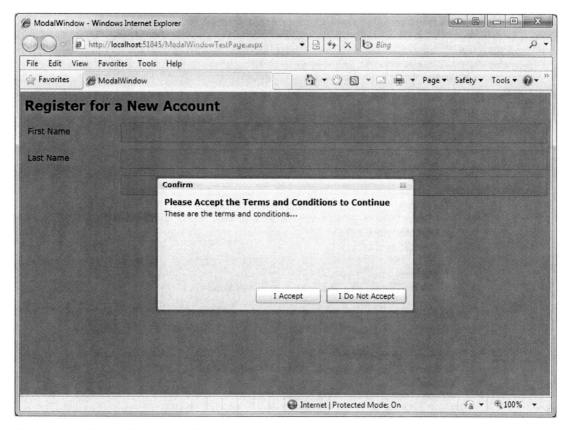

Figure 6-15. *The modified Child Window*

13. Now let's add code to retrieve results from the dialog. Open the
MainPage.xaml.cs file, and within the Button_Click event handler, wire up
another event handler for the Child Window's Closed()event. In this new event
handler, you need to get the Child Window's instance, which is sent to the
handler in the sender object. Once you have the window's instance, you can
retrieve the DialogResult property, which will contain true, false, or null.

```
public partial class MainPage : UserControl
{
    public MainPage()
    {
        InitializeComponent();
    }

    private void Button_Click(object sender, RoutedEventArgs e)
    {
        Confirm confirmDlg = new Confirm();
        confirmDlg.Closed += new EventHandler(confirmDlg_Closed);
```

```
        confirmDlg.Show();
    }

    void confirmDlg_Closed(object sender, EventArgs e)
    {
        Confirm confirmDlg = (Confirm)sender;

        if (confirmDlg.DialogResult == true)
        {
            this.Result.Text = "Terms and Conditions Accepted";
        }
        else if (confirmDlg.DialogResult == false)
        {
            this.Result.Text = "Terms and Conditions Not Accepted";
        }
    }
}
```

14. Run the application. Click the Register button to display the Child Window, and then press the I Accept button in the Child Window. You'll see that the Result TextBlock is updated to read "Terms and Conditions Accepted", as shown in Figure 6-16.

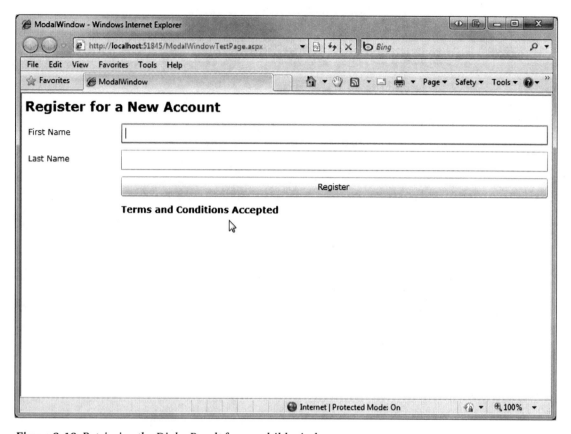

Figure 6-16. Retrieving the DialogResult from a child window

Summary

In this chapter, we looked at the Silverlight Toolkit, an excellent resource with a number of rich controls that Silverlight developers can use. What's even better is that the Toolkit provides the full source code, so developers can extend the controls and modify them to meet their specific needs. In the next chapter, we will look at data access and networking in Silverlight.

CHAPTER 7

Data Access and Networking

Data access in Silverlight applications works differently than it does in traditional applications. You'll need to be aware of how it works and the limitations. In this chapter, you will look at what makes data access different, and then explore mechanisms for accessing data in a Silverlight application.

Data Access in Silverlight Applications

As discussed in Chapter 1, Rich Internet Applications (RIAs) bridge the gap between Windows-based smart clients and web-based applications. When moving to this type of environment, data access and networking can be confusing.

In a Windows-based smart client, the application has access to the database at all times. It can create a connection to the database, maintain state with the database, and remain connected.

On the other hand, a web application is what is known as a *pseudo-conversational* environment, which is, for the most part, a completely stateless and disconnected environment. When a client makes a request to the web server, the web server processes the request and returns a response to the client. After that response has been sent, the connection between the client and the server is disconnected, and the server moves on to the next client request. No connection or state is maintained between the two.

In Silverlight applications, you have one additional layer of complexity. The application runs from the client's machine. However, it is still a disconnected environment because it is hosted within a web browser. There is no concept of posting back for each request or creating a round-trip to the server for data processing. Therefore, data access is limited to a small number of options.

In addition, a Silverlight application has a number of security restrictions placed on it to protect the users from the application gaining too much control over their machine. For instance, the Silverlight application has access to only an isolated storage space to store its disconnected data. It has no access whatsoever to the client's hard disk outside its *sandbox*. Silverlight's isolated storage is discussed in more detail in Chapter 9.

What are your options for accessing data in a Silverlight application? The following main mechanisms are available:

- The most common mechanism to access data from a Silverlight application is through web services, typically a Windows Communication Foundation (WCF) service.

- Silverlight applications can access data using ADO.NET Data Services, which provides access to data through a URI syntax.

- Silverlight also has built-in socket support, which allows applications to connect directly to a server through TCP sockets.

- Silverlight has out-of-the-box support for JavaScript Object Notation (JSON), as well as RSS 2.0 and Atom 1.0 syndication feed formats.

Of these mechanisms, I'll explore accessing WCF services from Silverlight in depth, and then give you a high-level look at using sockets. For examples and more information on accessing other data services, refer to *Pro Silverlight 5 in C#* by Matthew MacDonald (Apress, 2012).

Accessing Data Through Web Services

One of the ways that a Silverlight application can access data is through web services. These can be ASP.NET Web Services (ASMX), Windows Communication Foundation (WCF) services, or representational state transfer (REST) services. Here, you will concentrate on using a WCF service, which is the preferred way of accessing data in a Silverlight application through web services.

Try It Out: Accessing Data Through a WCF Service

To demonstrate accessing data from a WCF service, you will build the same application that you built in Chapter 5 to try out the DataGrid. (For more information about any part of this exercise regarding the DataGrid, refer back to Chapter 5.) The difference will be that the application will get the data through a web service.

As you'll recall, this application displays common starting hands in poker and the nicknames that have been given to those starting hands. The UI will have three columns: the first column will display two images of the cards in the hand, the second column will display the nickname, and the third column will contain notes about the hand. The completed application is shown in Figure 7-1.

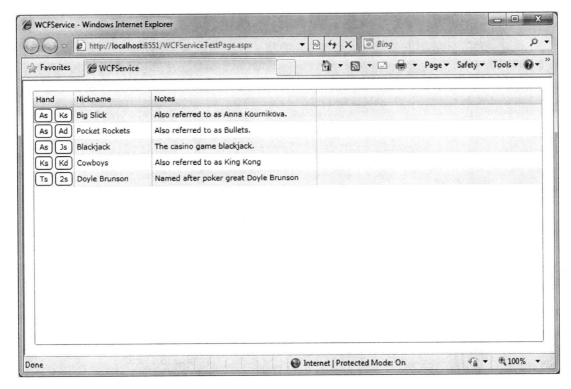

Figure 7-1. The poker starting hands application

1. Create a new Silverlight application in Visual Studio 2010. Call the application WCFService, and allow Visual Studio to create a Web Application project named WCFService.Web to host your application.

2. Right-click the WCFService.Web project, and select Add ➤ New Item. Create a new class with the Class Diagram template, as you saw in Chapter 2, or create a new empty Code File. Name the new class StartingHands.cs, as shown in Figure 7-2.

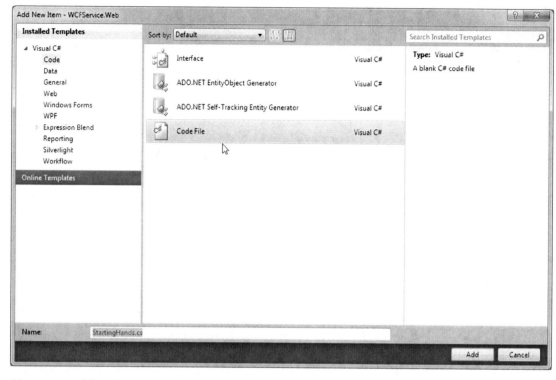

Figure 7-2. *Adding the StartingHands.cs class to the project*

3. Now you need to implement the StartingHands.cs class. It is very similar to
    the class used in Chapter 5's DataGrid example. To save yourself some typing,
    you can copy the code from that project. As shown in bold in the following
    code, the only differences are the namespace and the return type of the
    GetHands() method. Instead of using an ObservableCollection, it will return a
    simple List<StartingHands>.

■ **Note** In a real-world example, the StartingHands.cs class would be doing something like retrieving data from
a SQL Server database and executing some business logic rules on the data. For simplicity, this example just
returns a static collection.

```
using System;
using System.Collections.Generic;
using System.Linq;
using System.Web;
```

```csharp
namespace WCFService.Web
{
    public class StartingHands
    {
        public string Nickname { get; set; }
        public string Notes { get; set; }
        public string Card1 { get; set; }
        public string Card2 { get; set; }

        public static List<StartingHands> GetHands()
        {
            List<StartingHands> hands = new List<StartingHands>();

            hands.Add(
                new StartingHands()
                {
                    Nickname = "Big Slick",
                    Notes = "Also referred to as Anna Kournikova.",
                    Card1 = "As",
                    Card2 = "Ks"
                });

            hands.Add(
            new StartingHands()
            {
                Nickname = "Pocket Rockets",
                Notes = "Also referred to as Bullets.",
                Card1 = "As",
                Card2 = "Ad"
            });

            hands.Add(
                new StartingHands()
                {
                    Nickname = "Blackjack",
                    Notes = "The casino game blackjack.",
                    Card1 = "As",
                    Card2 = "Js"
                });

            hands.Add(
                new StartingHands()
                {
                    Nickname = "Cowboys",
                    Notes = "Also referred to as King Kong",
                    Card1 = "Ks",
                    Card2 = "Kd"
                });

            hands.Add(
                new StartingHands()
```

```
                                {
                                    Nickname = "Doyle Brunson",
                                    Notes = "Named after poker great Doyle Brunson",
                                    Card1 = "Ts",
                                    Card2 = "2s"
                                });


                        return hands;
                    }
                }
            }
```

4. Next, you need to add the WCF service that will call the StartingHands.
    GetHands() method. Right-click the WCFService.Web project, and select Add ➤
    New Item. In the Add New Item dialog box, select the template named
    "Silverlight-enabled WCF Service" and name it StartingHandService.svc, as
    shown in Figure 7-3. Then click the Add button.

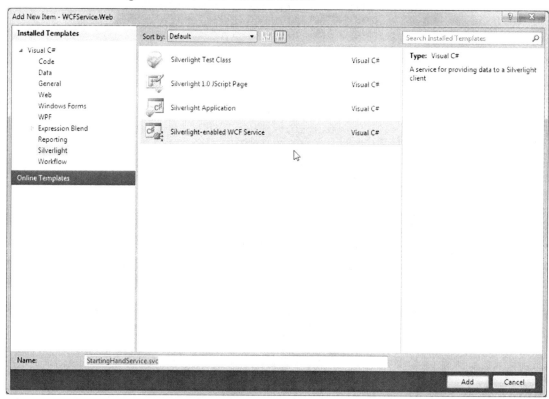

Figure 7-3. Adding the Silverlight-enabled WCF service

5. This adds a service named StartingHandService.svc to the project with an attached code-behind file named StartingHandService.svc.cs. View that code behind. You will see that Visual Studio has already created the base WCF service, including a sample method called DoWork(), as follows:

```
namespace WCFService.Web
{
    [ServiceContract(Namespace = "")]
    [SilverlightFaultBehavior]
    [AspNetCompatibilityRequirements(
        RequirementsMode = AspNetCompatibilityRequirementsMode.Allowed)]
    public class StartingHandService
    {
        [OperationContract]
        public void DoWork()
        {
            // Add your operation implementation here
            return;
        }

        // Add more operations here and mark them with [OperationContract]
    }
}
```

6. Replace the DoWork() method with a GetHands() method that returns a List<StartingHands> collection, as follows:

```
namespace WCFService.Web
{
    [ServiceContract(Namespace = "")]
    [AspNetCompatibilityRequirements(RequirementsMode =
        AspNetCompatibilityRequirementsMode.Allowed)]
    public class StartingHandService
    {
        [OperationContract]
        public List<StartingHands> GetHands()           {
                return StartingHands.GetHands();
        }
        // Add more operations here and mark them
        // with [OperationContract]
    }
}
```

This method simply returns the results from calling the StartingHands.GetHands() method. Note that you need to add a using statement for System.Collections.Generic.

7. Now that you have a Silverlight-enabled WCF service, you need to add a reference in your Silverlight project so that your Silverlight application can access the service. To do this, right-click References within the WCFService project in Solution Explorer and select Add Service Reference, as shown in Figure 7-4. This brings up the Add Service Reference dialog box.

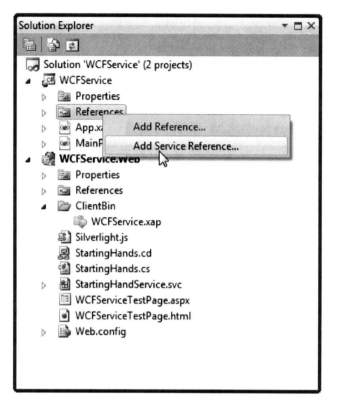

Figure 7-4. *Choosing to add a service reference*

8. In the Add Service Reference dialog box, click the Discover button, as shown in Figure 7-5.

9. Visual Studio will find the StartingHandService.svc and populate the Services list in the Add Service Reference dialog box. Note that you might need to build the solution before Visual Studio will find your service. Expand the StartingHandService.svc node to show the StartingHandService. Click StartingHandService to see the GetHands() web method in the Operations listing, as shown in Figure 7-6. Enter StartingHandServiceReference in the Namespace field, and then click OK to continue.

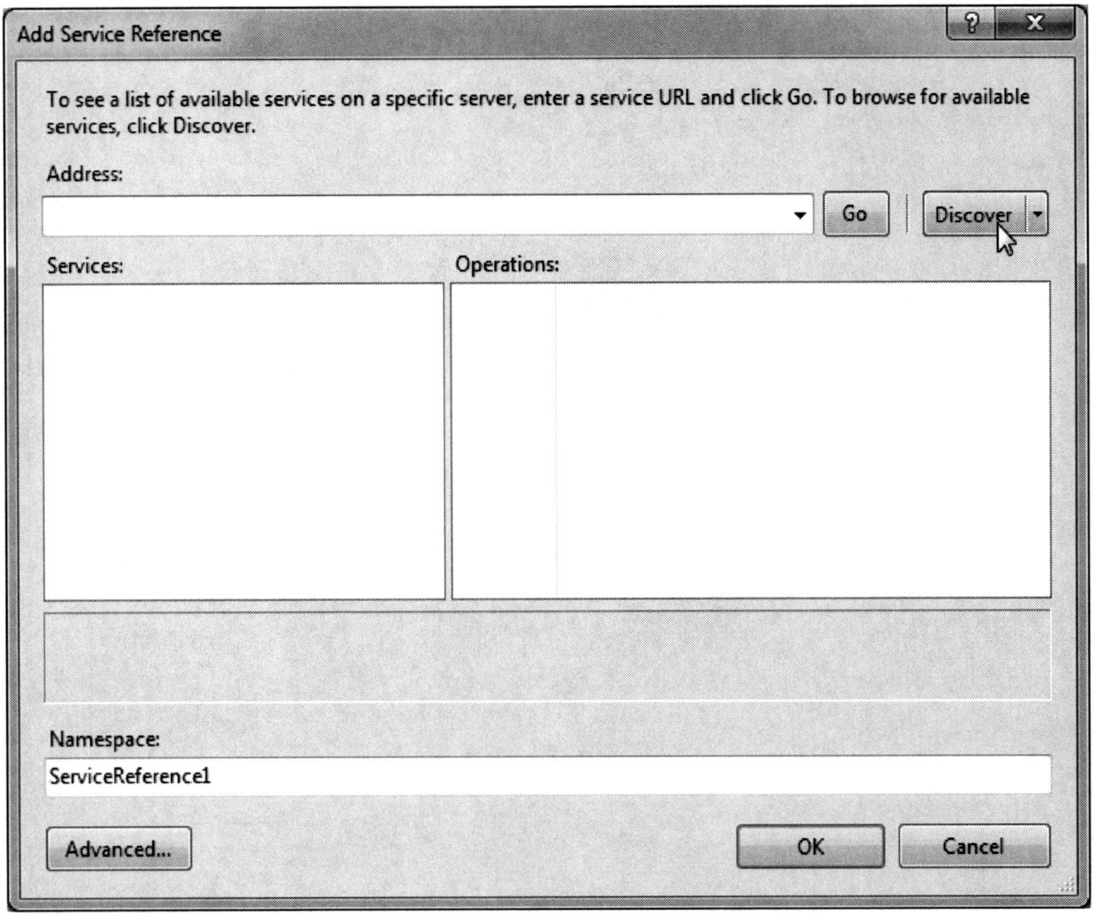

Figure 7-5. Finding the services in the solution

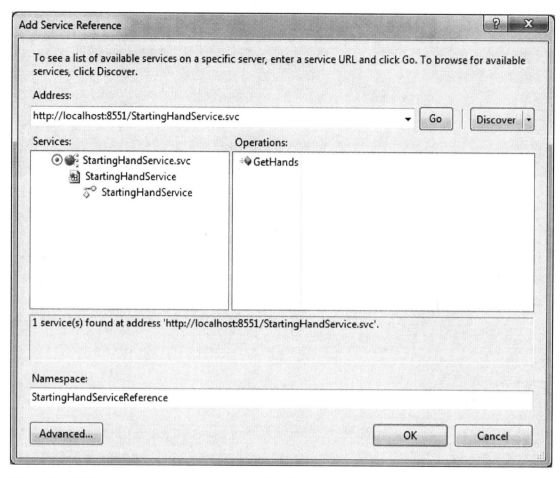

Figure 7-6. Adding a service reference for StartingHandService

10. Open the Visual Studio Object Browser by selecting View ➤ Object Browser from the main menu. Navigate to the WCFService entry, and expand the tree. You will find WCFService.StartingHandServiceReference under your project. Within that, you will see an object named StartingHandServiceClient. Select this object to examine it, as shown in Figure 7-7.

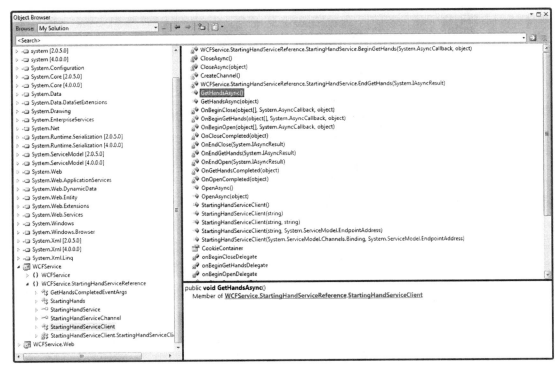

Figure 7-7. Object Browser for StartingHandService

11. Look at the members listed on the right side of the Object Browser. There are a number of items that are added, but take specific note of the method named GetHandsAsync() and the event named GetHandsCompleted. You need to use both of these in order to call your web service from Silverlight.

12. Now it's time to create the Silverlight application's UI. Open the MainPage.xaml file in Visual Studio. Place the cursor within the root Grid, and double-click the DataGrid control in the Toolbox. Once the DataGrid has been added, right-click on it in the designer and select Reset Layout ➤ All. This adds the following XAML:

```
<Grid x:Name="LayoutRoot" Background="White">
    <sdk:DataGrid AutoGenerateColumns="False" Name="dataGrid1" />
</Grid>
```

13. Rename the DataGrid to grdData, and set the Margin to 15. Next, add the following Column definitions, which are from the previous DataGrid exercise in Chapter 5. The DataGrid contains three columns: one template column containing the two cards in the hand, and two text columns containing the nickname and notes about the hand.

```xml
<sdk:DataGrid AutoGenerateColumns="False" Name="grdData" Margin="15">
    <sdk:DataGrid.Columns>
        <sdk:DataGridTemplateColumn Header="Hand">
            <sdk:DataGridTemplateColumn.CellTemplate>
                <DataTemplate>
                    <Grid>
                        <Grid.ColumnDefinitions>
                            <ColumnDefinition />
                            <ColumnDefinition />
                        </Grid.ColumnDefinitions>

                        <Border
                            Margin="2" CornerRadius="4"
                            BorderBrush="Black"
                            BorderThickness="1" />
                        <Rectangle
                            Margin="4" Fill="White"
                            Grid.Column="0" />
                        <Border
                            Margin="2" CornerRadius="4"
                            BorderBrush="Black"
                            BorderThickness="1"
                            Grid.Column="1" />
                        <Rectangle
                            Margin="4" Fill="White"
                            Grid.Column="1" />
                        <TextBlock
                            Text="{Binding Card1}"
                            HorizontalAlignment="Center"
                            VerticalAlignment="Center"
                            Grid.Column="0" />
                        <TextBlock
                            Text="{Binding Card2}"
                            HorizontalAlignment="Center"
                            VerticalAlignment="Center"
                            Grid.Column="1" />

                    </Grid>
                </DataTemplate>
            </sdk:DataGridTemplateColumn.CellTemplate>
        </sdk:DataGridTemplateColumn>

        <sdk:DataGridTextColumn
            Header="Nickname"
            Binding="{Binding Nickname}"  />
        <sdk:DataGridTextColumn
            Header="Notes"
            Binding="{Binding Notes}" />
```

```
        </sdk:DataGrid.Columns>
    </sdk:DataGrid>
```

14. Save the `MainPage.xaml` file, and navigate to the code behind for the application, located in the `MainPage.xaml.cs` file. Wire up the `Loaded` event handler for the page, as follows:

```
public partial class MainPage : UserControl
{
    public MainPage()
    {
        InitializeComponent();
        this.Loaded += new RoutedEventHandler(Page_Loaded);
    }

    void Page_Loaded(object sender, RoutedEventArgs e)
    {
        throw new NotImplementedException();
    }
}
```

15. Next, you need to call the WCF service. In Silverlight, web services can be called only asynchronously, so the browser's execution is not blocked by the transaction. To do this, you need to get an instance of the service reference (commonly referred to as the *web service proxy class*) named `StartingHandService`, which you added earlier. Then wire up an event handler for the service's `GetHandsCompleted` event, which you examined in the Object Browser (in step 8). This is the event handler that will be called when the service has completed execution. Finally, execute the `GetHandsAsync()` method.

▨ **Tip** In a real-world scenario, you will want to present the user with a progress bar or animation while the service is being called because the duration of a web service call can be lengthy.

---

16. Within the `Page_Loaded` event handler, first obtain an instance of `StartingHandService`. Then, in the `GetHandsCompleted` event handler, bind the `ItemsSource` of the `DataGrid` to the result returned from the service call, as shown in the following code. Note that normally you want to check the result to make certain that the web service call was successful and alert the user accordingly in case of failure.

```
using WCFService.StartingHandServiceReference;
...

public partial class MainPage : UserControl
{
    public MainPage()
    {
```

```
        InitializeComponent();
        this.Loaded += new RoutedEventHandler(Page_Loaded);
}

void Page_Loaded(object sender, RoutedEventArgs e)
{
    StartingHandServiceClient service = new StartingHandServiceClient();
    service.GetHandsCompleted += new
                EventHandler<GetHandsCompletedEventArgs>(
                service_GetHandsCompleted);
    service.GetHandsAsync();
}

void service_GetHandsCompleted(object sender, GetHandsCompletedEventArgs e)
{
    this.grdData.ItemsSource = e.Result;
}
}
```

17. Test your application. If all goes well, you should see the populated DataGrid, as shown earlier in Figure 7-1.

This example demonstrated how to use the Silverlight-enabled WCF service provided in Visual Studio to allow your Silverlight application to access data remotely. As noted earlier in the chapter in the section "Data Access in Silverlight Applications," this is one of the most common approaches to data access with Silverlight.

Accessing Services from Other Domains

In the previous example, the web service was on the same domain as your Silverlight application. What if you want to call a service that is on a different domain?

If you attempt to access a service from a different domain in Silverlight, you will notice that it fails. This is because, by default, a Silverlight application cannot call services that are on a different domain, unless it is permitted to do so by the service host. Silverlight determines if it has permission to access a service on a certain domain by looking for one of two files in the root of the target domain: clientaccesspolicy.xml or crossdomain.xml.

First, Silverlight looks for a file named clientaccesspolicy.xml in the domain's root. This is Silverlight's client-access policy file. If you are publishing your own services that you want to be accessible by Silverlight applications, this is the file you want to use, because it provides the most options for Silverlight application policy permissions. The following is a sample clientaccesspolicy.xml file:

```
<?xml version="1.0" encoding="utf-8"?>
<access-policy>
  <cross-domain-access>
    <policy>
      <allow-from http-request-headers="*">
        <domain uri="*"/>
      </allow-from>
      <grant-to>
        <resource path="/" include-subpaths="true"/>
      </grant-to>
```

```
    </policy>
  </cross-domain-access>
</access-policy>
```

The important elements are <allow-from> and <grant-to>. The <allow-from> element defines which domains are permitted to access the resources specified in the <grant-to> element.

If Silverlight cannot find a clientaccesspolicy.xml file at the root of the domain from which you are attempting to access a service, it then looks for a file named crossdomain.xml in the root. This is the XML policy file that has been used to provide access for Flash applications to access cross-domain services, and Silverlight supports this file as well. The following is an example of a crossdomain.xml file:

```
<?xml version="1.0"?>
<!DOCTYPE cross-domain-policy
    SYSTEM "http://www.macromedia.com/xml/dtds/cross-domain-policy.dtd">
<cross-domain-policy>
  <allow-http-request-headers-from domain="*" headers="*"/>
</cross-domain-policy>
```

Again, even though Silverlight supports crossdomain.xml, using clientaccesspolicy.xml for Silverlight applications is the preferred and best practice.

Accessing Data Through Sockets

In the majority of cases, your Silverlight applications accesses data through web services. However, Silverlight provides another mechanism that, though rarely used, can be quite powerful. This mechanism is socket communications. In this section, you will look at a greatly simplified example of communicating with a server via sockets and TCP. The main purpose here is to give you a taste of using sockets in Silverlight so that you have a basic understanding of the process and can consider whether you would like to take this approach. If so, you can refer to a more advanced resource, such as *Pro Silverlight 5 in C#* by Matthew MacDonald (Apress, 2012).

For this example, let's assume you have a socket server running at the IP address 192.168.1.100 on port 4500. The socket server simply accepts text inputs and does something with them. In Silverlight, you want to connect to that socket server and send it text from a TextBox control.

First, you make a connection to the socket server. To do this, create an instance of a System.Net.Sockets.Socket object for IP version 4 (AddressFamily.InterNetwork). The type will be Stream, meaning it will accept a stream of bytes, and the protocol will be TCP.

```
Socket socket;
socket = new Socket(
    AddressFamily.InterNetwork,
    SocketType.Stream,
    ProtocolType.Tcp);
```

You need to execute the socket's `ConnectAsync()` method, but first you must create an instance of `SocketAsyncEventArgs` to pass to the method, using a statement similar to the following:

```
SocketAsyncEventArgs socketArgs = new SocketAsyncEventArgs()
{
    RemoteEndPoint = new IPEndPoint(
        IPAddress.Parse("192.168.1.100"),
        4500)
};
```

This statement sets the target for the socket connection as 192.168.1.100 on port 4500.

In addition, because this is an asynchronous connection, you need to receive notification when the connection has been established. To get this notification, you wire up an event handler to be triggered on the `SocketAsyncEventArgs.Completed` event. Once you have that wired up, you simply call the `ConnectAsync()` method, passing it your `SocketAsyncEventArgs` instance:

```
socketArgs.Completed += new
    EventHandler<SocketAsyncEventArgs>(socketArgs_Completed);
socket.ConnectAsync(socketArgs);
```

The method for this event handler first removes the event handler, and then examines the response from the socket server. If it is successful, it sends a stream of bytes from your `TextBox` control to the socket server through your established connection.

```
void socketArgs_Completed(object sender, SocketAsyncEventArgs e)
{
    e.Completed -= socketArgs_Completed;

    if (e.SocketError == SocketError.Success)
    {
        SocketAsyncEventArgs args = new SocketAsyncEventArgs();
        args.SetBuffer(bytes, 0, bytes.Length);
        args.Completed += new EventHandler<SocketAsyncEventArgs>(OnSendCompleted);
        socket.SendAsync(args);
    }
}
```

Once again, because the calls to the socket are asynchronous, you wire up another event handler called `OnSendCompleted`, which fires when your `SendAsync()` method is completed. This event handler will do nothing more than close the socket:

```
void OnSendCompleted(object sender, SocketAsyncEventArgs e)
{
    socket.Close();
}
```

Although this seems pretty simple, it is complicated by client-access policy permissions. In the same way that a Silverlight application can call a web service on a separate domain only if it has the proper client-access policy permissions, a Silverlight application can call a socket server only if that server contains the proper client-access policy permissions. The following is an example of a client-access policy for a socket server:

```
<?xml version="1.0" encoding ="utf-8"?>
<access-policy>
  <cross-domain-access>
    <policy>
      <allow-from>
        <domain uri="*" />
      </allow-from>
      <grant-to>
        <socket-resource port="4500-4550" protocol="tcp" />
      </grant-to>
    </policy>
  </cross-domain-access>
</access-policy>
```

Recall that when you're using a web service, the client-access policy is contained in a file named clientaccesspolicy.xml, which is placed in the domain's root. In a socket access situation, things are a bit more complex.

Before Silverlight makes a socket request to a server on whatever port is requested by the application, it first makes a socket request of its own to the server on port 943, requesting a policy file. Therefore, your server must have a socket service set up to listen to requests on port 943 and serve up the contents of the client-access policy in order for Silverlight applications to be able to make a socket connection.

Summary

In this chapter, you focused on accessing data from your Silverlight applications through WCF services. I also discussed accessing data from different domains and cross-domain policy files. In addition, you looked at using sockets in Silverlight from a high level.

In the next chapter, you will look at Silverlight's Navigational Framework.

CHAPTER 8

Navigation Framework

The Navigation Framework is a feature in Silverlight that allows developers to implement a way to navigate through different pages within a Silverlight application, creating an experience similar to browsing through different pages of a web site. The framework also allows developers to create a history that can integrate with the browser, enabling users to navigate forward and backward through the history using the browser's back and forward buttons.

In this chapter, you will explore Silverlight's Navigation Framework and try out a couple of examples involving the different aspects of the framework.

Frame and Page Object

The two main objects that are contained in the Navigation Framework are the `Frame` and `Page` objects. (See Figure 8-1.) The `Frame` object is very similar to a `ContentPlaceHolder` in ASP.NET master pages and is the placeholder for the different views to be loaded onto the page.

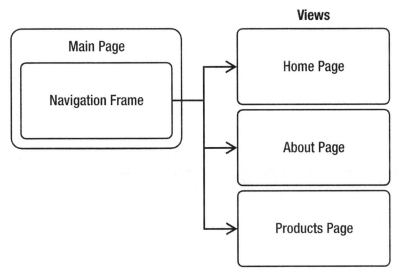

Figure 8-1. *Frame and Page objects*

Try It Out: Creating a Silverlight Navigation Application

This exercise demonstrates creating a Silverlight application with navigation support from scratch using the Navigation Framework. In the exercise, you will build a simple application that contains two HyperlinkButton elements and a Frame. Clicking the links loads one of two pages into the Frame. Let's get started:

1. Start Visual Studio 2010, and select File ➤ New ➤ Project from the main menu.

2. In the New Project dialog box, select Silverlight as the project type and Silverlight Application as the template. Name the project **NavAppFromScratch**, as shown in Figure 8-2.

Figure 8-2. *Creating a new Silverlight application*

3. When the New Silverlight Application dialog appears, select the default to host the Silverlight application in a new ASP.NET web application named NavAppFromScratch.Web. Click OK to continue.

4. By default, the MainPage.xaml file is created and opened for editing. You will start by editing that file. In the Grid definition, add ShowGridLines="True" so

that you can see how your cells are laid out. You can turn this property off later so that your application is cleaner.

5. Next you want to define the Grid cells. You will simply have two rows: one for the links and one for the navigated content.

```
<Grid ShowGridLines="True" x:Name="LayoutRoot" Background="White">

    <Grid.RowDefinitions>
        <RowDefinition Height="30" />
        <RowDefinition></RowDefinition>
    </Grid.RowDefinitions>

</Grid>
```

6. Now that you have the two rows, you want to add the HyperlinkButton elements that will be used to navigate to the different views. You will do this in a horizontal StackPanel. For the Click property, create an event handler called LinkClick:

```
<Grid ShowGridLines="True" x:Name="LayoutRoot" Background="White">

    <Grid.RowDefinitions>
        <RowDefinition Height="30" />
        <RowDefinition></RowDefinition>
    </Grid.RowDefinitions>

    <StackPanel Orientation="Horizontal" HorizontalAlignment="Center">

        <HyperlinkButton Content="View 1"
                         Click="LinkClick"
                         Padding="5" />
        <HyperlinkButton Content="View 2"
                         Click="LinkClick"
                         Padding="5" />

    </StackPanel>

</Grid>
```

7. The next step is to add support for the Navigation Framework in your project. First add a reference to System.Windows.Controls.Navigation.dll by right-clicking on the References folder in your Silverlight project and choosing Add Reference, as shown in Figure 8-3.

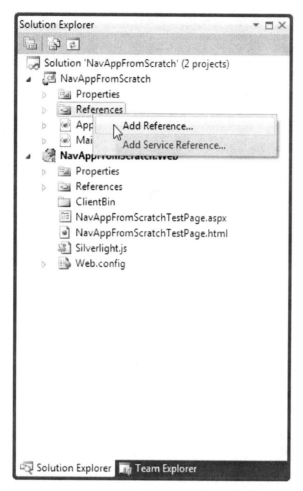

Figure 8-3. The Silverlight navigation application contents

8. When the Add Reference dialog appears, be sure the .NET tab is selected and then browse through the list until you find System.Windows.Controls.Navigation, as shown in Figure 8-4. Select the entry, and click OK to add the reference to the project.

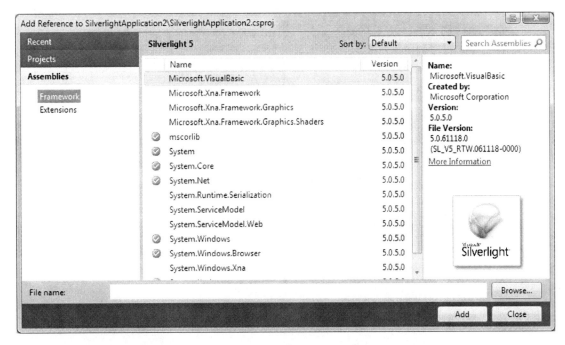

Figure 8-4. The Silverlight navigation application references

9. When the assembly is added, you will see it appear under References in the Solution Explorer, as shown in Figure 8-5.

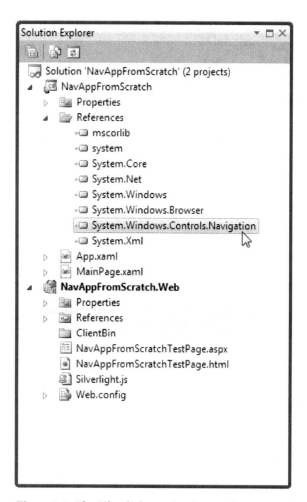

Figure 8-5. The Silverlight navigation application contents with reference

10. Now that you have added the reference to the Navigation Framework, you
    need to add the navigation objects to your application. You start by adding the
    XML namespace for System.Windows.Controls.Navigation to the UserControl
    definition:

```
<UserControl x:Class="NavAppFromScratch.MainPage"
    xmlns="http://schemas.microsoft.com/winfx/2006/xaml/presentation"
    xmlns:x="http://schemas.microsoft.com/winfx/2006/xaml"
    xmlns:d="http://schemas.microsoft.com/expression/blend/2008"
    xmlns:mc="http://schemas.openxmlformats.org/markup-compatibility/2006"
    xmlns:nav="clr-namespace:System.Windows.Controls;↵
assembly=System.Windows.Controls.Navigation"
    mc:Ignorable="d"
    d:DesignHeight="300" d:DesignWidth="400">
```

```
    <Grid x:Name="LayoutRoot" Background="White" ShowGridLines="True">
        <Grid.RowDefinitions>
            <RowDefinition Height="30" />
            <RowDefinition></RowDefinition>
        </Grid.RowDefinitions>
        <StackPanel Orientation="Horizontal" HorizontalAlignment="Center">
            <HyperlinkButton Content="View 1"
                        Click="LinkClick"
                        Padding="5" />
            <HyperlinkButton Content="View 2"
                        Click="LinkClick"
                        Padding="5" />
        </StackPanel>
    </Grid>

</UserControl>
```

11. Now add a Frame to the bottom row of the root Grid named ContentFrame. Set the HorizontalContentAlignment and VerticalContentAlignment to Stretch so that the Frame consumes the entire Grid cell. Also, give the Frame a 10-pixel Margin and a BorderThickness of 2 pixels:

```
<Grid x:Name="LayoutRoot" Background="White" ShowGridLines="True">
    <Grid.RowDefinitions>
        <RowDefinition Height="30" />
        <RowDefinition></RowDefinition>
    </Grid.RowDefinitions>
    <StackPanel Orientation="Horizontal" HorizontalAlignment="Center">

        <HyperlinkButton Content="View 1"
                    Click="LinkClick"
                    Tag="/View1.xaml"
                    Padding="5" />
        <HyperlinkButton Content="View 2"
                    Click="LinkClick"
                    Tag="/View2.xaml"
                    Padding="5" />
    </StackPanel>

    <nav:Frame x:Name="ContentFrame"
                HorizontalContentAlignment="Stretch"
                VerticalContentAlignment="Stretch"
                Margin="10"
                Grid.Row="1"
                BorderThickness="2"
                BorderBrush="Black" />
</Grid>
```

12. Next, add the different views to the project. Right-click on the Silverlight project, and select Add ➤ New Item.

13. In the New Item dialog, select the Silverlight Page template, name the page
View1.xaml, and click the Add button. (See Figure 8-6.)

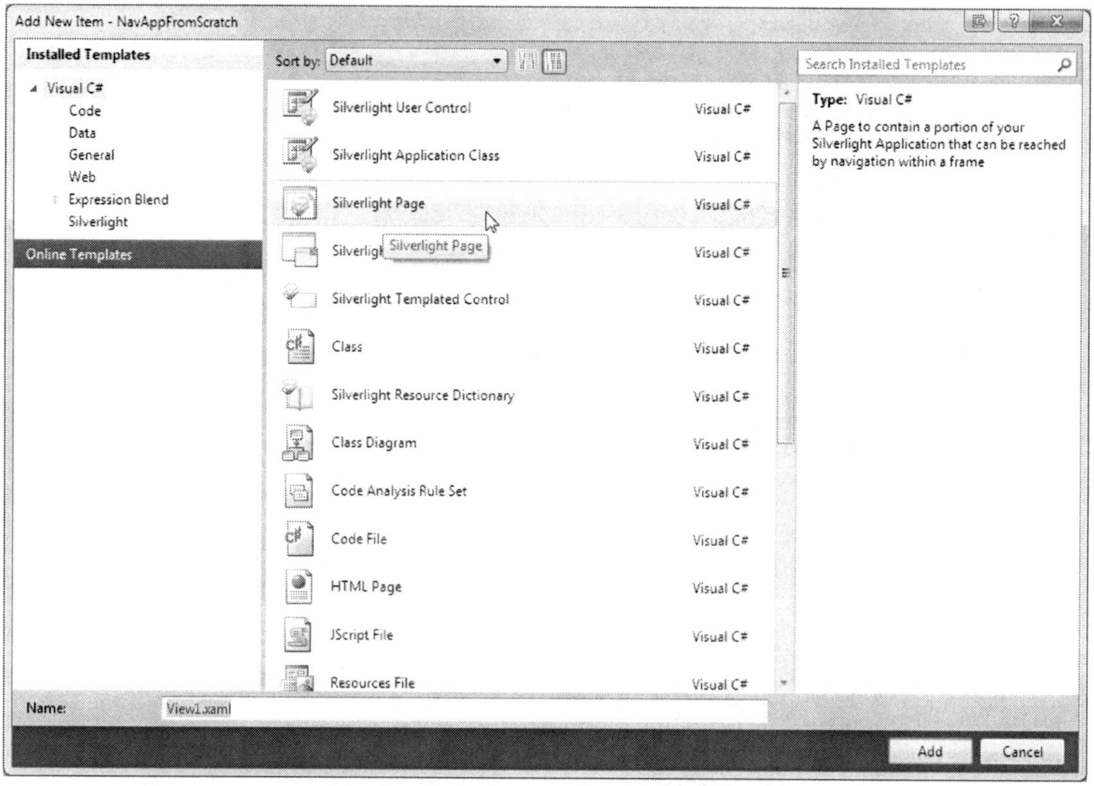

Figure 8-6. *Adding a Silverlight page*

14. Once View1.xaml has been added, repeat steps 12 and 13 to add another
Silverlight page named View2.xaml.

15. Open View1.xaml in design mode, and add the following XAML to the root
Grid:

```
<Grid x:Name="LayoutRoot">
    <TextBlock Text="View 1"
            FontSize="60"
            Foreground="Green"
            HorizontalAlignment="Center"
            VerticalAlignment="Center" />
</Grid>
```

16. Open View2.xaml in design mode, and add the following XAML to the root
Grid:

```
<Grid x:Name="LayoutRoot">
    <TextBlock Text="View 2"
            FontSize="60"
            Foreground="Red"
            HorizontalAlignment="Center"
            VerticalAlignment="Center" />
</Grid>
```

17. You now have the main page containing the Frame and the two views you will load into the Frame. Next, you need to actually load the views into the Frame. You do this on the click event of the two HyperlinkButtons you added in step 6. Although you can easily do this with two click event handlers, you will actually do it with one. Set the Tag property of the HyperlinkButton to be the page view source file. Then the click event handler will be able to retrieve the source file from the Tag:

```
<StackPanel Orientation="Horizontal" HorizontalAlignment="Center">

    <HyperlinkButton Content="View 1"
                Click="LinkClick"
                Tag="/View1.xaml"
                Padding="5" />
    <HyperlinkButton Content="View 2"
                Click="LinkClick"
                Tag="/View2.xaml"
                Padding="5" />
</StackPanel>
```

18. Right-click on LinkClick in the Click attribute, and select Navigate to Event Handler to create the LinkClick event handler. Within the event, add the following code to retrieve the view's source file:

```
private void LinkClick(object sender, RoutedEventArgs e)
{
    HyperlinkButton button = (HyperlinkButton)sender;
    string viewSource = button.Tag.ToString();
}
```

19. Now that you have the view's source file, you can use the Frame's Navigate method to navigate to the proper view:

```
private void LinkClick(object sender, RoutedEventArgs e)
{
    HyperlinkButton button = (HyperlinkButton)sender;
    string viewSource = button.Tag.ToString();
    ContentFrame.Navigate(new Uri(viewSource, UriKind.Relative));
}
```

20. You are now ready to run the solution. Select Debug ➤ Start Debugging, or press F5 to run the application. Internet Explorer will open and the application will be displayed, as shown in Figure 8-7.

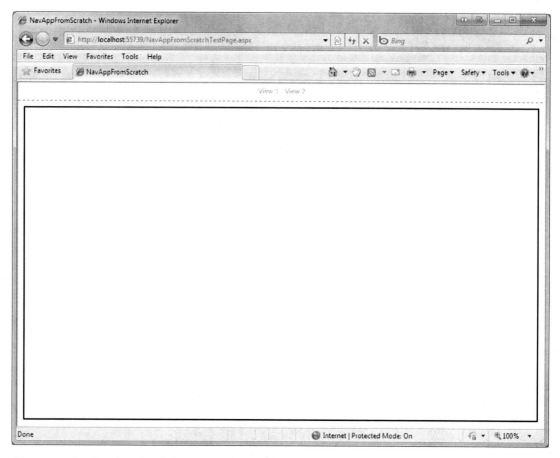

Figure 8-7. *Testing the Silverlight navigation application*

21. Click the View 1 HyperlinkButton at the top of the screen. The Content Frame navigates to the View1.xaml content, as shown in Figure 8-8.

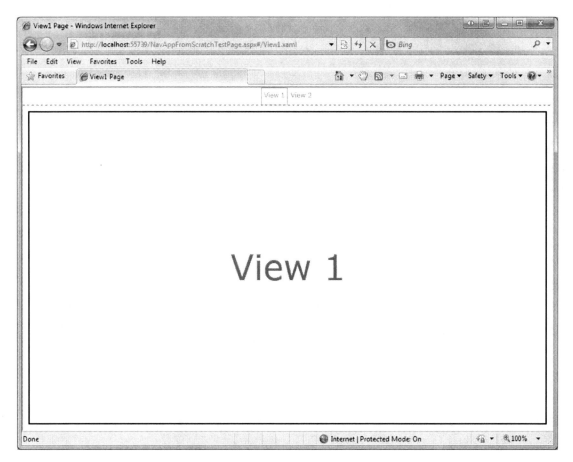

Figure 8-8. Testing the Silverlight navigation application template View 1

22. Then click on the View 2 link to see similar results, as shown in Figure 8-9.

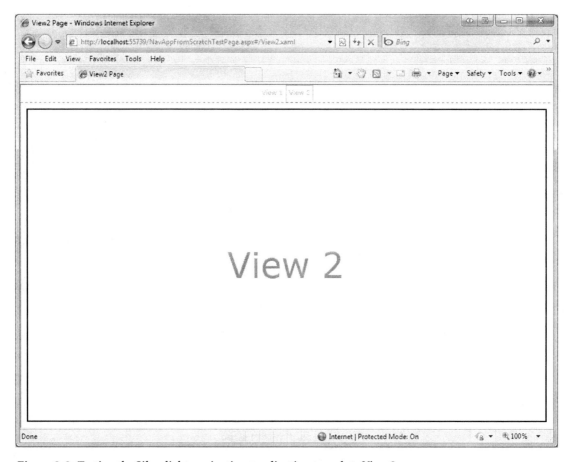

Figure 8-9. *Testing the Silverlight navigation application template View 2*

23. Notice that you can click the browser's back button to navigate backward in history from View 2 to View 1, and back to the default.

Benefits of the Navigation Framework

While the functionality of the Navigation Framework might have been achieved in previous versions of Silverlight, the amount of work it required was significant and normally required you to purchase a third-party control or library. Clearly, having this functionally built into Silverlight is a major advantage. It reduces the amount of code required to achieve the same affects and produces much cleaner and more maintainable code. In addition, it provides a number of additional benefits, such as browser history support and deep linking.

Deep Linking

Another benefit of the Navigation Framework in Silverlight is deep-linking support. *Deep linking* is the ability to link to an application at a specific state.

To illustrate deep linking, consider an application when it is loaded and the home page is displayed. When the user clicks on a link from the home page, the application navigates to the product listings page. The user can then click on a product to navigate to a page containing the details for that product. This application can be represented by the diagram shown in Figure 8-10.

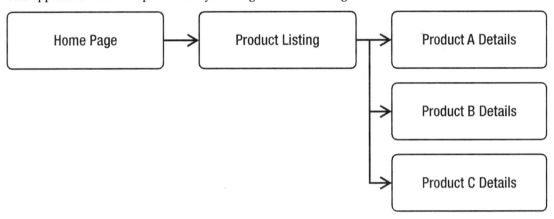

Figure 8-10. Deep linking in Silverlight

Let's say you wanted to generate a link directly to the Product B Details page in the application. With the Navigation Framework, Silverlight allows developers to link to different states in their application.

The NavigationService Object

As you saw earlier in this chapter, you change different views using the Frame object's Navigate method. There are times when you need to gain access to the Frame from within the page itself. For example, if you consider the diagram in Figure 8-11, you can easily navigate to View 1 from the Navigation Frame on the home page. However, if you want to navigate to Inner View 1 from the code behind on View 1, you need to get access to the Navigation Frame that is hosting View 1 in order to navigate to a different view.

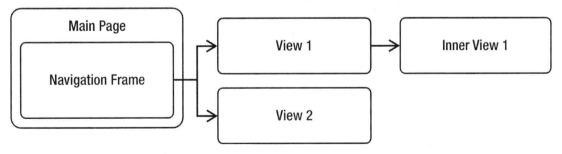

Figure 8-11. NavigationService object in Silverlight

Luckily, the Navigation Framework contains an object that allows a view to access its Hosting Frame. That object is the NavigationService. Let's explore the use of the NavigationService object by running through the following exercise.

Try It Out: Using the NavigationService Object

In this exercise, you will expand on the example you built earlier in the chapter. You add a button to the View 1 page and, on the click event of that button, you navigate to a new page called Inner View 1 using the NavigationService object. Let's get started:

1. Begin by opening the project NavAppFromScratch you just completed in the previous section.

2. Open the XAML for View1.xaml, and modify the source to include a button under the TextBlock:

```
<Grid x:Name="LayoutRoot">
    <StackPanel>
        <TextBlock Text="View 1"
                FontSize="60"
                Foreground="Green"
                HorizontalAlignment="Center"
                VerticalAlignment="Center" />
        <Button Click="Button_Click"
            Padding="10"
            Content="Navigate to Inner View"
            HorizontalAlignment="Center" />
    </StackPanel>
</Grid>
```

3. You now need to add the new view that you will navigate to using the NavigationService. Right-click on the Silverlight project, and choose Add ➤ New Item. Select Silverlight Page as the template, and name the file **InnerView1.xaml**.

4. In the XAML for InnerView1.xaml, add a simple TextBlock:

```
<Grid x:Name="LayoutRoot">
    <TextBlock Text="Inner View 1"
            FontSize="40"
            Foreground="Blue"
            HorizontalAlignment="Center"
            VerticalAlignment="Center" />
</Grid>
```

5. Next, add the Button_Click event handler in the View1.xaml code behind, and add the following code:

```
private void Button_Click(object sender, RoutedEventArgs e)
{
    NavigationService.Navigate(
            new Uri("/InnerView1.xaml", UriKind.Relative));
}
```

6. You are now ready to run the solution. Select Debug ➤ Start Debugging, or press F5 to run the application. When Internet Explorer opens the application, click on the View 1 link at the top. The application should appear as shown in Figure 8-12.

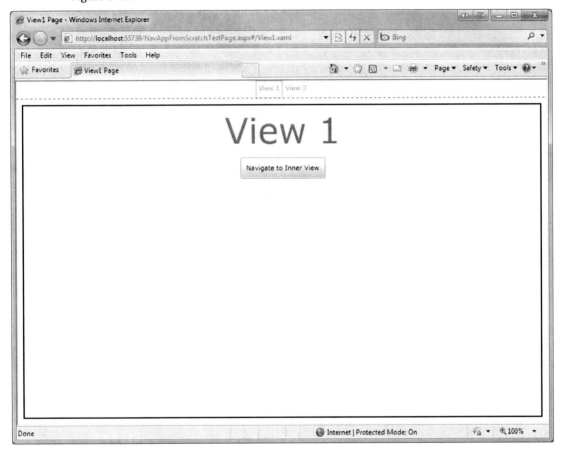

Figure 8-12. Testing the NavigationService object

7. If you click on the Navigate To Inner View button, the application now shows the InnerView1.xaml content in the top frame, as seen in Figure 8-13.

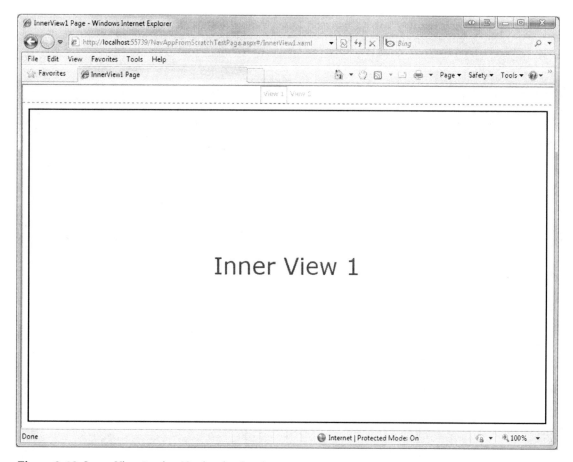

Figure 8-13. Inner View 1 using NavigationService

In this section, you learned how to use the NavigationService object to access the Navigation Frame from a Silverlight page. In the next section, you will learn how to pass data to navigation pages using another object contained in the Navigation Framework, the NetworkContext object.

Passing Data to Navigation Pages

In this section, you will discuss passing data to page views within a Navigation Framework solution. In HTML pages, data is passed to other pages using the QueryString. The same is true for pages within a Silverlight navigation application through the use of the NavigationContext object. As an example, if you want to retrieve the QueryString property ProductID, you use the following syntax:

```
string productId = NavigationContext.QueryString["ProductID"].ToString();
```

Let's explore how to use the NavigationContext object to pass data to views.

Try It Out: Passing Data to Navigation Pages

In this exercise, you will expand on the project you continued working on in the previous section. You pass some additional data to the InnerView1.xaml file, retrieve that data using the NavigationContext object, and then display the view content dependent on that data.

1. Begin by opening the project NavAppFromScratch you were working on in the previous section.

2. Open the XAML for View1.xaml, and modify the source to include a ComboBox under the Button:

```
<Grid x:Name="LayoutRoot">
    <StackPanel>
        <TextBlock Text="View 1"
                FontSize="60"
                Foreground="Green"
                HorizontalAlignment="Center"
                VerticalAlignment="Center" />
        <Button Click="Button_Click"
            Padding="10"
            Content="Navigate to Inner View"
            HorizontalAlignment="Center" />
        <ComboBox Padding="10" Margin="10" x:Name="Color" Width="100">
            <ComboBoxItem Content="Blue" IsSelected="True" />
            <ComboBoxItem Content="Red" />
            <ComboBoxItem Content="Green" />
        </ComboBox>
    </StackPanel>
</Grid>
```

3. Next open the code behind for View1.xaml, and edit the Button_Click event handler to pass the selected color in the query string of the URI passed to the Navigate method:

```
private void Button_Click(object sender, RoutedEventArgs e)
{
    string color = Color.SelectionBoxItem.ToString();

    NavigationService.Navigate(
        new Uri(string.Format("/InnerView1.xaml?Color={0}", color),
            UriKind.Relative));
}
```

4. Open the InnerView1.xaml file, and add a second TextBlock below the existing TextBlock using a StackPanel:

```
<Grid x:Name="LayoutRoot">
    <StackPanel Orientation="Vertical">
        <TextBlock Text="Inner View 1"
                x:Name="ViewHeader"
                FontSize="40"
                Foreground="Blue"
```

```
                            HorizontalAlignment="Center"
                            VerticalAlignment="Center" />
            <TextBlock Text="(Blue)"
                            x:Name="ViewColor"
                            FontSize="30"
                            Foreground="Blue"
                            HorizontalAlignment="Center"
                            VerticalAlignment="Center" />
        </StackPanel>
    </Grid>
```

5. Open the code behind for InnerView1.xaml, and retrieve the passed color using the NavigationContext object. Then add a switch statement to change the color of the TextBlocks, and edit the text for the second TextBlock:

```
protected override void OnNavigatedTo(NavigationEventArgs e)
{
    string color = NavigationContext.QueryString["Color"].ToString();
    Brush b;

    switch (color)
    {
        case "Red":
            b = new SolidColorBrush(Color.FromArgb(255, 255, 0, 0));
            ViewHeader.Foreground = b;
            ViewColor.Foreground = b;
            ViewColor.Text = "(Red)";
            break;

        case "Green":
            b = new SolidColorBrush(Color.FromArgb(255, 0, 255, 0));
            ViewHeader.Foreground = b;
            ViewColor.Foreground = b;
            ViewColor.Text = "(Green)";
            break;

        default:
            b = new SolidColorBrush(Color.FromArgb(255, 0, 0, 255));
            ViewHeader.Foreground = b;
            ViewColor.Foreground = b;
            ViewColor.Text = "(Blue)";
            break;
    }
}
```

6. You are now ready to run the solution. Select Debug ➤ Start Debugging, or press F5 to run the application. When Internet Explorer opens the application, click on the View 1 link at the top. The application should appear, as shown in Figure 8-14.

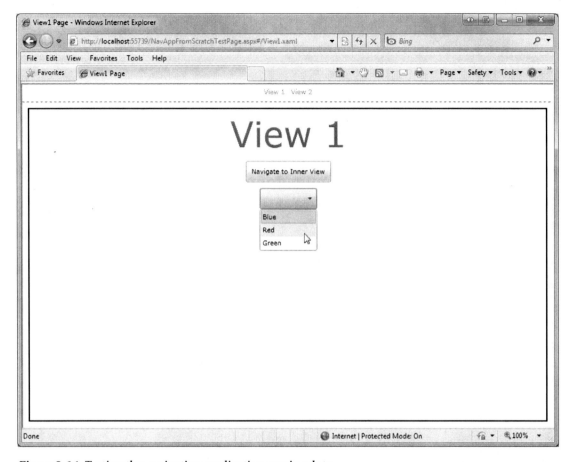

Figure 8-14. Testing the navigation application passing data

7. Select Red in the combo box, and click the Navigate To Inner View button. You will see the content of the InnerView1.xaml displayed with red text and with the text "(Red)" displayed, as shown in Figure 8-15.

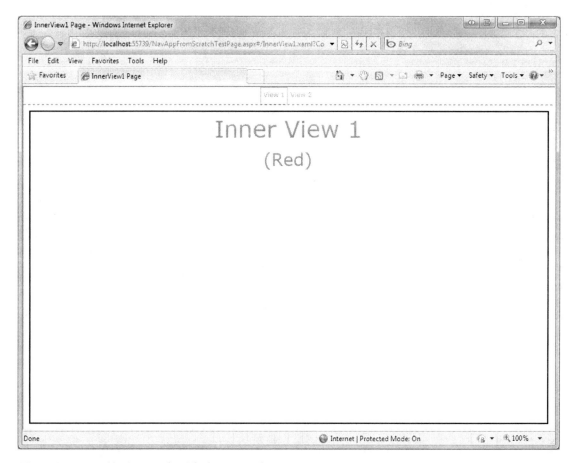

Figure 8-15. Navigation result with data passed

In this section, you learned how to use the `NavigationContext` object to pass data to navigation views using the query string. In the next section, I will discuss URI Mapping and how it can be used to create user-friendly URIs to your navigation views.

URI Mapping

In the preceding examples, you might have noticed the URL changing as you navigated to different views in a frame. You might have also noticed that the URLs were not very pretty and contained some information you might not want to display. As an example, consider the following URL:

`http://www.domain.com/Catalog.aspx#ProductDetails.xaml?ID=4`

For starters, this URL is not very pleasant to look at, and it's not very user-friendly either. It also might contain information you prefer not to provide the user, such as the exact file name and the query string name. A much more appropriate URL would look like the following:

```
http://www.domain.com/Catalog.aspx#Product/4
```

This URL is much easier to read and is more user friendly. In addition, it doesn't give away any details about your solution. You can obtain this URL using a feature known as URI Mapping. Let's work through an example to further explore URI Mapping with the Navigation Framework.

Try It Out: URI Mapping and the Navigation Framework

In this example, you will work through implementing URI Mapping with the project you have been working with earlier in the chapter.

1. Begin by opening the project NavAppFromScratch you were working on in the previous section.

2. There are three views in your solution you will add a URI Mapping for: View1.xaml, View2.xaml, and InnerView1.xaml. For these views, you add simple URI maps that point them to View1, View2, and InnerView. Start by opening the App.xaml file and adding the xml namespace for the Navigation Framework:

    ```
    <Application xmlns="http://schemas.microsoft.com/winfx/2006/xaml/presentation"
        xmlns:x="http://schemas.microsoft.com/winfx/2006/xaml"
        xmlns:nav="clr-
    namespace:System.Windows.Navigation;assembly=System.Windows.Controls.Navigation"
        x:Class="NavAppFromScratch.App"
        >
        <Application.Resources>

        </Application.Resources>
    </Application>
    ```

3. Now that the namespace is added, you need to add the UriMapper section to the application resources:

    ```
    <Application.Resources>
        <nav:UriMapper x:Key="uriMapper">

        </nav:UriMapper>
    </Application.Resources>
    ```

4. Within the UriMapper section, you now need to add two UriMapping elements: one for View1.xaml and one for View2.xaml. Each mapping contains two attributes: the Uri attribute is the name representing the mapping that will appear in the browser address bar, and the MappedUri attribute represents the actual URI mapped to by the UriMapping:

    ```
    <Application.Resources>
        <nav:UriMapper x:Key="uriMapper">
            <nav:UriMapping Uri="View1" MappedUri="/View1.xaml" />
            <nav:UriMapping Uri="View2" MappedUri="/View2.xaml" />
        </nav:UriMapper>
    </Application.Resources>
    ```

5. Update MainPage.xaml to navigate to the views using the UriMappings:

```
<StackPanel Orientation="Horizontal" HorizontalAlignment="Center">

    <HyperlinkButton Content="View 1"
            Click="LinkClick"
            Tag="View1"
            Padding="5" />
    <HyperlinkButton Content="View 2"
            Click="LinkClick"
            Tag="View2"
            Padding="5" />
</StackPanel>
```

6. Next, shift your attention to the InnerView1.xaml. If you recall in the previous section on passing data to a navigation view, you are passing the color to InnerView1.xaml via the QueryString. Because of this, you need that to be taken into account in your UriMapping. Open up the code behind for View1.xaml, and modify the Button_Click method so that it navigates to InnerView/{0}:

```
private void Button_Click(object sender, RoutedEventArgs e)
{
    string color = Color.SelectionBoxItem.ToString();

    NavigationService.Navigate(
        new Uri(string.Format("InnerView/{0}", color),
            UriKind.Relative));
}
```

7. For the navigation to work, you need to add an additional UriMapping to the Application.Resources in the App.xaml file:

```
<Application.Resources>
    <nav:UriMapper x:Key="uriMapper">
        <nav:UriMapping Uri="View1" MappedUri="/View1.xaml" />
        <nav:UriMapping Uri="View2" MappedUri="/View2.xaml" />
        <nav:UriMapping Uri="InnerView/{c}"
                    MappedUri="/InnerView1.xaml?Color={c}" />
    </nav:UriMapper>
</Application.Resources>
```

8. Next, in the MainPage.xaml, add the UriMapper property to the Navigation Frame object:

```
<nav:Frame x:Name="ContentFrame"
                HorizontalContentAlignment="Stretch"
                VerticalContentAlignment="Stretch"
                Margin="10"
                Grid.Row="1"
                BorderThickness="2"
                BorderBrush="Black"
                UriMapper="{StaticResource uriMapper}" />
```

9. You are now ready to run the solution. Select Debug ➤ Start Debugging, or press F5 to run the application. When Internet Explorer opens the application, click on the View 1 link at the top. Notice that the URL now reads as follows:

```
NavAppFromScratchTestPage.aspx#
```

10. Now select Red, click on Navigate To Inner View, and once again inspect the URL:

```
NavAppFromScratchTestPage.aspx#InnerView/Red
```

As you saw in this example, UriMapping provides a way to create more user-friendly URL addresses and to keep application-specific information from appearing in your application.

URI ROUTING

In addition to URI Mapping, the Navigation Framework in Silverlight supports URI Routing. For example, if you place all of your navigation views in a subdirectory named Views, you can follow a naming convention that you set. Then set up URI routes such as the following:

```
<nav:UriMapping Uri="{}{p}" MappedUri="/Views/{p}.xaml" />
```

This mapping will map all files within the Views directory to its file name minus the extension. For example, */Views/View1.xaml* would map to *View1* and */Views/AboutPage.xaml* would map to *AboutPage*. As you can see, if you are able to set a naming convention that you can follow, URI Routing can really help you handle default mappings with the Navigation Framework.

Silverlight Navigation Application Template

Although you can use the Navigation Framework from within a standard Silverlight application, Visual Studio 2010 contains a project template that creates a base Silverlight Navigation Application.

Try It Out: Using the Silverlight Navigation Application Template

In this example, you will create a base Silverlight application with navigation support using the built-in Silverlight Navigation Application template included in Visual Studio 2010:

1. Start Visual Studio 2010, and select File ➤ New ➤ Project from the main menu.

2. In the New Project dialog box, select Silverlight as the project type and Silverlight Navigation Application as the template. Name the project **NavTemplate**, as shown in Figure 8-16.

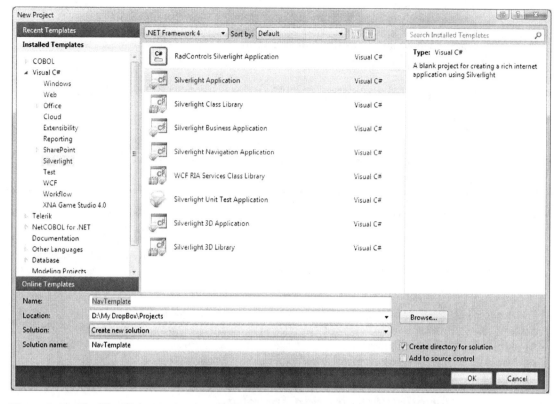

Figure 8-16. The Silverlight Navigation Application project template

3. When the New Silverlight Application dialog appears, select the default to host the Silverlight application in a new ASP.NET web application named NavTemplate.Web. Click OK to continue.

4. When the project is created by Visual Studio, you will notice that a number of pages have already been created for you, as shown in Figure 8-17. The base navigation project contains a main page called MainPage.xaml that hosts the navigation frame and has two navigation pages in the Views folder: About.xaml and Home.xaml. In addition, there is a ErrorWindow.xaml page view that is created.

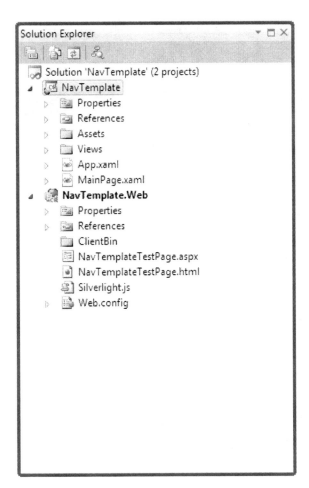

Figure 8-17. The base navigation project

5. Select Debug ➤ Start Debugging, or press F5 to run the application. Internet Explorer will open and the application will be displayed, as shown in Figure 8-18.

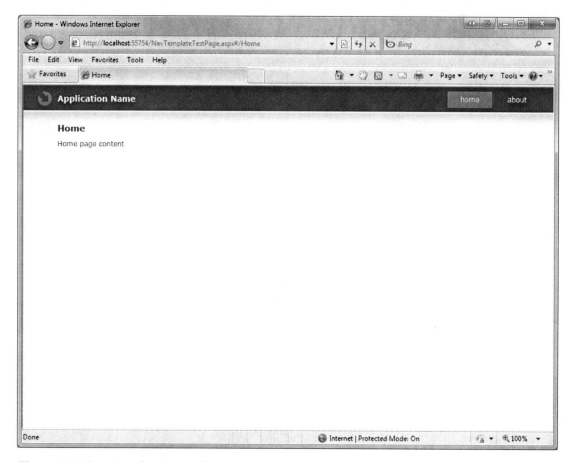

Figure 8-18. *Creating a hosting application*

6. Notice at the top right-hand corner of the application there are two links: home and about. Click the about button, and the navigation frame loads the AboutPage.xaml page into the white content box, as shown in Figure 8-19.

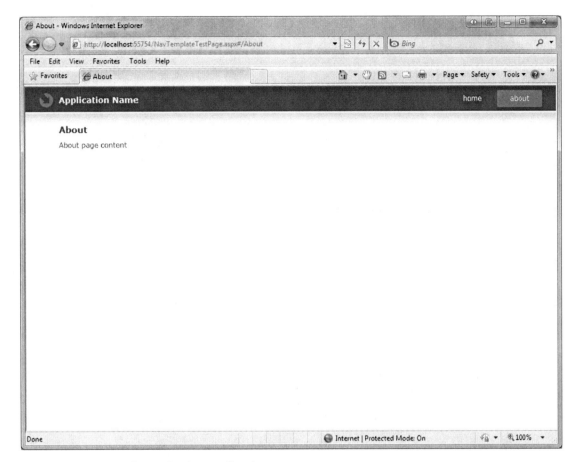

Figure 8-19. *Testing the navigation application*

As you have seen, the Silverlight Navigation Application template can be used to give you a base application with navigation support to build on.

Using Multiple Frames

In all the examples you have worked through in this chapter, you have dealt only with a single Frame. However, there is no limit on the number of Frames you can include in your application. There are some restrictions, though. First of all, only one Frame can integrate with the browser. Because of this, if you use multiple Frames, you need to indicate what Frame will be integrated with the browser. This is done using the JournalOwnership property on the Frame object. Consider the following example:

```
<navigation:Frame x:Name="ContentFrame"  />
<navigation:Frame x:Name="BottomFrame" JournalOwnership="OwnsJournal" />
```

In the preceding example, the ContentFrame has full integration with the browser, but the BottomFrame does not. Let's see this in action in the following exercise.

Try It Out: Using Multiple Frames

In this example, you will add a second Frame to the project you have been working on throughout this chapter:

1. Begin by opening the project NavAppFromScratch you were working on in the earlier section.

2. Add a new view to the project. Right-click on the Silverlight project, and choose Add ➤ New Item. Select Silverlight Page as the template, and name the file **BottomView.xaml**.

3. In the XAML for BottomView.xaml, add a simple TextBlock:

```
<Grid x:Name="LayoutRoot">
    <TextBlock Text="Bottom View 1"
            FontSize="30"
            Foreground="Green"
            HorizontalAlignment="Center"
            VerticalAlignment="Center" />
</Grid>
```

4. With the new view created, you now need to edit the MainPage.xaml file to add a third row to the Grid and add a new Frame within that new row. The second Frame will not integrate with the browser, so set the JournalOwnership property to OwnsJournal:

```
<Grid x:Name="LayoutRoot" Background="White" ShowGridLines="True">
    <Grid.RowDefinitions>
        <RowDefinition Height="30" />
        <RowDefinition></RowDefinition>
        <RowDefinition Height="65" />
    </Grid.RowDefinitions>
    <StackPanel Orientation="Horizontal" HorizontalAlignment="Center">

        <HyperlinkButton Content="View 1"
                Click="LinkClick"
                Tag="View1"
                Padding="5" />
        <HyperlinkButton Content="View 2"
                Click="LinkClick"
                Tag="View2"
                Padding="5" />
    </StackPanel>

    <nav:Frame x:Name="ContentFrame"
            HorizontalContentAlignment="Stretch"
            VerticalContentAlignment="Stretch"
            Margin="10"
            Grid.Row="1"
            BorderThickness="2"
            BorderBrush="Black"
            UriMapper="{StaticResource uriMapper}" />
```

```
<nav:Frame x:Name="BottomFrame"
        HorizontalContentAlignment="Stretch"
        VerticalContentAlignment="Stretch"
        Margin="10"
        Grid.Row="2"
        JournalOwnership="OwnsJournal"
        BorderThickness="2"
        BorderBrush="Black" />
```

```
</Grid>
```

5. Next, view the code behind for MainPage.xaml, and add a Navigate call for BottomFrame:

```
private void LinkClick(object sender, RoutedEventArgs e)
{
    HyperlinkButton button = (HyperlinkButton)sender;
    string viewSource = button.Tag.ToString();
    ContentFrame.Navigate(new Uri(viewSource, UriKind.Relative));
    BottomFrame.Navigate(new Uri("/BottomView.xaml", UriKind.Relative));
}
```

6. You are now ready to run the solution. Select Debug ➤ Start Debugging, or press F5 to run the application. Click on the View 1 link at the top and the application will appear, as shown in Figure 8-20 with the second Frame at the bottom.

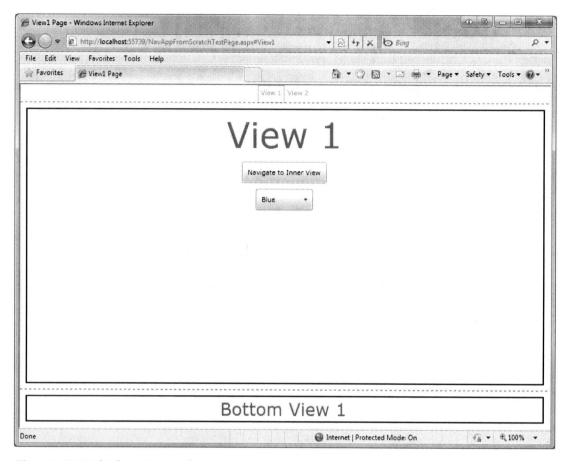

Figure 8-20. Multiple navigation frames

Summary

In this chapter, you looked at the Navigation Framework in depth and saw how it can be used to build Silverlight applications that contain multiple page views. You explored the different objects within the Navigation Framework, such as the `NavigationContext` and `NavigationService`, as well as how to implement URI Mapping within your applications.

CHAPTER 9

Isolated Storage in Silverlight

Localized storage in Silverlight is handled by its *isolated storage* feature, which is a virtual file system that can be used to store application data on the client's machine. As just a few examples, you might use local storage in your application to store user settings, undo information or shopping cart contents, or use it as a local cache for your commonly used objects. Implementations of this feature are really limited only by your imagination.

In this chapter, you will explore Silverlight's isolated storage. I will walk you through building a virtual storage explorer to view the directories and files contained within isolated storage for an application. In addition, you will look at the isolated storage quota and how to increase the quota size for your Silverlight applications.

Note Silverlight allows developers to create out-of-browser applications with elevated security. With this elevated access comes the ability to access the client's local hard drive. In this chapter, we are discussing the isolated storage features of Silverlight only. For more information on creating applications with elevated security, see Chapter 16.

Working with Isolated Storage

Storing application information has always been a challenge for developers of traditional web applications. Often, implementing such storage means storing information in cookies or on the server, which requires using a postback to retrieve the data. In the case of desktop applications, implementing storage for application information is significantly easier because developers have more access to the user's hard drive. Once again, Silverlight bridges the gap between desktop applications and web applications by offering isolated storage.

Using the Silverlight classes for working with isolated storage, you can not only store settings locally, but also create files and directories, as well as read and write files within isolated storage.

Using the Isolated Storage API

The classes for accessing isolated storage are contained within the System.IO.IsolatedStorage namespace. This namespace contains the following three classes:

- IsolatedStorageFile

- IsolatedStorageFileStream

- IsolatedStorageSettings

You'll look at each class to see what it represents.

IsolatedStorageFile

The IsolatedStorageFile class represents the isolated storage area, and the files and directories contained within it. This class provides the majority of the properties and methods used when working with isolated storage in Silverlight. As an example, to get an instance of the user's isolated storage for a given application, use the static method GetUserStoreForApplication(), as follows:

```
using (var store = IsolatedStorageFile.GetUserStoreForApplication())
{
    //...
}
```

Once the storage instance has been retrieved, a number of operations are available, including CreateDirectory(), CreateFile(), GetDirectoryNames(), and GetFileNames(). Also, the class has properties, such as Quota and AvailableFreeSpace. The following example creates a directory in isolated storage called Directory1, and then it retrieves the total and available free space in isolated storage:

```
using (var store = IsolatedStorageFile.GetUserStoreForApplication())
{
    store.CreateDirectory("Directory1");
    long quota = store.Quota;
    long availableSpace = store.AvailableFreeSpace;
}
```

IsolatedStorageFileStream

The IsolatedStorageFileStream class represents a given file. It is used to read, write, and create files within isolated storage. The class extends the FileStream class, and in most cases, developers will use a StreamReader and StreamWriter to work with the stream. As an example, the following code creates a new file named TextFile.txt and writes a string to the file:

```
using (var store = IsolatedStorageFile.GetUserStoreForApplication())
{
    IsolatedStorageFileStream stream = store.CreateFile("TextFile.txt");
    System.IO.StreamWriter sw = new System.IO.StreamWriter(stream);
    sw.Write("Contents of the File");
    sw.Close();
}
```

IsolatedStorageSettings

The IsolatedStorageSettings class allows developers to store key/value pairs in isolated storage. The key/value pairs are user-specific and provide a very convenient way to store settings locally. The following example demonstrates storing the user's name in IsolatedStorageSettings:

```
public partial class MainPage : UserControl
{
    private IsolatedStorageSettings isSettings =
        IsolatedStorageSettings.ApplicationSettings;

    public MainPage()
    {
        InitializeComponent();
        this.Loaded += new RoutedEventHandler(Page_Loaded);
        this.cmdSave.Click += new RoutedEventHandler(cmdSave_Click);
    }

    void cmdSave_Click(object sender, RoutedEventArgs e)
    {
        isSettings["name"] = this.txtName.Text;
        SetWelcomeMessage();
    }

    void Page_Loaded(object sender, RoutedEventArgs e)
    {
        SetWelcomeMessage();
    }

    private void SetWelcomeMessage()
    {
        if (isSettings.Contains("name"))
        {
            string name = (string)isSettings["name"];
            this.txtWelcome.Text = "Welcome " + name;
        }
        else
        {
            txtWelcome.Text =
                "Welcome! Enter Your Name and Press Save.";
        }
    }
}
```

The first time users access the application, they see the message "Welcome! Enter Your Name and Press Save." They can then enter their name and click the Save Name button. The name is saved in local storage under the key/value pair called name. The next time the user accesses the application, his name will still be stored in local storage, and he will see the friendly welcome message, as shown in Figure 9-1.

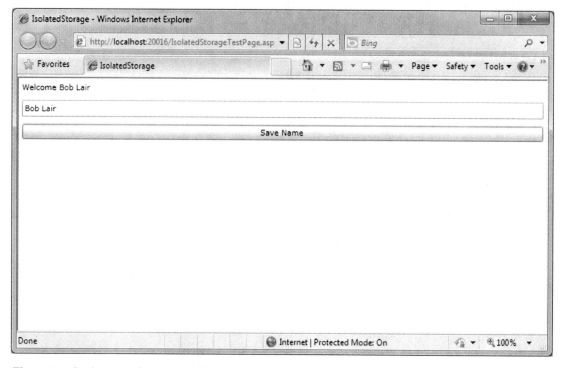

Figure 9-1. *Saving a user's name with IsolatedStorageSettings*

Now that you have briefly looked at some of the key classes associated with Silverlight's isolated storage, let's try building an application that uses this storage.

Try It Out: Creating a File Explorer for Isolated Storage

In this example, you will create a file explorer that allows a user to navigate through an application's virtual storage within Silverlight's isolated storage. The file explorer will allow users to view, modify, and create new files within the given directories. Keep in mind that each Silverlight application has its own isolated storage, so the file explorer will be unique to the application. The end result will appear as shown in Figure 9-2.

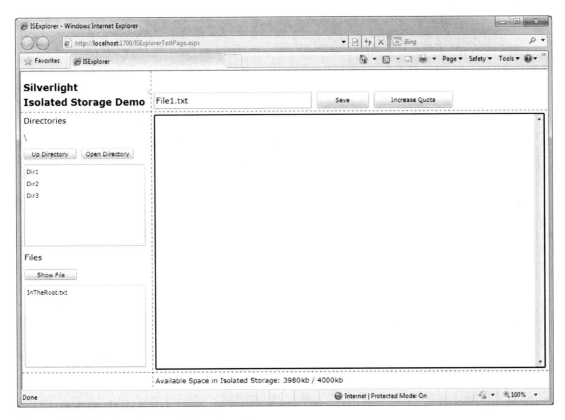

Figure 9-2. *The isolated storage file explorer demo*

Creating the Application Layout

Let's get started by setting up the application layout.

1. Create a new Silverlight application in Visual Studio 2010. Name it ISExplorer, and allow Visual Studio to create an ASP.NET Web Application called ISExplorer.Web to host your application.

2. Next, you need to define the Grid layout. You will use the LayoutRoot grid that is already added by default, and then add two columns and three rows. Set the Width property of the first column to 1* and the Width of the second column to 3*. Set the Height for the rows to 75, *, and 30 from top to bottom.

```
<Grid x:Name="LayoutRoot" Background="White" ShowGridLines="True">
    <Grid.ColumnDefinitions>
        <ColumnDefinition Width="250" />
        <ColumnDefinition />
    </Grid.ColumnDefinitions>
    <Grid.RowDefinitions>
```

```
            <RowDefinition Height="75" />
            <RowDefinition />
            <RowDefinition Height="30" />
        </Grid.RowDefinitions>
    </Grid>
```

3. Next, double click on GridSplitter in the toolbox to add a GridSplitter (see Chapter 4 for details) to allow the user to resize the left and right columns. Set the Grid.RowSpan to 3 and HorizontalAlignment to Right.

```
<Grid x:Name="LayoutRoot" Background="White" ShowGridLines="True">
    <Grid.ColumnDefinitions>
        <ColumnDefinition Width="250" />
        <ColumnDefinition />
    </Grid.ColumnDefinitions>
    <Grid.RowDefinitions>
        <RowDefinition Height="75" />
        <RowDefinition />
        <RowDefinition Height="30" />
    </Grid.RowDefinitions>

    <sdk:GridSplitter
        Grid.RowSpan="3"
        HorizontalAlignment="Right" />
</Grid>
```

4. Now you will start filling the Grid cells with controls. You will add quite a few controls, using nested StackPanel components to assist you in getting the desired layout. These controls were discussed in detail in Chapters 4 and 5, and you can refer back to those chapters for more information about any of the controls used here.

5. Run your application. It should look like Figure 9-3.

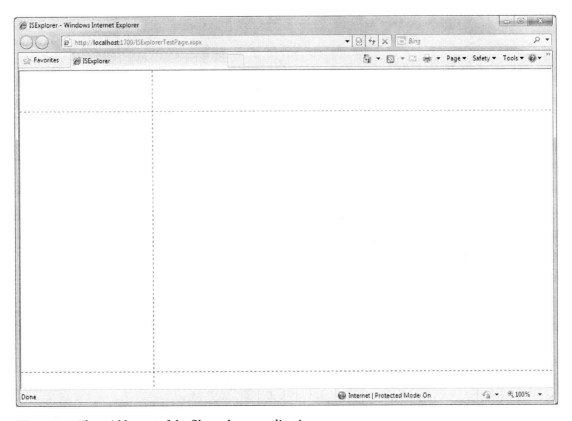

Figure 9-3. The grid layout of the file explorer application

6. In `Grid.Row` and `Grid.Column` (0,0), place a `StackPanel` that contains a couple cosmetic `TextBlock` controls that will serve as your application title, as follows (with some of the existing code omitted for brevity):

```
<Grid x:Name="LayoutRoot" Background="White" ShowGridLines="True">
    ...
    <basics:GridSplitter ...

    <StackPanel
        VerticalAlignment="Bottom"
        Orientation="Vertical"
        Margin="5">

        <TextBlock
            FontSize="18"
            FontWeight="Bold"
            Text="Silverlight">
        </TextBlock>
        <TextBlock
```

```
            FontSize="18"
            FontWeight="Bold"
            Text="Isolated Storage Demo">
        </TextBlock>

    </StackPanel>
</Grid>
```

7. Referring to Figure 9-2, notice that the content is divided into two sections: one for directories (top) and one for files (bottom). Let's first take care of the section for directories.

8. In Grid.Row and Grid.Column (1,0), place another StackPanel, which spans two rows, with a couple TextBlock controls, three Button controls, and two ListBox controls. The XAML should appear as follows (again, with some of the source code omitted, but with the changes shown):

```
<Grid x:Name="LayoutRoot" Background="White" ShowGridLines="True">
    ...
    <basics:GridSplitter ...

    <StackPanel
        VerticalAlignment="Bottom"
        Orientation="Vertical"
        Margin="5">

        <TextBlock
            FontSize="18"
            FontWeight="Bold"
            Text="Silverlight 2">
        </TextBlock>
        <TextBlock
            FontSize="18"
            FontWeight="Bold"
            Text="Isolated Storage Demo">
        </TextBlock>

    </StackPanel>

    <StackPanel
        Grid.Row="1"
        Grid.RowSpan="2"
        Orientation="Vertical">

        <TextBlock
            FontSize="15"
            Text="Directories"
            Margin="5">
        </TextBlock>

        <TextBlock
            x:Name="lblCurrentDirectory"
```

```xml
                    FontSize="13"
                    Text="Selected Directory"
                    Margin="5">
                </TextBlock>

                <StackPanel Orientation="Horizontal">
                    <Button
                        x:Name="btnUpDir"
                        Margin="5"
                        Click="btnUpDir_Click"
                        Content="Up Directory"
                        Width="100"
                        Height="20" />
                    <Button
                        x:Name="btnOpenDir"
                        Margin="5"
                        Click="btnOpenDir_Click"
                        Content="Open Directory"
                        Width="100"
                        Height="20" />
                </StackPanel>

                <ListBox Height="150"
                    x:Name="lstDirectoryListing"
                    Margin="5,5,13,5">
                </ListBox>
            </StackPanel>
        </Grid>
```

9. First is a simple cosmetic TextBlock for the section title. This is followed by the TextBlock named lblCurrentDirectory, which will be filled with the current directory. As the users navigate through the directories, it will be important to inform them which directory they are in.

10. Next are two Button controls (btnUpDir and btnOpenDir), which will be used for navigating through the directories. This functionality is simplified into two basic tasks: moving up a directory and opening the currently selected directory. To get the buttons to appear visually as desired, they are contained in a StackPanel with horizontal orientation.

11. The final ListBox will be populated with directories named lstDirectoryListing. As the users navigate through the directories using the btnUpDir and btnOpenDir buttons, this ListBox will be repopulated automatically with the directories contained in the user's current location.

12. Next, still within Grid.Row and Grid.Column (1,0), add the files section, as follows:

```xml
<Grid x:Name="LayoutRoot" Background="White" ShowGridLines="True">

    ...
        <ListBox Height="100"
```

```
                x:Name="lstDirectoryListing"
                Margin="5,5,13,5">
        </ListBox>

        <TextBlock
            FontSize="15"
            Text="Files"
            Margin="5">
        </TextBlock>

        <StackPanel Orientation="Horizontal">
            <Button
                x:Name="btnOpenFile"
                Margin="5"
                Click="btnOpenFile_Click"
                Content="Show File"
                Width="100"
                Height="20" />
        </StackPanel>

        <ListBox Height="150"
            x:Name="lstFileListing"
            Margin="5,5,13,5">
        </ListBox>

    </StackPanel>
</Grid>
```

13. As with the previous section, the first TextBlock holds the section title. Next is a Button control called btnOpenFile. Notice that even though there is only one button, it is still placed within a StackPanel for consistency. In the future, if you want to extend this application—for example, to add file-deletion functionality—you might want to add buttons to this StackPanel. This is purely a matter of user preference; the StackPanel really was not required in this instance.

14. Finally, you have the ListBox that will be filled with the files in the current directory, in the same way that the directories ListBox will be filled in the top section.

15. To see what you have so far, press F5 (or choose Debug Start Debugging from the menu bar) to start your Silverlight application.

16. Notice that Visual Studio compiles successfully and opens the browser instance. However, just when you think everything is going great and you are excited to see your beautiful form coming to life, you get an XamlParseException with the following cryptic message:

    AG_E_PARSER_BAD_PROPERTY_VALUE [Line: 66 Position: 34].

17. This is caused by the fact that, within the code behind, you have not declared the delegates that are referred to in your XAML.

> ■ **Note** The line and position noted in the error message you see might be slightly different from those shown here, depending on the spacing you included when adding the controls to the code.

18. Stop debugging by clicking the Stop button. Press F7, or select View ▸ View Code. Sure enough, there are no event handlers.

19. At this point, you could go through and manually add the handlers in the code. But I think you've done enough typing already, so let's have Visual Studio do it for you.

20. Return to your XAML by clicking the MainPage.xaml file in the Files tab. Look at the controls you added. Notice that the code refers to three event handlers, one for each of the buttons: btnUpDir_Click, btnOpenDir_Click, and btnOpenFile_Click.

21. Find the first reference, btnUpDir_Click. Right-click it, and select the Navigate To Event Handler option, as shown in Figure 9-4. Visual Studio automatically creates the event handler in the code behind, as follows:

```
public partial class MainPage : UserControl
{
    public MainPage()
    {
        InitializeComponent();
    }

    private void btnUpDir_Click(object sender, RoutedEventArgs e)
    {

    }
}
```

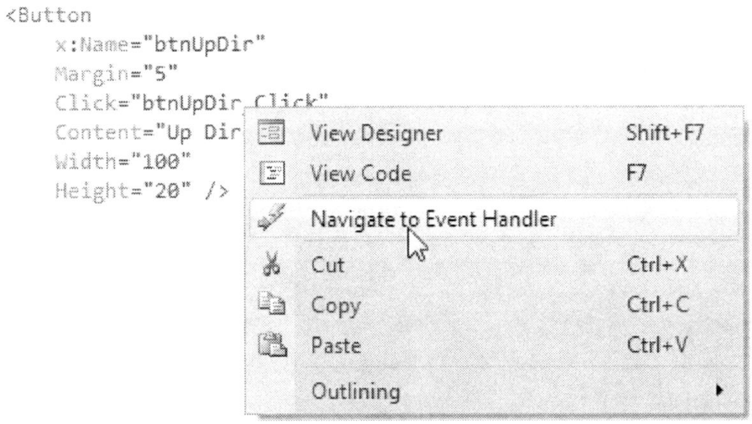

Figure 9-4. Choosing the Navigate to Event Handler option in Visual Studio

22. Repeat step 11 for the other two event handlers. At this point, your code behind should look as follows:

```
public partial class MainPage : UserControl
{
    public MainPage()
    {
        InitializeComponent();
    }

    private void btnUpDir_Click(object sender, RoutedEventArgs e)
    {

    }

    private void btnOpenDir_Click(object sender, RoutedEventArgs e)
    {

    }
    private void btnOpenFile_Click(object sender, RoutedEventArgs e)
    {

    }
}
```

23. Run the application. Once again, press F5 to start debugging. Barring any typos, the Silverlight application should appear as shown in Figure 9-5.

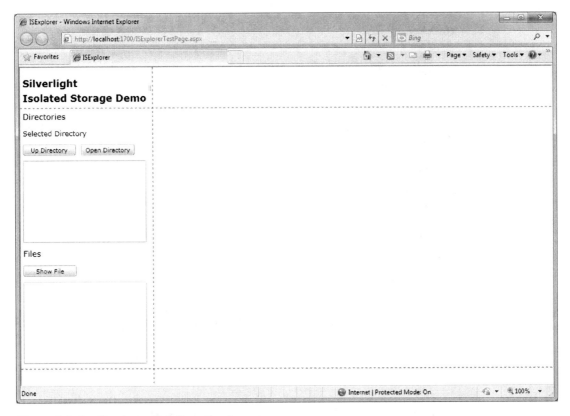

Figure 9-5. *Application with left portion layout*

24. It's looking good so far! You are almost finished with the application layout. Now, let's move on to the right column and add the final controls.

25. At the bottom of your Grid definition within Grid.Row and Grid.Column (0,1), place another StackPanel. Within it, add a TextBox named txtFileName that will contain the name of the file being edited, along with a Button control named btnSave, which will save the file referred to in txtFileName. Your XAML should look as follows:

```
<Grid x:Name="LayoutRoot" Background="White" ShowGridLines="True">

    ...

    </StackPanel>

    <StackPanel
        VerticalAlignment="Bottom"
        Orientation="Horizontal"
        Grid.Row="0"
        Grid.Column="1">
```

```
<TextBox
    x:Name="txtFileName"
    Text="File1.txt"
    Margin="5"
    Width="300"
    Height="30"
    FontSize="15">
</TextBox>
<Button
    x:Name="btnSave"
    Margin="5"
    Content="Save"
    Width="100"
    Height="30"
    Click="btnSave_Click">
</Button>

        </StackPanel>

    </Grid>
```

26. While you are at it, go ahead and have Visual Studio create the event handler for btnSave_Click. Right-click it, and choose the Navigate to Event Handler option to add the following handler:

```
public partial class MainPage : UserControl
{
    ...

    private void btnSave_Click(object sender, RoutedEventArgs e)
    {

    }
}
```

27. Navigate back to the XAML. Within Grid.Row and Grid.Column (1,1), add a TextBox named txtContents, which will display the contents of the opened file, as follows:

```
<Grid x:Name="LayoutRoot" Background="White" ShowGridLines="True">

    ...

    </StackPanel>

<TextBox
    x:Name="txtContents"
    VerticalScrollBarVisibility="Visible"
    HorizontalScrollBarVisibility="Auto"
    AcceptsReturn="True"
    BorderBrush="Black" BorderThickness="2"
```

```
            Margin="5" Grid.Column="1" Grid.Row="1"
            FontSize="15" FontFamily="Courier">
        </TextBox>

    </Grid>
```

28. Since this should be a multiline TextBox, you set the AcceptsReturn property to True. You also set the VerticalScrollBarVisibility property to Visible, which makes it always appear, and the HorizontalScrollBarVisibility property to Auto, which makes it appear only when there is enough text to require left and right scrolling.

29. Within Grid.Row and Grid.Column (1,2), place a StackPanel that contains five TextBlock controls—some that are simply cosmetic, and some that will be populated in the application's code—as follows:

```
<Grid x:Name="LayoutRoot" Background="White" ShowGridLines="True">

    ...

    </StackPanel>

    <TextBox
        x:Name="txtContents"
        VerticalScrollBarVisibility="Visible"
        HorizontalScrollBarVisibility="Auto"
        AcceptsReturn="True"
        BorderBrush="Black" BorderThickness="2"
        Margin="5" Grid.Column="1" Grid.Row="1"
        FontSize="15" FontFamily="Courier">
    </TextBox>

    <StackPanel
        VerticalAlignment="Bottom" Orientation="Horizontal"
        Margin="5" Grid.Column="1" Grid.Row="2">

        <TextBlock FontSize="13"
            Text="Available Space in Isolated Storage: " />
        <TextBlock x:Name="txtAvalSpace" FontSize="13" Text="123" />
        <TextBlock FontSize="13" Text="kb / " />
        <TextBlock x:Name="txtQuota" FontSize="13" Text="123" />
        <TextBlock FontSize="13" Text="kb" />

    </StackPanel>

</Grid>
```

With this, you are finished creating the application layout! You can now turn your attention to the code behind.

Coding the File Explorer

Now let's add the functionality that demonstrates accessing Silverlight's isolated storage.

1. When the file explorer is started, it does two things. First, it loads some sample directories and files in isolated storage. Second, it populates the ListBox controls and updates the informative TextBlock controls. You will encapsulate these tasks into two methods: LoadFilesAndDirs()and GetStorageData().Create a Loaded event handler, and add these two method calls to the event:

```csharp
public partial class MainPage : UserControl
{
    public MainPage()
    {
        InitializeComponent();
        this.Loaded += new RoutedEventHandler(Page_Loaded);
    }

    void Page_Loaded(object sender, RoutedEventArgs e)
    {
        LoadFilesAndDirs();
        GetStorageData();
    }

    private void LoadFilesAndDirs()
    {

    }

    private void GetStorageData()
    {

    }

    private void btnUpDir_Click(object sender, RoutedEventArgs e)
    {

    }

    private void btnOpenDir_Click(object sender, RoutedEventArgs e)
    {

    }

    private void btnOpenFile_Click(object sender, RoutedEventArgs e)
    {

    }

    private void btnSave_Click(object sender, RoutedEventArgs e)
    {
```

```
    }
}
```

2. Next, add a using statement for the two namespaces for your application. Also, create a global string variable called currentDir, which will store the current directory:

```
using ...
using System.IO;
using System.IO.IsolatedStorage;

namespace ISExplorer
{
    public partial class MainPage : UserControl
    {
        private string currentDir = "";

        public MainPage()
        {
            InitializeComponent();
            this.Loaded += new RoutedEventHandler(Page_Loaded);
        }

        ...
    }
}
```

3. Let's implement the LoadFilesAndDirs() method. The first step is to get an instance of the user's isolated storage for the application using the IsolatedStorageFile class's GetUserStoreForApplication() method. You do this within a C# using statement so that the instance is disposed of automatically:

```
private void LoadFilesAndDirs()
{
    using (var store =
        IsolatedStorageFile.GetUserStoreForApplication())
    {
    }
}
```

4. Now that you have an instance of the isolated storage, create three root-level directories and three subdirectories, one in each of the root-level directories. Use the CreateDirectory() method to create the directories, as follows:

```
private void LoadFilesAndDirs()
{
    using (var store =
        IsolatedStorageFile.GetUserStoreForApplication())
    {
        // Create three directories in the root.
        store.CreateDirectory("Dir1");
        store.CreateDirectory("Dir2");
```

```
        store.CreateDirectory("Dir3");

        // Create three subdirectories under Dir1.
        string subdir1 = System.IO.Path.Combine("Dir1", "SubDir1");
        string subdir2 = System.IO.Path.Combine("Dir2", "SubDir2");
        string subdir3 = System.IO.Path.Combine("Dir3", "SubDir3");
        store.CreateDirectory(subdir1);
        store.CreateDirectory(subdir2);
        store.CreateDirectory(subdir3);
    }
}
```

5. Next, create two files: one in the root and one in a subdirectory. To do this, use the CreateFile() method, which returns an IsolatedStorageFileStream object. For now, you will leave the files empty, so after creating the files, simply close the stream.

```
private void LoadFilesAndDirs()
{
    using (var store =
        IsolatedStorageFile.GetUserStoreForApplication())
    {
        // Create three directories in the root.
        store.CreateDirectory("Dir1");
        store.CreateDirectory("Dir2");
        store.CreateDirectory("Dir3");

        // Create three subdirectories under Dir1.
        string subdir1 = System.IO.Path.Combine("Dir1", "SubDir1");
        string subdir2 = System.IO.Path.Combine("Dir2", "SubDir2");
        string subdir3 = System.IO.Path.Combine("Dir3", "SubDir3");
        store.CreateDirectory(subdir1);
        store.CreateDirectory(subdir2);
        store.CreateDirectory(subdir3);

        // Create a file in the root.
        IsolatedStorageFileStream rootFile =
            store.CreateFile("InTheRoot.txt");
        rootFile.Close();

        // Create a file in a subdirectory.
        IsolatedStorageFileStream subDirFile =
            store.CreateFile(
                System.IO.Path.Combine(subdir1, "SubDir1.txt"));
        subDirFile.Close();
    }
}
```

Caution Notice the Path.Combine() method call here is fully qualified (specified with the namespace). This is because there is another Path class in System.Windows.Shapes. If you don't fully qualify Path, the ambiguous name will cause an error.

---

6. That completes the LoadFilesAndDirs() method. Next, you will implement the GetStorageData() method, which displays the storage information in the application.

7. Because you are populating the ListBox controls, you need to make sure you clear them each time the GetStorageData() method is called. You do this by calling the Items.Clear() method on the two ListBox controls. Then you get an instance of the user's isolated storage, in the same way as you did in the LoadFilesAndDirs() method:

```
private void GetStorageData()
{
    this.lstDirectoryListing.Items.Clear();
    this.lstFileListing.Items.Clear();

    using (var store =
        IsolatedStorageFile.GetUserStoreForApplication())
    {

    }
}
```

8. Next, you want to list all of the directories that are contained in the directory passed to the method. In order to do this, you will construct a search string using the System.IO.Path.Combine() method. You will then call the GetDirectoryNames() method along with the search string. This will return a string array, which you can then step through to manually populate the ListBox.

```
private void GetStorageData()
{
    this.lstDirectoryListing.Items.Clear();
    this.lstFileListing.Items.Clear();

    using (var store =
        IsolatedStorageFile.GetUserStoreForApplication())
    {
        string searchString =
            System.IO.Path.Combine(currentDir, "*.*");

        string[] directories =
            store.GetDirectoryNames(searchString);

        foreach (string sDir in directories)
```

```
        {
            this.lstDirectoryListing.Items.Add(sDir);
        }
    }
}
```

9. Now populate the ListBox You do this in the same way that you populated the ListBox, except this time, use the GetFileNames() method, which similarly returns a string array:

```
private void GetStorageData()
{
    this.lstDirectoryListing.Items.Clear();
    this.lstFileListing.Items.Clear();

    using (var store =
        IsolatedStorageFile.GetUserStoreForApplication())
    {
        string searchString =
            System.IO.Path.Combine(currentDir, "*.*");

        string[] directories =
            store.GetDirectoryNames(searchString);

        foreach (string sDir in directories)
        {
            this.lstDirectoryListing.Items.Add(sDir);
        }

        string[] files = store.GetFileNames(searchString);

        foreach (string sFile in files)
        {
            this.lstFileListing.Items.Add(sFile);
        }
    }
}
```

10. Now that the two ListBox controls are populated, you want to populate three additional TextBlock controls. One will show the current directory. The other two will display the amount of free space remaining in isolated storage and the available quota for the application. You get this information by using the Quota and AvailableFreeSpace properties, which return the total and free space in bytes, respectively:

```
private void GetStorageData()
{
    this.lstDirectoryListing.Items.Clear();
    this.lstFileListing.Items.Clear();

    using (var store =
        IsolatedStorageFile.GetUserStoreForApplication())
    {
```

```csharp
            string searchString =
                System.IO.Path.Combine(currentDir, "*.*");

            string[] directories =
                store.GetDirectoryNames(searchString);

            foreach (string sDir in directories)
            {
                this.lstDirectoryListing.Items.Add(sDir);
            }

            string[] files = store.GetFileNames(searchString);

            foreach (string sFile in files)
            {
                this.lstFileListing.Items.Add(sFile);
            }

            long space = store.AvailableFreeSpace;
            txtAvalSpace.Text = (space / 1000).ToString();

            long quota = store.Quota;
            txtQuota.Text = (quota / 1000).ToString();

            this.lblCurrentDirectory.Text =
                String.Concat("\\", currentDir);
        }
    }
```

■ **Note** For simplicity, you are dividing by 1000 instead of 1024. Therefore, the calculation will not be exact, but it will be close enough for the purposes of this example.

---

11. Run the application. You will see that the current directory is set to \, and that the three directories and the file you created at the root level are displayed in the ListBox controls, as shown in Figure 9-6.

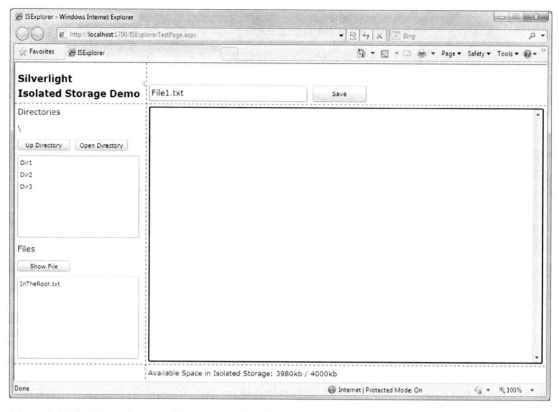

Figure 9-6. *The file explorer application showing the root directory*

12. Now you can implement the Button events, starting with the Up Directory and Open Directory buttons.

13. When the user clicks the Up Directory button, the system finds the current directory's parent directory using System.IO.Path.GetDirectoryName(), sets the current directory to be the parent directory, and re-executes the GetStorageData() method:

```
private void btnUpDir_Click(object sender, RoutedEventArgs e)
{
    if (currentDir != "")
    {
        currentDir =
            System.IO.Path.GetDirectoryName(currentDir);
    }

    GetStorageData();
}
```

14. When the user clicks the Open Directory button, you combine the current directory with the selected directory from the directory ListBox using the System.IO.Path.Combine() method, set the current directory to that new directory, and once again re-execute the GetStorageData() method:

```
private void btnOpenDir_Click(object sender, RoutedEventArgs e)
{
    if (this.lstDirectoryListing.SelectedItem != null)
    {
        currentDir =
            System.IO.Path.Combine(
                currentDir,
                this.lstDirectoryListing.SelectedItem.ToString());
    }
    GetStorageData();
}
```

15. Next, implement the Show File button's Click event, as follows:

```
private void btnOpenFile_Click(object sender, RoutedEventArgs e)
{
    if (this.lstFileListing.SelectedItem != null)
    {
        this.txtFileName.Text =
            this.lstFileListing.SelectedItem.ToString();

        using (var store =
            IsolatedStorageFile.GetUserStoreForApplication())
        {
            string filePath =
                System.IO.Path.Combine(
                    currentDir,
                    this.lstFileListing.SelectedItem.ToString());

            IsolatedStorageFileStream stream =
                store.OpenFile(filePath, FileMode.Open);
            StreamReader sr = new StreamReader(stream);

            this.txtContents.Text = sr.ReadToEnd();
            sr.Close();
        }
    }
}
```

16. When a user clicks the Show File button, the file from isolated storage opens, and its contents are displayed in txtContents. You achieve this by first getting an instance of the user's isolated storage, and then generating the path to the file by combining the current directory with the file name provided in txtFileName. After you construct the full file path, you open the file using OpenFile(), which returns a Stream containing the file contents. You attach a StreamReader to the Stream to assist in working with the stream, and then

display the contents of the Stream using the StreamReader's ReadToEnd()
method.

17. Finally, wire up the Save button, which will save the contents of txtContents to
the file name specified in txtFileName. You want to make it so that if the user
enters a file name that doesn't exist, the application will create a new file. If the
user enters one that does exist, the application will override the contents of
that file. Although this is not perfect for use in the real world, it serves as a fine
demo for using isolated storage.

```
private void btnSave_Click(object sender, RoutedEventArgs e)
{
    string fileContents = this.txtContents.Text;

    using (var store =
        IsolatedStorageFile.GetUserStoreForApplication())
    {
        IsolatedStorageFileStream stream =
            store.OpenFile(
                System.IO.Path.Combine(
                    currentDir,
                    this.txtFileName.Text),
                FileMode.OpenOrCreate);

        StreamWriter sw = new StreamWriter(stream);
        sw.Write(fileContents);
        sw.Close();
        stream.Close();
    }

    GetStorageData();
}
```

18. This method is similar to the ShowFile() method. Basically, you get the
isolated storage instance, and open the file using the OpenFile() method,
passing it the full file path. However, this time, you pass the OpenFile()
method FileMode.OpenOrCreate. This way, if the file doesn't exist, the
application will create it. You then attach the returned stream to a
StreamWriter, and write the contents to the Stream using the StreamWriter's
Write() method.

19. After writing the file, you clean up the objects and call the GetStorageData()
method, which will cause the newly created file to appear in the files ListBox
(in the event a new file was created).

At this point, you're ready to test your completed application.

Testing the File Explorer

Now let's try out your new file explorer.

1. Fire up the application by pressing F5. If all goes well, you should see the application.

2. Highlight Dir1 in the Directories list box, and click the Open Directory button. The application navigates to that directory and refreshes the list boxes to show the directories and files contained within that file.

3. Enter the file name SampleTextFile.txt in the txtFileName text box. For the contents, enter some arbitrary data. If you have Microsoft Word, you can generate a ton of random text by typing =Rand(10,20) into a blank document and then paste the result into the text box.

4. After you enter the contents, click the Save button. You will see the file appear in the Files list box, as shown in Figure 9-7.

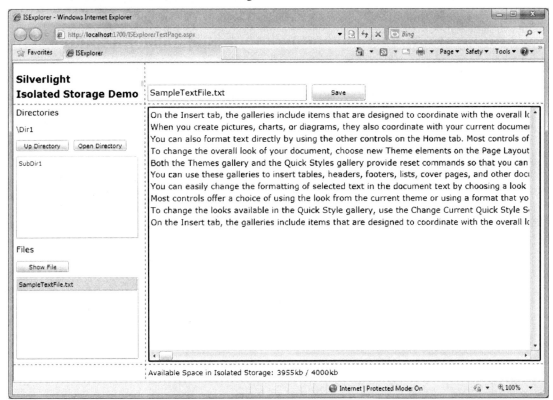

Figure 9-7. Testing the completed file explorer

5. Click the Up Directory button to navigate back to the root. You will notice that the current directory changes, as do the contents of the list boxes. For kicks, click Save again. This time, the application saves the same file in the root directory.

6. Highlight the InTheRoot.txt file, and click the Show File button. Because you left the file empty, nothing appears in the txtContents box. You can enter some text in the text box and click Save.

7. Highlight SampleTextFile.txt, and click Show File. The contents of your file are still there. It really works!

8. Try adding some files (preferably with a large amount of text). Take a look at the display of the current free space and the quota of the isolated storage at the bottom of the application. You should see the amount of free space decrease.

9. Stop debugging. Now restart debugging. Notice anything? Your files are still there! That is because isolated storage is persistent data, and that data will remain until the user clears the isolated storage, as explained in the next section.

This exercise demonstrated how Silverlight's isolated storage works and how you can access it. In the following section, you will learn how to manage isolated storage, including changing its quota.

Managing Isolated Storage

By default, the amount of isolated storage space available for a Silverlight application is 1 MB. You can view the available storage, clear it, and increase its size.

Viewing and Clearing Isolated Storage

In order to view the isolated storage saved on your machine, simply right-click any Silverlight application and select Silverlight from the pop-up menu. This displays the Microsoft Silverlight Configuration window. Navigate to the Application Storage tab, as shown in Figure 9-8. There, you can see your test application in the listing, and depending on what other Silverlight applications you have accessed, you might see other web sites listed.

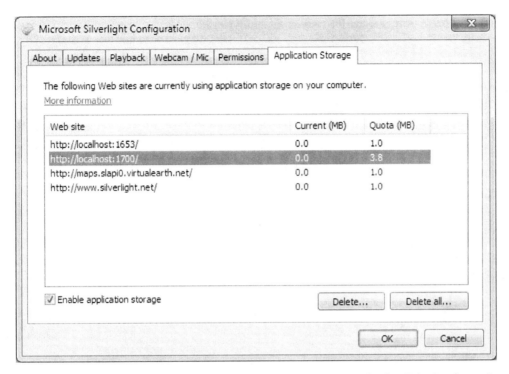

Figure 9-8. Viewing application storage information in the Microsoft Silverlight Configuration window

If users want to clear the storage space, they simply need to highlight the site they want to clear data for and click Delete. This displays a confirmation dialog box, as shown in Figure 9-9.

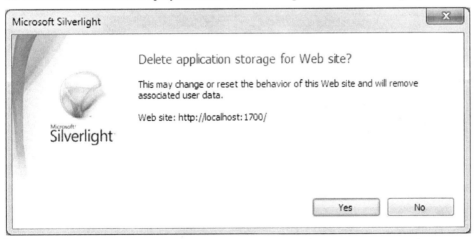

Figure 9-9. Deleting an application's isolated storage

What if you want more storage space for your application? Developers can request additional storage space by using the TryIncreaseQuotaTo() method. A restriction placed on this task is that it can be executed only in a user-triggered event, such as a Button control's Click event. This restriction is in place to prevent the application from increasing the quota without the user's knowledge.

Try It Out: Increasing the Isolated Storage Quota

To demonstrate how to increase the isolated storage quota, let's add a button to the file explorer demo to increase the quota to 4 MB.

1. Open the ISExplorer project that you created in the previous exercise.

2. In the MainPage.xaml file, locate the definition of the Save button and add a new Button control called btnIncreaseQuota, with the caption Increase Quota, as follows:

```
<StackPanel
    VerticalAlignment="Bottom"
    Orientation="Horizontal"
    Grid.Row="0"
    Grid.Column="1">

    <TextBox
        x:Name="txtFileName"
        Text="File1.txt"
        Margin="5"
        Width="300"
        Height="30"
        FontSize="15">
    </TextBox>
    <Button
        x:Name="btnSave"
        Margin="5"
        Content="Save"
        Width="100"
        Height="30"
        Click="btnSave_Click">
    </Button>
    <Button
        x:Name="btnIncreaseQuota"
        Margin="5"
        Content="Increase Quota"
        Width="150"
        Height="30"
        Click="btnIncreaseQuota_Click">
    </Button>

</StackPanel>
```

3. You have wired up the Click event to a new event handler created by Visual Studio. Navigate to the code behind's definition of that event handler:

```
private void btnIncreaseQuota_Click(object sender, RoutedEventArgs e)
{
}
```

4. Next, you want to get an instance of the user's isolated storage, just as you did numerous times in creating the file explorer. Then call the IncreaseQuotaTo() method, passing it 4000000, which is roughly 4 MB. Add the following to event handler:

```
private void btnIncreaseQuota_Click(object sender, RoutedEventArgs e)
{
    using (var store =
        IsolatedStorageFile.GetUserStoreForApplication())
    {
        if (store.IncreaseQuotaTo(4000000))
        {
            GetStorageData();
        }
        else
        {
            // The user rejected the request to increase the quota size
        }
    }
}
```

▪ **Note** These numbers are not exact, which is fine for the demonstration here. You can increase the quota to 4 MB exactly by multiplying 1024 by 4.

---

5. Notice that the IncreaseQuotaTo() method returns a Boolean value. Depending on whether the user accepted the application's request to increase the quota size, true or false will be returned. If the user accepted the request, you will want to redisplay the information displayed for the quota. The easiest way to do this is to simply call the GetStorageData() method, as you did in the event handler here.

6. Try out your new addition by running your application and clicking the new Increase Quota button. You will see the dialog box shown in Figure 9-10.

Figure 9-10. Dialog box to request to increase available storage

7. Click Yes. You will notice that the available quota is now increased in your
    application, as shown in Figure 9-11.

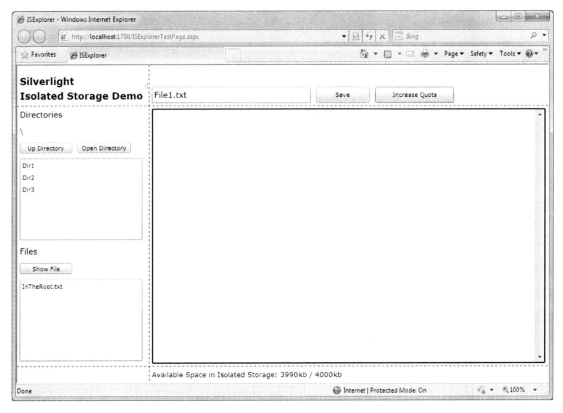

Figure 9-11. *File explorer showing additional storage space*

This completes the file explorer. Now you can apply these concepts to your own persistent storage implementations in your Silverlight applications.

Summary

In this chapter, you looked at Silverlight's isolated storage feature. As you saw, it is very straightforward to store user-specific data for your application and have that data persist over browser instances. This provides a very convenient way for developers to add offline content or save user settings.

In the next chapter, you will look at Microsoft Expression Blend 4, an application created for the sole purpose of visually editing XAML.

CHAPTER 10

System Integration and Device Support

Silverlight includes a number of features that allow developers to integrate their applications with a user's system. These features include notifications, interaction with legacy COM applications and libraries, access to a user's web camera and microphone, and better access to the operating system, such as enabling the Silverlight application as a drop target. In this chapter, we will discuss and try out a number of these features.

Notification (Toast) API

A *toast* is a small informational window you can display to notify users of various events, typically in the bottom-right corner of the screen (in Windows) and the upper right corner (in Mac OS). Let's take a look at toast notifications in Silverlight and run through an example.

Try It Out: Implementing Toast Notifications

In this example, you will create an application with a single button. When the button is pressed, it displays a toast window for five seconds.

1. Create a new Silverlight application in Visual Studio 2010. Name it NotifyApplication, and allow Visual Studio to create an ASP.NET Web Application called NotifyApplication.Web to host your application.

2. Add a Button to the LayoutRoot grid, and set its Width to 200, Height to 30, and Content to Display Notify Window. Right-click the event name in the XAML, and select Navigate To Event Handler to wire up the click event to Button_Click.

```
<Grid x:Name="LayoutRoot" Background="White">
    <Button
        Height="30"
        Width="200"
        Content="Display Notify Window"
        Click="Button_Click" />
</Grid>
```

3. Now you need to define the toast notification window. To do this, you'll create a new user control that defines the layout of the window. To start, add a new user control to the Silverlight project by right-clicking on the NotifyApplication project and selecting Add ➤ New Item. When the Add New Item dialog appears, select Silverlight User Control and name the user control NotifyWindow.xaml, as shown in Figure 10-1.

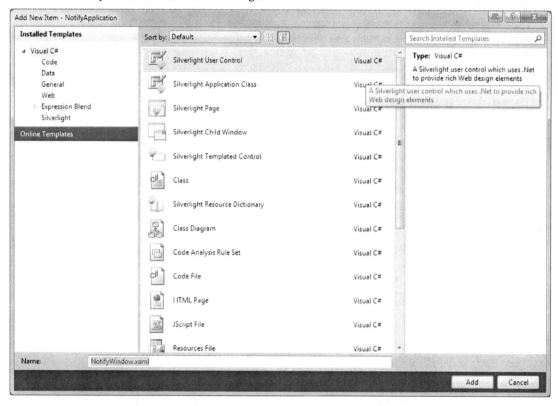

Figure 10-1. *Adding the NotifyWindow user control*

4. After you create NotifyWindow, you can start defining the layout. First, set the Height of the user control to 75 and the Width to 300.

```
<UserControl x:Class="NotifyApplication.NotifyWindow"
    xmlns="http://schemas.microsoft.com/winfx/2006/xaml/presentation"
    xmlns:x="http://schemas.microsoft.com/winfx/2006/xaml"
    xmlns:d="http://schemas.microsoft.com/expression/blend/2008"
    xmlns:mc="http://schemas.openxmlformats.org/markup-compatibility/2006"
    mc:Ignorable="d"
    Height="75" Width="300">

    <Grid x:Name="LayoutRoot" Background="White">

    </Grid>
</UserControl>
```

5. Next, add a Border to the LayoutRoot grid, set the Background to #DDDDDD, the
    BorderBrush to Black, and the BorderThickness to 2. Within the Border, add
    another Grid control with three rows defined:

```
<Grid x:Name="LayoutRoot" Background="White">
    <Border
        Background="#DDDDDD"
        BorderBrush="Black"
        BorderThickness="2">

        <Grid>
            <Grid.RowDefinitions>
                <RowDefinition Height="0.113*"/>
                <RowDefinition Height="0.306*"/>
                <RowDefinition Height="0.582*"/>
            </Grid.RowDefinitions>

        </Grid>
    </Border>
</Grid>
```

6. Now you'll add four more controls to the nested grid: a Rectangle and a
    TextBlock, which are completely cosmetic, and two additional TextBlocks, one
    for the toast notification header and one for the description. Add these
    controls, and set the properties as indicated in the following code. The result
    should look like what you see in Figure 10-2.

```
<Grid x:Name="LayoutRoot" Background="White">
    <Border
        Background="#DDDDDD"
        BorderBrush="Black"
        BorderThickness="2">

        <Grid>
            <Grid.RowDefinitions>
                <RowDefinition Height="0.113*"/>
                <RowDefinition Height="0.306*"/>
                <RowDefinition Height="0.582*"/>
            </Grid.RowDefinitions>
```

```xml
                    <Rectangle
                        Fill="#FF747474"
                        Stroke="White"
                        StrokeThickness="0"
                        Grid.ColumnSpan="2"/>

                    <TextBlock
                        TextWrapping="Wrap"
                        Text="x"
                        HorizontalAlignment="Right"
                        Margin="0,0,5,0"
                        Grid.Row="1"
                        FontFamily="Verdana"
                        FontWeight="Bold"
                        FontSize="13"/>

                    <TextBlock
                        Name="Header"
                        TextWrapping="Wrap"
                        Text="Header Text"
                        Grid.Row="1"
                        FontWeight="Bold"
                        VerticalAlignment="Bottom"
                        FontSize="13"
                        Margin="5,0,5,0"
                        FontFamily="Tahoma"/>

                    <TextBlock
                        Name="Description"
                        TextWrapping="Wrap"
                        Text="Notification Text"
                        Grid.Row="2"
                        FontSize="11"
                        FontFamily="Verdana"
                        Margin="5,0,5,0"/>
                </Grid>
            </Border>
        </Grid>
```

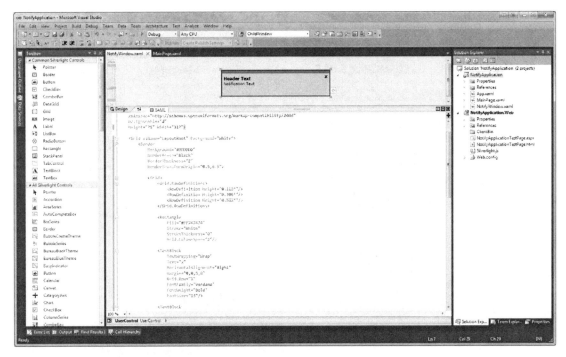

Figure 10-2. *The finished NotifyWindow user control*

7. Now you can turn your attention to the MainPage.xaml.cs code-behind file—in particular, to the Button_Click delegate you wired up earlier. First you need to make certain that the application is running outside of the browser. You can do that by checking the Boolean property App.Current.IsRunningOutOfBrowser:

```
private void Button_Click(object sender, RoutedEventArgs e)
{
    if (App.Current.IsRunningOutOfBrowser)
    {

    }
}
```

8. Next you'll create an instance of the NotificationWindow class, and then you'll create an instance of the NotifyWindow user control and set the Text of the Header and Description. To make sure the NotificationWindow is set to the correct size, set the height and width equal to the NotifyWindow height and width. Finally, set the content of the NotificationWindow to the instance of your NotifyWindow user control, and execute the NotificationWindow's Show method, passing it 5000, which indicates the window should display for five seconds.

```
private void Button_Click(object sender, RoutedEventArgs e)
{
    if (App.Current.IsRunningOutOfBrowser)
    {
        NotificationWindow notify = new NotificationWindow();

        NotifyWindow win = new NotifyWindow();
        win.Header.Text = "Custom Message Header";
        win.Description.Text = "This is a custom description.";

        notify.Width = win.Width;
        notify.Height = win.Height;

        notify.Content = win;
        notify.Show(5000);
    }
}
```

9. You are now ready to test the application. However, because Silverlight notification works only with applications running outside of the browser, you must enable out-of-browser support for the application. To do this, open the project properties for the NotifyApplication Silverlight project and select the Enable Running Application Out Of The Browser check box, as shown in Figure 10-3.

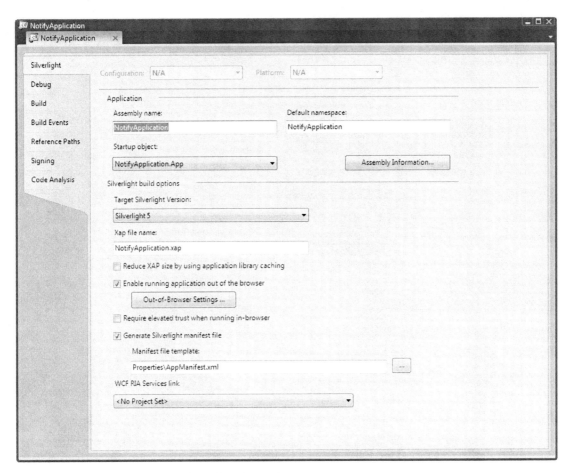

Figure 10-3. Settings for the NotifyApplication project

10. At this point, if you run the project, the application will be installed
automatically for out-of-browser use. To debug the application when using it
out of the browser, click on the Debug tab on the project properties dialog. On
that screen, select Out-Of-Browser Application for the Start Action. Next, save
the project settings, right-click on the NotifyApplication project in Solution
Explorer, and select Set As StartUp Project. Press F5 to test the application.
When the application opens outside of the browser, click the Display Notify
Window button. If all goes well, you should see the notification window in the
bottom-right corner of your screen, as shown in Figure 10-4. Note that the "x"
in the top-right corner of the notification message is only cosmetic—you
would have to add additional logic to implement actual close functionality.

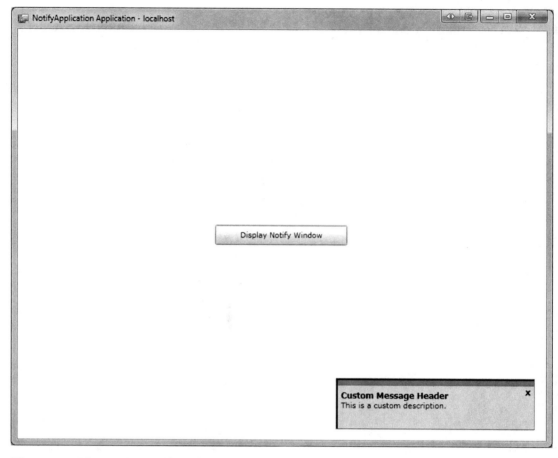

Figure 10-4. The running NotifyApplication application

Webcam/Microphone Access

Silverlight supports capture from web cams and microphones installed on the local user's machine. In this section, we'll explore this feature and walk through an example.

CaptureDeviceConfiguration Class

The CaptureDeviceConfiguration class provides developers with some helper functionality related to web cam and microphone access, including the ability to list the different audio and video capture devices installed on the user's machine. In addition, it provides functions that verify and request permission to access the local devices. For example, if you want to request device access, you can call the RequestDeviceAccess method, or if you need to check whether access has already been granted, you can inspect the AllowedDeviceAccess property.

CaptureSource Class

The CaptureSource class provides audio and video capture functionality from a given capture device, including methods for starting and stopping capture as well as for taking static images from the captured video. To explore these methods, let's work through an example.

Try It Out: Accessing a User's Web Camera and Microphone

In this example, you'll access the web camera and microphone installed on the local user's machine, capture the source from those devices, and display it in your Silverlight application. Let's get started!

1. Create a new Silverlight application in Visual Studio 2010. Name it CameraAccess, and allow Visual Studio to create an ASP.NET Web Application called CameraAccess.Web to host your application.

2. Define two columns and two rows as shown in the following code, and set the Background of the grid to #333333.

```xml
<Grid x:Name="LayoutRoot" Background="#333333">

    <Grid.ColumnDefinitions>
        <ColumnDefinition Width="*" />
        <ColumnDefinition Width="*" />
    </Grid.ColumnDefinitions>
    <Grid.RowDefinitions>
        <RowDefinition Height="240*" />
        <RowDefinition Height="60*" />
    </Grid.RowDefinitions>

</Grid>
```

3. Add a Rectangle to the first row that spans both columns. Next, add a Button with the Content "Start Capture" to the first column of the second row. Add another Button with the Content "Stop Capture" to the second column of the second row. Set the Margin for all three controls to 5 to provide some spacing between the controls. Also, set the Click event to StartCapture and StopCapture, appropriately. The completed user interface should appear as shown in Figure 10-5.

```xml
<Grid x:Name="LayoutRoot" Background="#333333">

    <Grid.ColumnDefinitions>
        <ColumnDefinition Width="*" />
        <ColumnDefinition Width="*" />
    </Grid.ColumnDefinitions>
    <Grid.RowDefinitions>
        <RowDefinition Height="240*" />
        <RowDefinition Height="60*" />
    </Grid.RowDefinitions>

    <Rectangle
        Name="CaptureDisplay"
```

```
        Fill="White"
        Grid.ColumnSpan="2"
        Margin="5" />

    <Button
        Click="StartCapture"
        Content="Start Capture"
        Grid.Row="1"
        Grid.Column="0"
        Margin="5" />

    <Button
        Click="StopCapture"
        Content="Stop Capture"
        Grid.Row="1"
        Grid.Column="1"
        Margin="5" />

</Grid>
```

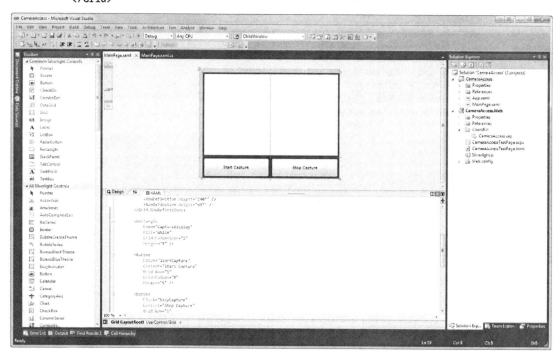

Figure 10-5. The finished CameraAccess project UI

4. Make certain the two click events have the delegates in the code-behind file, MainPage.xaml.cs, as shown next. In addition, add a variable for CaptureSource named source.

```
public partial class MainPage : UserControl
{
    CaptureSource source;

    public MainPage()
    {
        InitializeComponent();
    }
    private void StartCapture(object sender, RoutedEventArgs e)
    {

    }

    private void StopCapture(object sender, RoutedEventArgs e)
    {

    }
}
```

5. Now you'll add the logic to the StartCapture delegate. First check to see if there is already a capture source established; if so, you need to stop it. Next, create a new instance of the CaptureSource, and then set VideoCaptureDevice to the system default video capture device and AudioCaptureDevice to the default audio capture device.

```
private void StartCapture(object sender, RoutedEventArgs e)
{
    if (source != null)
    {
        source.Stop();
    }

    source = new CaptureSource();
    source.VideoCaptureDevice =
        CaptureDeviceConfiguration.GetDefaultVideoCaptureDevice();
    source.AudioCaptureDevice =
        CaptureDeviceConfiguration.GetDefaultAudioCaptureDevice();
}
```

6. With the capture devices set, you now need to create a VideoBrush, which will be used to fill your Rectangle control. Set the source of the VideoBrush to the capture source, and set the Fill property to the VideoBrush.

```
    private void StartCapture(object sender, RoutedEventArgs e)
    {
        if (source != null)
        {
            source.Stop();
        }

        source = new CaptureSource();
        source.VideoCaptureDevice =
            CaptureDeviceConfiguration.GetDefaultVideoCaptureDevice();
        source.AudioCaptureDevice =
            CaptureDeviceConfiguration.GetDefaultAudioCaptureDevice();

        VideoBrush video = new VideoBrush();
        video.SetSource(source);
        CaptureDisplay.Fill = video;
    }
```

7. Next you need to see if you have permission to access the client's capture device. If not, you'll try to request access. If you gain access, you'll start the capture source.

```
    private void StartCapture(object sender, RoutedEventArgs e)
    {
        if (source != null)
        {
            source.Stop();
        }

        source = new CaptureSource();
        source.VideoCaptureDevice =
            CaptureDeviceConfiguration.GetDefaultVideoCaptureDevice();
        source.AudioCaptureDevice =
            CaptureDeviceConfiguration.GetDefaultAudioCaptureDevice();

        VideoBrush video = new VideoBrush();
        video.SetSource(source);
        CaptureDisplay.Fill = video;

        if (CaptureDeviceConfiguration.AllowedDeviceAccess ||
            CaptureDeviceConfiguration.RequestDeviceAccess())
        {
            source.Start();
        }
    }
```

8. You now have logic to start the capture, but you need a way to stop it. This is much more straightforward. First, you check whether a source exists; if it does, you execute the Stop method.

```
private void StopCapture(object sender, RoutedEventArgs e)
{
    if (source != null)
    {
        source.Stop();
    }
}
```

9. Press F5 to start the application. When it is displayed as shown in Figure 10-6, click the Start Capture button.

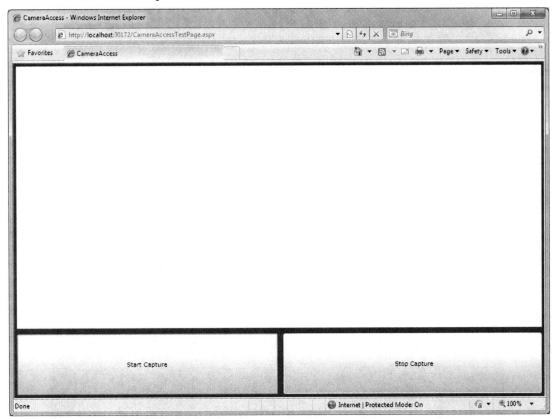

Figure 10-6. The web camera capture application

10. If access hasn't already been granted, you'll be prompted with the consent dialog shown in Figure 10-7, asking for permission to access the camera and microphone.

Figure 10-7. *Consent dialog for camera and microphone access*

11. If all goes well, you should see video captured as shown in Figure 10-8. When you are ready to stop the capture, simply click the Stop Capture button.

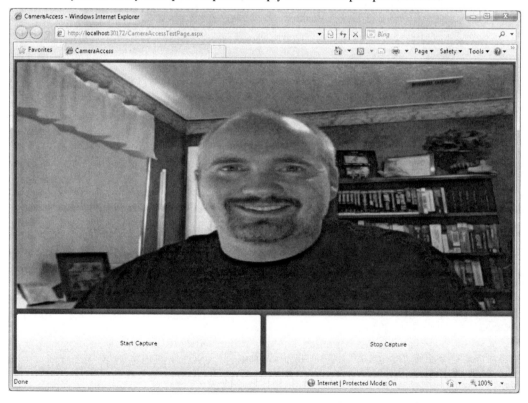

Figure 10-8. *CameraAccess application capturing audio and video*

Working with Captured Streams

If you're interested in actually working with the raw audio and video stream, or if you'd like to save the stream data, you need to create a class that implements the AudioSink and VideoSink classes. When implementing these classes, you need to provide overrides to a number of callbacks, including OnCaptureStarted, OnCaptureStopped, OnFormatChange, and OnSample. The specifics of working with the raw streams from an audio or video capture are outside the scope of this book. For more information on this topic, I recommend *Pro Silverlight 5 in C#* by Matthew MacDonald (Apress, 2012).

COM Interoperability

When building a rich client application, there might be times you'd like to leverage existing applications and libraries installed on the local user's machine. In Silverlight, you have access to COM objects installed locally. For the most part, this is exposed through a new class called AutomationFactory, which allows you to perform a CreateObject that activates and returns a reference to a registered COM object. Let's run through an example.

Try It Out: Executing an EXE

In this example, you'll execute an executable with Silverlight using the new COM interoperability feature. To illustrate, open the Notepad application.

1. Create a new Silverlight application in Visual Studio 2010. Name it InvokeNotepad, and allow Visual Studio to create an ASP.NET Web Application called InvokeNotepad.Web to host your application.

2. When the project is created, you should be looking at the MainPage.xaml file. Within the LayoutRoot grid of the Silverlight page, add a Button and set its attributes as follows, wiring up the Click event as well:

    ```
    <Grid x:Name="LayoutRoot" Background="White">
        <Button
            Content="Invoke Notepad"
            Width="100"
            Height="30"
            Name="button1"
            Click="button1_Click" />
    </Grid>
    ```

3. Add a reference to the Microsoft.CSharp in the Silverlight project, and then in the code behind, MainPage.xaml.cs, check that the application has elevated permissions. Next, add a using statement at the top of the code to System.Runtime.InteropServices.Automation. Now you'll create an instance of the WScript.Shell COM object using the AutomationFactory's CreateObject method. You can then execute the Run command and pass it the location for Notepad.exe.

    ```
    private void button1_Click(object sender, RoutedEventArgs e)
    {
        if (App.Current.HasElevatedPermissions)
        {
    ```

```
using (dynamic cmd = AutomationFactory.CreateObject("WScript.Shell"))
{
    cmd.Run(@"C:\WINDOWS\NOTEPAD.EXE", 1, true);
}
    }
}
```

4. Because the COM interoperability feature requires elevated permissions, open the properties of your Silverlight project, InvokeNotepad. Within the project properties, select the Require Elevated Trust When Running In-Browser check box, as shown in Figure 10-9.

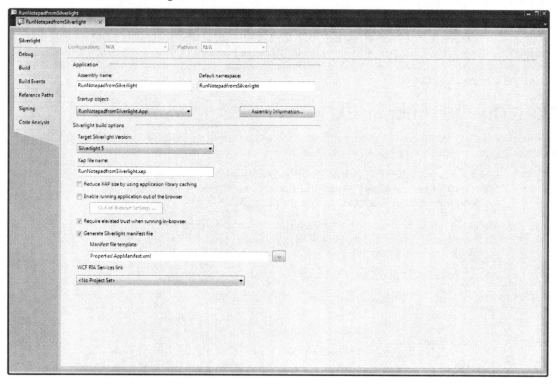

Figure 10-9. Project properties for InvokeNotepad

5. Press F5 to test the application. When the application is displayed, click the Invoke Notepad button. If all goes well, you should see Notepad open, as shown in Figure 10-10.

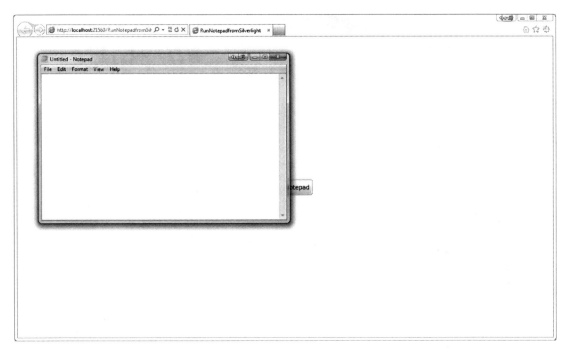

Figure 10-10. Opening Notepad from Silverlight

Dropping Files on a Silverlight Application

A feature that users have grown very accustomed to in desktop applications is the ability to drag files directly onto the application and have some action take place. With web applications, in contrast, you've always been restricted to browse functionality, which is not efficient or intuitive to users. Silverlight, however, supports the ability to drag files directly onto a Silverlight application. Currently, this is limited to files, but you can see from the API that future releases of Silverlight will most likely support additional types.

To enable drop functionality in your application, you need to enable only one property on your UI element, `AllowDrop`. If you set `AllowDrop` to `true` on your element, your application can immediately access the drop-target functionality.

Once `AllowDrop` has been set, you have a number of events that will allow you to work with file(s) dropped onto your application. The `DragEnter`, `DragLeave`, and `DragOver` events are fired during the drag process, but the primary event you are concerned with is the `Drop` event that occurs when a file is actually dropped onto your control.

Drop Event

The `Drop` event occurs when a file is dropped onto a control with `AllowDrop` enabled. This is the primary event that is used in enabling Silverlight as a drop target. From within the `Drop` event, you can get information about the file list from the `DropEventArgs.Data` property.

Let's get a closer look at enabling file drop in a Silverlight application by running through an example.

Try It Out: Enabling an Application as a Drop Target

In this example, you'll create a simple Silverlight application that contains a TextBlock. You will then enable the application as a drop target. When a file is dropped, if it is a text document with the extension *.txt, you will display the contents of the file in the TextBlock control. Let's get started.

1. Create a new Silverlight application in Visual Studio 2010. Name it SilverlightDropTarget, and allow Visual Studio to create an ASP.NET Web Application called SilverlightDropTarget.Web to host your application.

2. When the project is created, you should be looking at the MainPage.xaml file. First, set the AllowDrop property for the grid to True. Then, within the LayoutRoot grid of the Silverlight page, add a TextBlock named FileContents, and set the Margin to 10 and the TextWrapping property to Wrap.

```
<Grid AllowDrop="True" x:Name="LayoutRoot" Background="White">
    <TextBlock
        Margin="10"
        TextWrapping="Wrap"
        Name="FileContents" />
</Grid>
```

3. Now turn your attention to the code behind, MainPage.xaml.cs. First add a using reference to the System.IO namespace, and then wire up the Drop event in the constructor.

```
public MainPage()
{
    InitializeComponent();
    LayoutRoot.Drop += new DragEventHandler(LayoutRoot_Drop);
}
```

4. Next, in the LayoutRoot_Drop event, you'll start to work with the dropped file(s). First, make certain that the data dropped on the application is not null. Next, create an IDataObject set to the DragEventArgs.Data property passed into the event. You can then get the collection of files dropped using the GetData method.

```
void LayoutRoot_Drop(object sender, DragEventArgs e)
{
    if (e.Data != null)
    {
        IDataObject obj = e.Data;
        FileInfo[] files = obj.GetData(DataFormats.FileDrop) as FileInfo[];

    }
}
```

5. Once you have a collection of files, you can create a foreach statement to step through each file within your collection. For each instance, you'll inspect the file extension. If the extension is .txt, open the file using a StreamReader and read the contents of the file. Once you have read the contents, set that to the Text property of the FileContents TextBlock.

```
void LayoutRoot_Drop(object sender, DragEventArgs e)
{
    if (e.Data != null)
    {
        IDataObject obj = e.Data;
        FileInfo[] files = obj.GetData(DataFormats.FileDrop) as FileInfo[];

        foreach (FileInfo file in files)
        {
            if (file.Extension.Equals(".txt"))
            {
                using (Stream stream = file.OpenRead())
                {
                    using (StreamReader reader = new StreamReader(stream))
                    {
                        FileContents.Text = reader.ReadToEnd();
                    }
                }
            }
        }
    }
}
```

6. Now you'll test the application, but first inspect the file you are going to drop onto your application. The file name is DropMe.txt, and it contains the text shown in Figure 10-11.

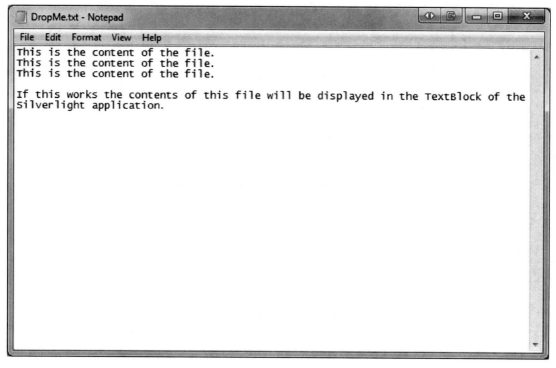

Figure 10-11. Contents of the DropMe.txt file

7. Press F5 to start the application. Once the application is open, drag DropMe.txt onto the application. You should see the cursor displayed as shown in Figure 10-12.

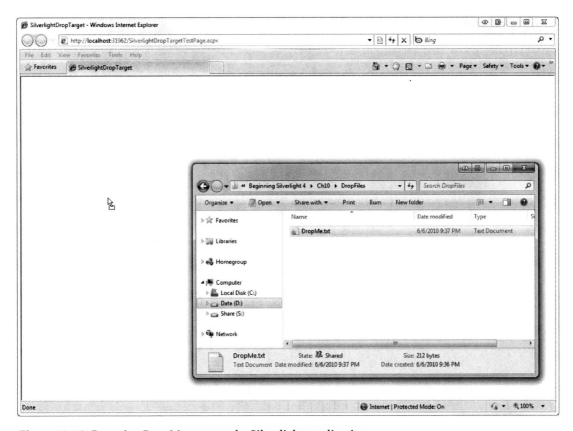

Figure 10-12. Dragging DropMe.txt onto the Silverlight application

8. After you drop the file, if all goes well you should see the contents of the file displayed in the TextBlock as shown in Figure 10-13.

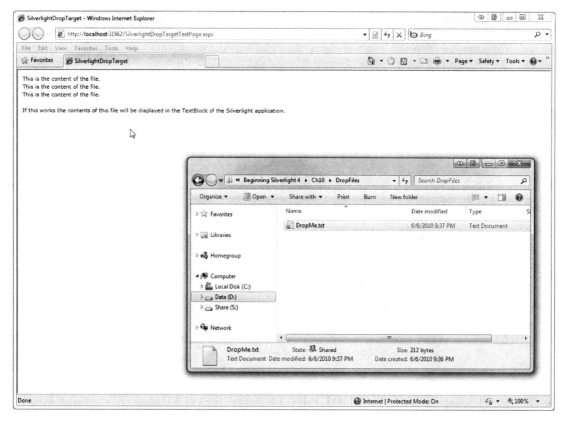

Figure 10-13. File successfully dropped onto the Silverlight application

Summary

In this chapter, you looked at a number of new features in Silverlight that enable developers to gain access to user machine devices and operating-system functionality. These features let developers make their Silverlight applications very rich and user friendly. In the next chapter, we will start to look at Expression Blend, a new tool for designing XAML-based applications.

Introduction to Expression Blend

So far in this book, the primary focus has been on using Visual Studio 2010 to create Silverlight applications. Visual Studio provides developers with a strong integrated development environment (IDE) for developing rich interactive (or Internet) applications (RIAs). However, you may want your Silverlight applications to contain some complicated design elements, and in these cases, it's not much fun to edit the XAML manually. To address this problem, Microsoft created Expression Blend, a product built to edit XAML documents visually.

Whereas Visual Studio has been designed to cater to the developer, Expression Blend has been built for the designer. As you've seen, Silverlight does a fantastic job of separating the appearance and logic of an application, so developers and designers can work side by side. ASP.NET took a few strides toward achieving this separation, but it still fell short in many ways. I think you will find that Silverlight has reached a new layer in this separation, making it much more practical for designers and developers to truly work in parallel in designing applications.

The first reaction most ASP.NET software developers will have when opening Expression Blend is shock. "Wow, this looks like no Microsoft development product I have ever seen!" And it is true that Expression Blend is quite different from the standard Visual Studio IDE. The Microsoft developers have finally provided a product for the graphic designer audience, and they have attempted to make it very similar to the tools that designers are accustomed to using. As software developers, we may need to play around a bit in Expression Blend to get the feel of it. I have found it quite cool to learn and use, and I think you will, too.

This chapter will get you started with Expression Blend. You'll learn about its key features and its workspace. Finally, I'll walk you through creating a grid layout with Expression Blend.

Key Features in Expression Blend

In this section, you will look at some of the notable features in Expression Blend, including the following:

- Visual XAML editor

- Visual Studio 2010 integration

- Split-view mode

- Visual State Manager and template editing support

- Timeline

> ▓ **Note** One of the things Microsoft has done better and better over the past few years is documentation. Expression Blend's documentation is quite comprehensive. For additional information about any of the items discussed in this chapter, refer to the User Guide provided with Expression Blend.

Visual XAML Editor

Clearly, the biggest feature of Expression Blend is that it provides a WYSIWYG editor for XAML. XAML is a very clean language, but it can also get quite complex quickly when you are working with your applications. This is especially true when you start to add animations and transformations, which are covered in Chapter 13.

Although it is possible to edit your XAML files completely in Visual Studio using IntelliSense, there is no substitute for a visual editor. In addition, the XAML that Expression Blend creates is very clean and developer-friendly. This should make developers happy, considering the terrible memories of earlier versions of FrontPage, where every change you made resulted in your code being mangled beyond recognition.

In addition, when you start working with styles (covered in Chapter 12), IntelliSense support in Visual Studio becomes limited, so the XAML is very difficult to edit manually. Expression Blend provides an extremely quick and easy way to edit and create styles, which is another reason it is an invaluable tool for editing your Silverlight applications.

Visual Studio 2010 Integration

Due to the strong push for developers and designers to work in parallel, and given that XAML files are included directly within Visual Studio 2010 projects, a valid concern is how well Expression Blend and Visual Studio work together. If there were conflicts between the two IDEs, there could be conflicts between the developers and designers, resulting in resistance to working in parallel.

The good news is that Expression Blend integrates with Visual Studio. Visual Studio 2010 projects can be opened directly in Expression Blend and vice versa. In addition, although Expression Blend creates Visual Studio 2010 projects by default, it is also capable of opening Visual Studio 2008 and 2005 projects.

Split-View Mode

As shown in Figure 11-1, Expression Blend allows you to work in design and source (XAML) mode simultaneously. For example, you can draw an object at the top of the screen in design mode, and the XAML in the source window will be updated automatically. In addition, you can just as easily edit the XAML, and the change will be reflected automatically in the design window.

Figure 11-1. Expression Blend's split-view mode

Visual State Manager and Template Editing Support

One of the cool features of Silverlight is that all controls released with it support the new "Parts and State" model, which requires strict separation between a control's logic and appearance. Microsoft recommends that all custom controls also support this model.

By separating the logic from the appearance of a control, a developer or designer can completely change the appearance of a control without affecting its behavior. This process is known as creating a template, or *skinning*, and it is regulated by Visual State Manager (VSM). Expression Blend provides a very clean way to create and edit these parts and states, which makes skinning your applications a relatively simple task. You'll learn more about VSM and skinning in *Pro Silverlight 5 in C#* by Matthew MacDonald (Apress, 2012).

World-Class Timeline

In Silverlight, animations are based on keyframes within a storyboard. These keyframes are set on a timeline, and they define the start and end points of a smooth visual transition. Figure 11-2 shows the Expression Blend timeline, which is located in the Objects And Timeline panel.

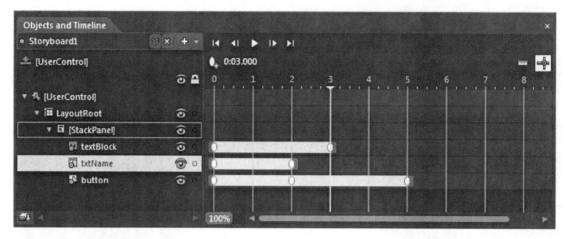

Figure 11-2. The Expression Blend timeline

The timeline provides you with structure for all of the animation sequences in your Silverlight application. Instead of the timeline being based on abstract frames, it is based on time, which makes it very straightforward and easy to understand. Also, as you develop your animations, you can quickly navigate to any given time on the timeline to check the appearance of your application at that point.

Try It Out: Working with Projects in Expression Blend

As you've learned, one of the key features of Expression Blend is that it integrates directly with Visual Studio 2010 projects. This exercise demonstrates how you can use the two products side by side while creating and editing projects.

1. Open Expression Blend. By default, when you open Expression Blend, you will see the splash screen shown in Figure 11-3. If you do not want this screen to appear when you start Expression Blend, you can simply deselect the Run At Startup check box at the bottom left. For now, if this screen appears, click Close to continue with the example.

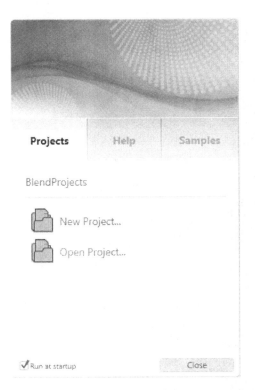

Figure 11-3. Startup screen for Expression Blend

2. You should now have an empty Expression Blend workspace. From the main menu, click File ➤ New Project. This displays the New Project dialog box.

3. In the New Project dialog box, select Silverlight Application + Website for the project type, and then enter BlendProjects for the project name, as shown in Figure 11-4. Click OK to create the new project.

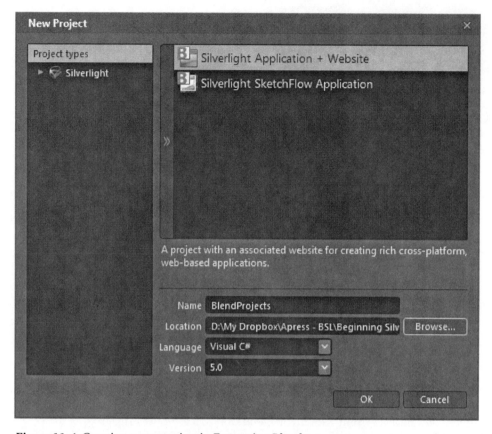

Figure 11-4. Creating a new project in Expression Blend

4.   By default, Expression Blend opens the `MainPage.xaml` file for editing. In the upper-right portion of the artboard (which contains the XML) are options to switch between the design, XAML, and split-mode views. Click Split to see both the XAML and the design view at the same time, as shown in Figure 11-5.

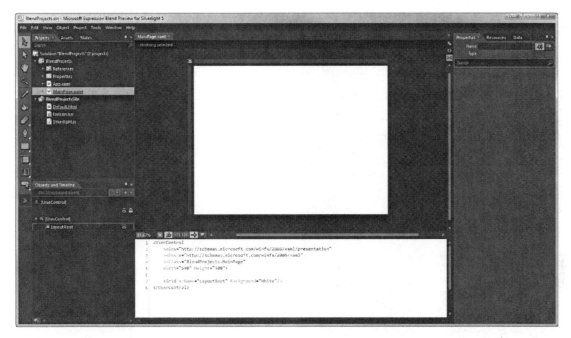

Figure 11-5. *Split-view mode in Expression Blend*

5. Now edit this project in Visual Studio. In the Project panel, right-click the
    BlendProjects project and select Edit in Visual Studio, as shown in Figure 11-6.
    This automatically starts Visual Studio 2010 and opens your project.

■ **Note** Step 5 assumes that you have already installed Visual Studio 2010. If not, you need to install that to
continue.

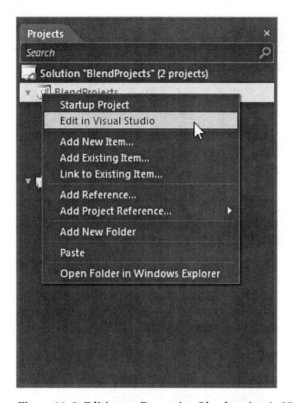

Figure 11-6. Editing an Expression Blend project in Visual Studio

6. In Visual Studio 2010, double-click MainPage.xaml in Solution Explorer. Let's make a simple change to the application in Visual Studio.

7. Modify the root Grid to add the following code shown in bold, to define a StackPanel with a TextBlock, TextBox, and Button:

```
<UserControl
      xmlns="http://schemas.microsoft.com/winfx/2006/xaml/presentation"
      xmlns:x="http://schemas.microsoft.com/winfx/2006/xaml"
      x:Class="BlendProjects.MainPage"
      Width="640" Height="480">

    <Grid x:Name="LayoutRoot" Background="White">
        <StackPanel Margin="20" Orientation="Vertical">
            <TextBlock Margin="5" Text="Enter Your Name:" />
            <TextBox Margin="5" x:Name="txtName" />
            <Button Margin="5" Content="Click Me!" />
        </StackPanel>
    </Grid>

</UserControl>
```

8. From the main menu, click File ➤ Save All, just to make sure everything is saved.

9. Switch back to Expression Blend. It prompts you with the File Modified dialog box, as shown in Figure 11-7. Click Yes. You will see Expression Blend refresh the project so that it reflects the changes you made in Visual Studio 2010.

Figure 11-7. File-modification notification in Expression Blend

Pretty nifty, right? The same file modification is offered when you do the reverse: make a change in Expression Blend and then go back into Visual Studio. Feel free to try this out yourself.

As this exercise demonstrated, Expression Blend and Visual Studio work together seamlessly. You can switch back and forth between the two products without fear of data loss or conflicts.

Note Although Expression Blend usually will be used with Visual Studio, Expression Blend actually picks up on changes to open files caused by edits in any editor.

Exploring the Workspace

Now that I have briefly discussed some of the key features of Expression Blend, let's take a look at the different elements of its workspace. Despite Expression Blend's radical appearance, developers will find many similarities between Visual Studio and Expression Blend.

Let's start out by looking at Expression Blend in Animation workspace mode. You enter this mode by selecting Window ➤ Workspaces ➤ Animation from the main menu. Starting at the left, you will see the Toolbox and the artboard, which contains the application and the XAML source. On the right is the Properties panel. Docked with the Properties panel are the Project and Resources panels. At the bottom of the workspace, you will see the VSM panel and the Objects And Timeline panel. Let's take a closer look at some of these workspace elements.

Toolbox

The Expression Blend Toolbox provides the tools for adding and manipulating objects within your application. As shown in Figure 11-8, it is divided into five primary sections: selection tools, view tools, brush tools, object tools, and asset tools. The object tool group includes six submenus, which contain path tools, shape tools, layout tools, text controls, and common controls.

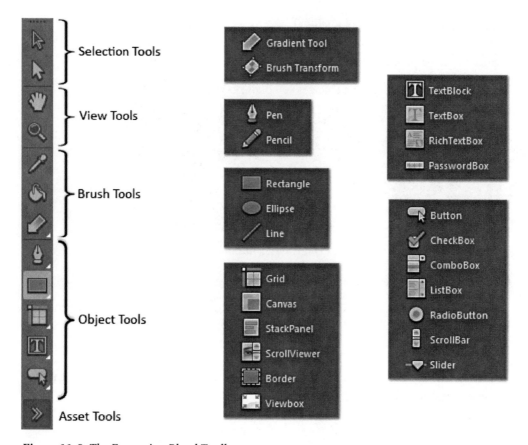

Figure 11-8. *The Expression Blend Toolbox*

Clicking the Asset Tools icon at the very bottom of the Toolbox opens the Asset Library window, which lists the Silverlight system controls, as shown in Figure 11-9.

Figure 11-9. The Asset Library window

Project Panel

The Project panel is very similar to Solution Explorer in Visual Studio. It lists all the files associated with the project.

The Project panel also displays project references and properties. See Figure 11-6 earlier in the chapter for an example of the Project panel.

Properties Panel

The Properties panel allows you to view and modify the properties of objects on the artboard. Figure 11-10 shows an example of the Properties panel when an Ellipse control is selected.

The Properties panel is divided into a number of sections to help you easily find specific properties. The sections displayed depend on the object you have selected. In addition, the Search box at the top of the Properties panel allows you to filter the listing by typing in the property name. Figure 11-11 shows an example of the Properties panel after searching for the Margin property.

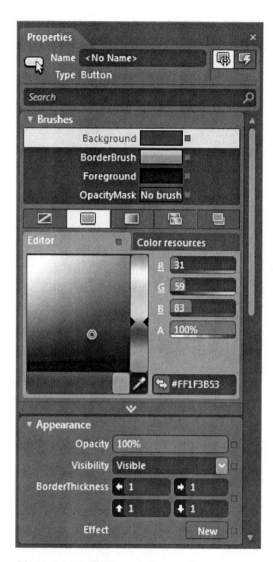

Figure 11-10. The Properties panel

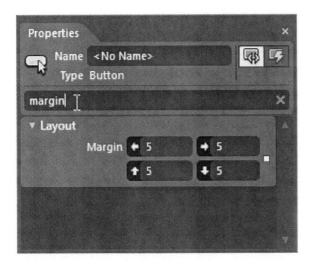

Figure 11-11. *Filtering the Properties panel*

Objects And Timeline Panel

All objects that are added to your Silverlight application are represented in the Objects And Timeline panel. Because items can be nested within other objects, a type of layering takes place. For objects that contain additional objects, an arrow appears to the left of the item. Click this arrow to expand and collapse the display of the nested objects.

When animation is added to your Silverlight application, storyboards are created. Storyboards are represented in the timeline, as shown earlier in Figure 11-2. You'll learn more about the timeline in Chapter 13.

Laying Out an Application with Expression Blend

As discussed in Chapter 3, you have a number of options when it comes to laying out your Silverlight application. Although these layout controls can be added manually, Expression Blend offers a visual option. In this section, you will look at how Expression Blend can be used to easily work with the Grid layout control.

Working with the Grid Control in Expression Blend

In Expression Blend, you place dividers to create columns and rows in the grid. When a Grid control is defined, Expression Blend shows blue rulers above and to the left of the grid. When you move your cursor over the blue rulers, a row divider appears. Clicking the blue ruler places the divider, and dragging a placed divider moves it. You will have a chance to try this out in a moment.

In the top-left corner of the window is an icon that determines the grid's edit mode. There are two layout editing modes for a grid within Expression Blend:

- *Canvas layout mode*: In canvas layout mode, when column and row dividers are moved, elements inside those rows and columns stay in place.

- *Grid layout mode*: In grid layout mode, the elements move with the column and row dividers.

Try It Out: Editing a Layout Grid with Expression Blend

Let's give layout in Expression Blend a try. In this exercise, you will create a simple grid layout with three rows and two columns. Then you will nest a secondary grid within the right-center cell, and place two more rows within that grid. The end product will look like Figure 11-12.

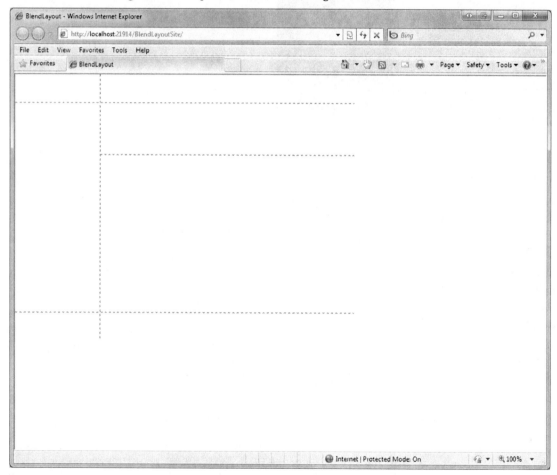

Figure 11-12. The completed grid layout

1. In Expression Blend, create a new Silverlight Application + Website project named BlendLayout. The MainPage.xaml file opens automatically, and as usual, a root Grid named LayoutRoot will be present.

2.   First, create the column definitions. To do this, at about 25% from the left of
     the top blue grid ruler, click the ruler to place a grid divider, as shown in Figure
     11-13. If you examine the XAML, you will notice that the
     `<Grid.ColumnDefinitions>` element has been added, along with two
     `<ColumnDefinition>` elements, as follows (note that your percentages do not
     need to be exact):

```
<UserControl
        xmlns="http://schemas.microsoft.com/winfx/2006/xaml/presentation"
        xmlns:x="http://schemas.microsoft.com/winfx/2006/xaml"
        x:Class="BlendLayout.MainPage"
        Width="640" Height="480">

        <Grid x:Name="LayoutRoot" Background="White">
                <Grid.ColumnDefinitions>
                        <ColumnDefinition Width="0.251*"/>
                        <ColumnDefinition Width="0.749*"/>
                </Grid.ColumnDefinitions>
        </Grid>
</UserControl>
```

Figure 11-13. Adding column defintions

3.   Next, create the rows. In the blue grid ruler on the left, click at about 10% from
     the top and 10% from the bottom to place two dividers. Your grid should now
     look like the one shown in Figure 11-14.

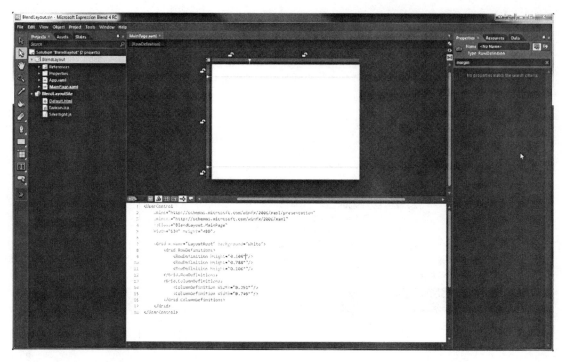

Figure 11-14. *Adding row definitions*

4. The source for the `MainPage.xaml` file should be very similar to the following (the actual heights and widths do not need to be exact):

```
<UserControl
        xmlns="http://schemas.microsoft.com/winfx/2006/xaml/presentation"
        xmlns:x="http://schemas.microsoft.com/winfx/2006/xaml"
        x:Class="BlendLayout.MainPage"
        Width="634" Height="480">

        <Grid x:Name="LayoutRoot" Background="White">
                <Grid.RowDefinitions>
                        <RowDefinition Height="0.106*"/>
                        <RowDefinition Height="0.788*"/>
                        <RowDefinition Height="0.106*"/>
                </Grid.RowDefinitions>
                <Grid.ColumnDefinitions>
                        <ColumnDefinition Width="0.251*"/>
                        <ColumnDefinition Width="0.749*"/>
                </Grid.ColumnDefinitions>
        </Grid>
</UserControl>
```

5. At this point, you have created a number of cells. Now, let's create a nested grid within the right-center cell. To do this, make certain that the LayoutRoot is selected in the Objects And Timeline panel, and then double-click the Grid control in the Toolbox. This adds a Grid of the default size to your application, as shown in Figure 11-15.

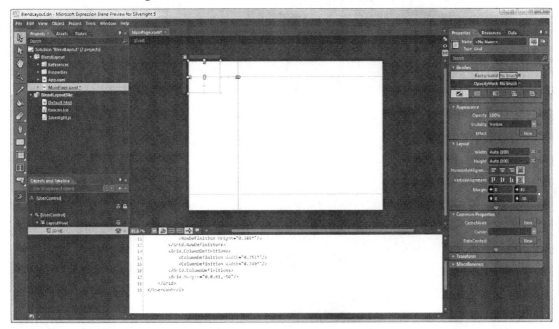

Figure 11-15. Adding a nested grid

6. With this new grid selected, edit its properties. In the Properties panel, set the properties as shown in Figure 11-16.

7. The nested grid should now take up the entire right-center cell. In the Objects And Timeline panel, double-click the innerGrid object you just added. The top and left grid rulers will now appear for the inner grid, as shown in Figure 11-17.

8. At this point, you could easily add rows and columns using the rulers, as you did with the LayoutRoot, but let's try a different method.

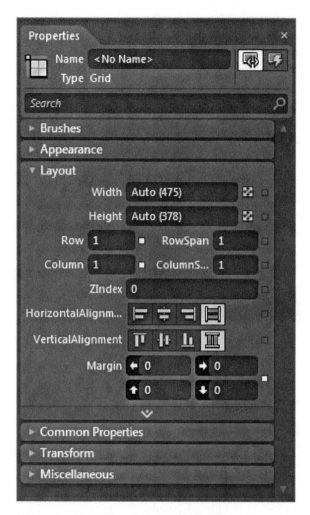

Figure 11-16. *Setting the nested grid properties*

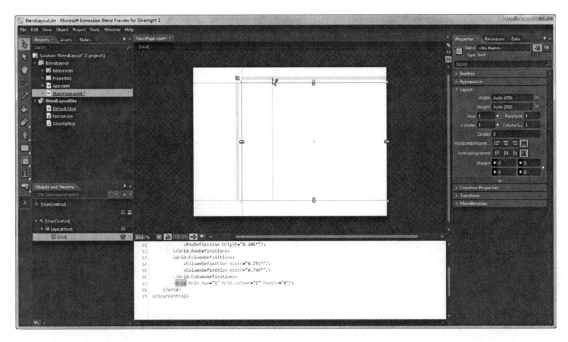

Figure 11-17. Nested grid with row and column rulers

9. With `innerGrid` selected, in the Properties panel's Search box, type
   Definitions. This displays the `RowDefinitions` and `ColumnDefinitions`
   properties, as shown in Figure 11-18.

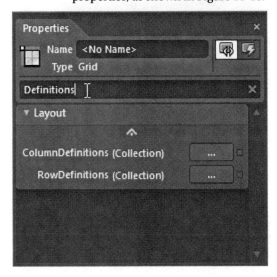

Figure 11-18. RowDefinition and ColumnDefinition property collections

10. Click the button to the right of RowDefinitions (Collection) to bring up the RowDefinition Collection Editor dialog box.

11. Click the Add Another Item button near the bottom of the RowDefinition Collection Editor dialog box and add two RowDefinition items. Set the Height property for the first RowDefinition to 25 (Star) and the Height property for the second RowDefinition to 75 (Star), as shown in Figure 11-19. Then click OK to close the editor.

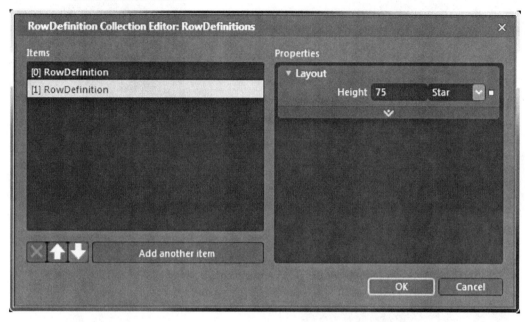

Figure 11-19. Adding RowDefinition items in the RowDefinition Collection Editor

12. In the Properties panel, set the ShowGridLines property for both Grids to True. The final XAML should look like the following (again, the heights and widths only need to be close):

```xml
<UserControl
        xmlns="http://schemas.microsoft.com/winfx/2006/xaml/presentation"
        xmlns:x="http://schemas.microsoft.com/winfx/2006/xaml"
        x:Class="BlendLayout.MainPage"
        Width="634" Height="480">

        <Grid x:Name="LayoutRoot" Background="White" ShowGridLines="True">
                <Grid.RowDefinitions>
                        <RowDefinition Height="0.106*"/>
                        <RowDefinition Height="0.788*"/>
                        <RowDefinition Height="0.106*"/>
                </Grid.RowDefinitions>
                <Grid.ColumnDefinitions>
```

```
                    <ColumnDefinition Width="0.251*"/>
                    <ColumnDefinition Width="0.749*"/>
            </Grid.ColumnDefinitions>
            <Grid Margin="0" Grid.Row="1" Grid.Column="1" ShowGridLines="True">
                    <Grid.RowDefinitions>
                            <RowDefinition Height="25*"/>
                            <RowDefinition Height="75*"/>
                    </Grid.RowDefinitions>
            </Grid>
        </Grid>
    </UserControl>
```

13. Press F5 to test your application. The result should appear, as shown earlier in Figure 11-12.

As you can see, once you get used to working with Expression Blend, it can save you quite a bit of typing. This makes laying out your applications a much faster and easier task.

Summary

In this chapter, you took a first look at Expression Blend and how it can be used alongside Visual Studio 2010 to help you design your Silverlight applications. You also looked at working with the Grid layout control to create complex layouts for your applications.

The upcoming chapters explain how to use Expression Blend to style your Silverlight applications, as well as add transformations and animations to your applications.

CHAPTER 12

Styling in Silverlight

Of course, you will want to create a rich appearance for your Silverlight application. You'll make choices about your design. What font size and family will you use? How much space will you place between your objects? What size of text boxes and buttons will you use?

As you'll learn in this chapter, you can control the styles of your Silverlight application's UI elements in several ways. The first approach you'll explore is the straightforward use of inline properties. Then you'll look at how to define and apply Silverlight styles.

Inline Properties

You can simply define style properties directly in the object definitions. As an example, the following code snippet sets the FontFamily, FontSize, FontWeight, and Margin properties within the TextBlock itself:

```
<TextBlock
    Grid.Row="0"
    Grid.Column="0"
    Text="First Name"
    FontFamily="Verdana"
    FontSize="16"
    FontWeight="Bold"
    Margin="5" />
```

You can set inline properties using either Visual Studio or Expression Blend. Let's try out both.

Try It Out: Setting Inline Properties with Visual Studio

The following exercise demonstrates how to use Visual Studio 2010 to define the appearance of your Silverlight applications with inline properties. In this exercise, you will create the UI for a simple data-input application. You will not add any logic to the application because the focus is on the appearance of the controls.

1. Open Visual Studio 2010, and create a new Silverlight application named VSInlineStyling. Allow Visual Studio to create a Web Application project to host the application.

2. When the project is created, you should be looking at the MainPage.xaml file. If you do not see the XAML source, switch to that view. Start by adjusting the size of the UserControl to get some additional space in which to work. Set Height to 400 and Width to 600, as follows:

```
<UserControl x:Class="VSInlineStyling.MainPage"
    xmlns="http://schemas.microsoft.com/winfx/2006/xaml/presentation"
    xmlns:x="http://schemas.microsoft.com/winfx/2006/xaml"
    Width="600" Height="400">
    <Grid x:Name="LayoutRoot" Background="White">

    </Grid>
</UserControl>
```

3. Add four rows and two columns to the root Grid. Set the width of the left column to 150, leaving the rest of the row and column definitions unspecified, as follows:

```
<Grid x:Name="LayoutRoot" Background="White">
    <Grid.RowDefinitions>
        <RowDefinition />
        <RowDefinition />
        <RowDefinition />
        <RowDefinition />
    </Grid.RowDefinitions>
    <Grid.ColumnDefinitions>
        <ColumnDefinition Width="150" />
        <ColumnDefinition />
    </Grid.ColumnDefinitions>
</Grid>
```

4. Next, add TextBlock controls in the three top-left columns and TextBox controls in the top-right columns, with the text First Name, Last Name, and Age. Then add three Button controls within a horizontal StackPanel in the bottom-right column. Give these buttons the labels Save, Next, and Delete. (Again, you won't be adding any logic to these controls; you will simply be modifying their appearance.) The code for this layout follows:

```
<Grid x:Name="LayoutRoot" Background="White">
    <Grid.RowDefinitions>
        <RowDefinition />
        <RowDefinition />
        <RowDefinition />
        <RowDefinition />
    </Grid.RowDefinitions>
    <Grid.ColumnDefinitions>
        <ColumnDefinition Width="150" />
        <ColumnDefinition />
    </Grid.ColumnDefinitions>

    <TextBlock Grid.Row="0" Grid.Column="0" Text="First Name" />
    <TextBlock Grid.Row="1" Grid.Column="0" Text="Last Name" />
    <TextBlock Grid.Row="2" Grid.Column="0" Text="Age" />

    <TextBox Grid.Row="0" Grid.Column="1" />
    <TextBox Grid.Row="1" Grid.Column="1" />
    <TextBox Grid.Row="2" Grid.Column="1"  />
```

```
    <StackPanel Grid.Row="3" Grid.Column="2" Orientation="Horizontal">
        <Button Content="Save" />
        <Button Content="Next" />
        <Button Content="Delete" />
    </StackPanel>
</Grid>
```

5. Press F5 to start the application. You will see that the UI you created is far from
    attractive, as shown in Figure 12-1. So let's make this ugly UI look a bit nicer by
    adding some styling.

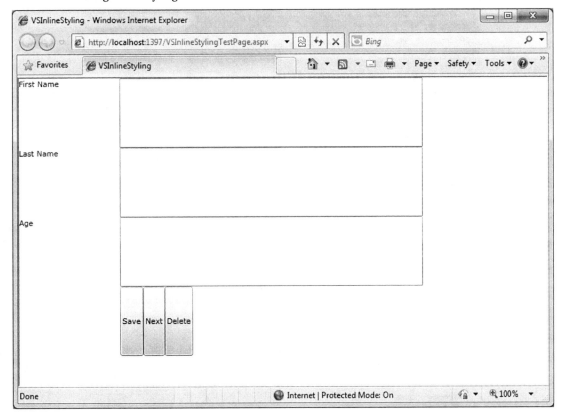

Figure 12-1. Default input form without styling

6. Start with the three TextBlock controls. Within Visual Studio, set the
    FontFamily, FontSize, FontWeight, and Margin properties directly within each
    TextBlock definition, as shown in the following code snippet. As you type the
    property names, you will notice that IntelliSense makes this task a bit less
    tedious. After you set the four properties on the First Name TextBlock, copy
    and paste the properties to the other two TextBlock controls:

```
<TextBlock Grid.Row="0" Grid.Column="0" Text="First Name"
    FontFamily="Verdana"
    FontSize="16"
    FontWeight="Bold"
    Margin="5" />
<TextBlock Grid.Row="1" Grid.Column="0" Text="Last Name"
    FontFamily="Verdana"
    FontSize="16"
    FontWeight="Bold"
    Margin="5" />
<TextBlock Grid.Row="2" Grid.Column="0" Text="Age"
    FontFamily="Verdana"
    FontSize="16"
    FontWeight="Bold"
    Margin="5" />
```

7. Run the application again. You can see the changes that were made to the TextBlock labels, as shown in Figure 12-2.

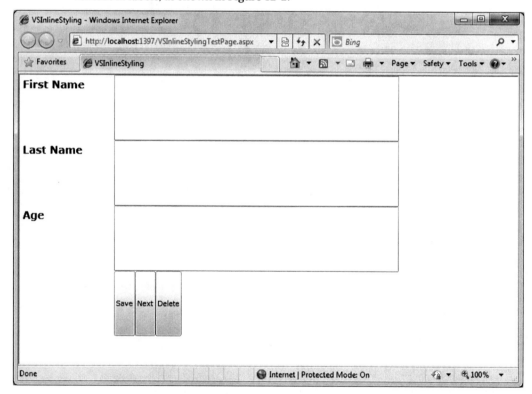

Figure 12-2. Input form with styled TextBlock labels

8. Now let's focus on the TextBox controls. Add the following style attributes to these controls:

```xml
<TextBox Grid.Row="0" Grid.Column="1"
    VerticalAlignment="Top"
    Height="24"
    Margin="5"
    FontSize="14"
    FontFamily="Verdana"
    Foreground="Blue"
    Background="Wheat" />

<TextBox Grid.Row="1" Grid.Column="1"
    VerticalAlignment="Top"
    Height="24"
    Margin="5"
    FontSize="14"
    FontFamily="Verdana"
    Foreground="Blue"
    Background="Wheat" />

<TextBox Grid.Row="2" Grid.Column="1"
    VerticalAlignment="Top"
    Height="24"
    Margin="5"
    FontSize="14"
    FontFamily="Verdana"
    Foreground="Blue"
    Background="Wheat" />
```

9. Run the application to see the effect. It should look like Figure 12-3.

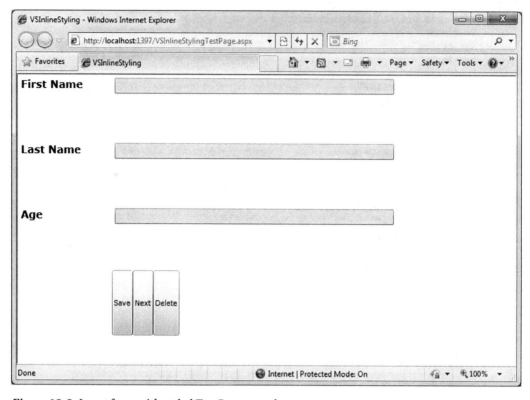

Figure 12-3. Input form with styled TextBox controls

10. Notice that the spacing between the rows is too large. Ideally, the spaces should be only large enough to allow the margins of the controls to provide the separation. To adjust this spacing, on each RowDefinition, change the Height property to Auto, as follows:

```
<Grid.RowDefinitions>
    <RowDefinition Height="Auto" />
    <RowDefinition Height="Auto" />
    <RowDefinition Height="Auto" />
    <RowDefinition Height="Auto" />
</Grid.RowDefinitions>
<Grid.ColumnDefinitions>
    <ColumnDefinition Width="150" />
    <ColumnDefinition />
</Grid.ColumnDefinitions>
```

11. Once more, run the application to see how it looks at this point. Figure 12-4 shows the results of the automatic height settings.

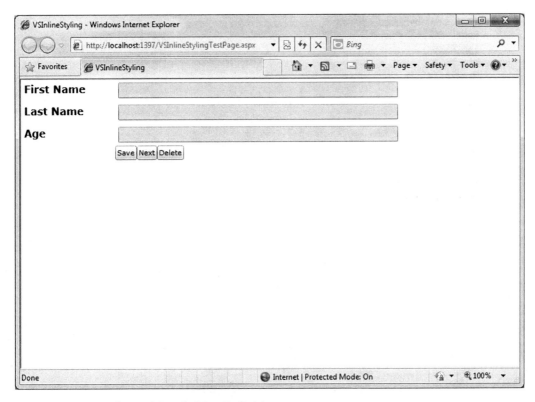

Figure 12-4. Input form with styled RowDefinitions

12. The next elements to tackle are the Button controls. Add the following style attributes to these three controls:

```
<Button Content="Save"
    FontFamily="Verdana"
    FontSize="11"
    Width="75"
    Margin="5" />

<Button Content="Next"
    FontFamily="Verdana"
    FontSize="11"
    Width="75"
    Margin="5" />

<Button Content="Delete"
    FontFamily="Verdana"
    FontSize="11"
    Width="75"
    Margin="5" />
```

13. Run the application to see the effect. It should look like Figure 12-5.

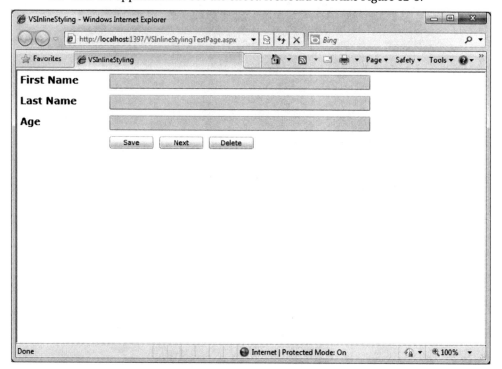

Figure 12-5. Input form with styled buttons

14. Finally, it would be nice to add a margin around the entire application. To do this, simply add a Margin property definition to the root Grid, as follows:

```
<Grid x:Name="LayoutRoot" Background="White" Margin="25">
```

15. Press F5. The final product is a UI that looks pretty nice, as shown in Figure 12-6.

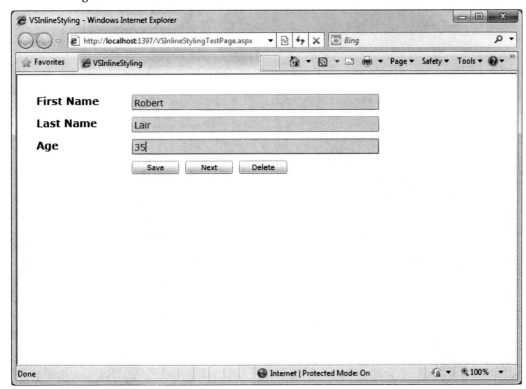

Figure 12-6. Final input form styled with inline properties

As you saw in this exercise, the process of setting inline properties in Visual Studio is simple and straightforward. However, the sample application contained only nine controls. You will look at some better options later in this chapter, in the "Silverlight Styles" section. Next, let's see how to set inline properties within Expression Blend.

Try It Out: Setting Inline Properties with Expression Blend

The previous example used Visual Studio to set the inline properties of an application's controls. If you are not a big fan of a lot of typing, you might find that Expression Blend is a better place to set these properties. In this next exercise, you will perform the same styling as in previous exercise, but you'll do it using Expression Blend to set the properties, rather than Visual Studio 2010. Let's give it a try!

1. Open Expression Blend, and create a new Silverlight application named BlendStyling.

2. The UserControl is 640 by 480 by default when created in Expression Blend, so you can leave that size. The first thing to do is add the column and row definitions. You can copy and paste the grid definitions from the previous exercise, or you can add the columns and rows using Expression Blend's grid editor, as described in Chapter 9. The result should look like Figure 12-7.

3. Next, add the controls to the form. In the Toolbox, double-click the TextBlock control three times to add three TextBlock controls to the grid. Then double-click the TextBox control three times, which will add three TextBox controls below the TextBlock controls.

4. Double-click the StackPanel layout control. Once the StackPanel is added, double- click it in the Objects And Timeline panel so that it is outlined, as shown in Figure 12-8.

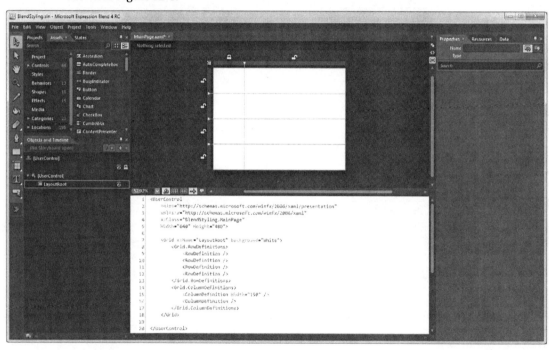

Figure 12-7. Completed grid layout

Figure 12-8. Selecting the StackPanel in the Objects And Timeline panel

5. With the StackPanel selected, double-click the Button control three times. The three Button controls will appear within the StackPanel, as shown in Figure 12-9.

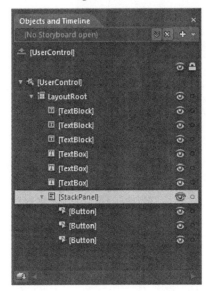

Figure 12-9. The Button controls added to the StackPanel

6. By default, Expression Blend adds a number of properties that you don't need. In the next steps, you'll remove the properties shown in bold in the following XAML:

```xml
<Grid x:Name="LayoutRoot" Background="White" >
    <Grid.RowDefinitions>
        <RowDefinition/>
        <RowDefinition/>
        <RowDefinition/>
        <RowDefinition/>
    </Grid.RowDefinitions>
    <Grid.ColumnDefinitions>
        <ColumnDefinition Width="150"/>
        <ColumnDefinition/>
    </Grid.ColumnDefinitions>
    <TextBlock HorizontalAlignment="Left"
        VerticalAlignment="Top" Text="TextBlock" TextWrapping="Wrap"/>
    <TextBlock HorizontalAlignment="Left"
        VerticalAlignment="Top" Text="TextBlock" TextWrapping="Wrap"/>
    <TextBlock HorizontalAlignment="Left"
        VerticalAlignment="Top" Text="TextBlock" TextWrapping="Wrap"/>
    <TextBox HorizontalAlignment="Left"
        VerticalAlignment="Top" Text="TextBox" TextWrapping="Wrap"/>
    <TextBox HorizontalAlignment="Left"
        VerticalAlignment="Top" Text="TextBox" TextWrapping="Wrap"/>
    <TextBox HorizontalAlignment="Left"
        VerticalAlignment="Top" Text="TextBox" TextWrapping="Wrap"/>
    <StackPanel Margin="0,0,50,20">
        <Button Content="Button"/>
        <Button Content="Button"/>
        <Button Content="Button"/>
    </StackPanel>
</Grid>
```

7. In the Objects And Timeline panel, highlight all of the TextBlock and TextBox controls, as shown in Figure 12-10. You can highlight multiple items in the Objects And Timeline panel by holding down the Shift or Ctrl key as you click.

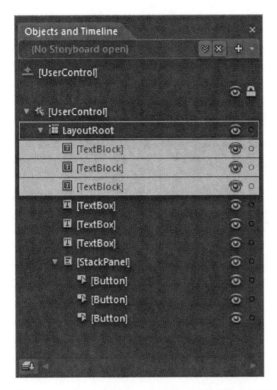

Figure 12-10. Selecting multiple objects in the Objects and Timeline panel

8. With these six controls selected, look in the Properties panel. Notice that any property that is set in the XAML has a white dot to its right. (Properties you cannot edit have a gray dot.) You can easily remove these properties from the XAML and reset the code by clicking the white dot and selecting Reset. Start out by resetting the HorizontalAlignment property located in the Layout section of the Properties panel, as shown in Figure 12-11. Then reset the VerticalAlignment property. This removes the HorizontalAlignment and VerticalAlignment property definitions in the XAML.

Figure 12-11. *Resetting the HorizontalAlignment property*

9. The TextWrapping property is located in the Text Section of the Properties panel, but you must extend the section to see it. I figured that this would be a good opportunity to show you another feature of the Properties panel. At the top of the Properties panel, type TextWrapping into the Search box. That will filter the Properties panel to show only the TextWrapping property. Click and reset that property as well.

10. Next, highlight the StackPanel and reset its Margin property in the same way. When you have finished all of these steps, the XAML should contain the following source code:

```
<Grid x:Name="LayoutRoot" Background="White" >
    <Grid.RowDefinitions>
      <RowDefinition/>
       <RowDefinition/>
       <RowDefinition/>
       <RowDefinition/>
    </Grid.RowDefinitions>
    <Grid.ColumnDefinitions>
        <ColumnDefinition Width="150"/>
        <ColumnDefinition/>
    </Grid.ColumnDefinitions>
    <TextBlock Text="TextBlock"/>
    <TextBlock Text="TextBlock"/>
    <TextBlock Text="TextBlock"/>
    <TextBox Text="TextBox"/>
    <TextBox Text="TextBox"/>
    <TextBox Text="TextBox"/>
    <StackPanel>
        <Button Content="Button"/>
        <Button Content="Button"/>
        <Button Content="Button"/>
    </StackPanel>
</Grid>
```

11. Now you need to place these controls in the proper cells in your grid. Click to highlight the control in the Objects And Timeline panel. In the Layout section of the Properties panel, you will see Row and Column properties. Set their values so that you have the following result:

```
<Grid x:Name="LayoutRoot" Background="White" >
    <Grid.RowDefinitions>
        <RowDefinition/>
        <RowDefinition/>
        <RowDefinition/>
        <RowDefinition/>
    </Grid.RowDefinitions>
    <Grid.ColumnDefinitions>
        <ColumnDefinition Width="150"/>
        <ColumnDefinition/>
    </Grid.ColumnDefinitions>
    <TextBlock Text="TextBlock"/>
    <TextBlock Text="TextBlock" Grid.Row="1"/>
    <TextBlock Text="TextBlock" Grid.Row="2"/>
    <TextBox Text="TextBox" Grid.Column="1"/>
    <TextBox Text="TextBox" Grid.Column="1" Grid.Row="1"/>
    <TextBox Text="TextBox" Grid.Row="2" Grid.Column="1"/>
    <StackPanel Grid.Column="1" Grid.Row="3">
        <Button Content="Button"/>
```

```
            <Button Content="Button"/>
            <Button Content="Button"/>
        </StackPanel>
    </Grid>
```

12. Go through each of the TextBlock controls to set the Text properties to First Name, Last Name, and Age. Next, set the Text property of the TextBox controls to blank (or just reset the property). Then set the Orientation property for the StackPanel to Horizontal. Finally, set the Content property for the Button controls to Save, Next, and Delete. The result should be the following:

```
<Grid x:Name="LayoutRoot" Background="White" >
    <Grid.RowDefinitions>
        <RowDefinition/>
        <RowDefinition/>
        <RowDefinition/>
        <RowDefinition/>
    </Grid.RowDefinitions>
    <Grid.ColumnDefinitions>
        <ColumnDefinition Width="150"/>
        <ColumnDefinition/>
    </Grid.ColumnDefinitions>
    <TextBlock Text="First Name"/>
    <TextBlock Text="Last Name" Grid.Row="1"/>
    <TextBlock Text="Age" Grid.Row="2"/>
    <TextBox Grid.Column="1"/>
    <TextBox Grid.Column="1" Grid.Row="1"/>
    <TextBox Grid.Row="2" Grid.Column="1"/>
    <StackPanel Grid.Column="1" Grid.Row="3" Orientation="Horizontal">
        <Button Content="Save"/>
        <Button Content="Next"/>
        <Button Content="Delete"/>
    </StackPanel>
</Grid>
```

13. Run the solution, and you will see the initial layout, which should look the same as what you started with in the previous exercise (which was shown in Figure 12-1). The next thing to do is set the style properties for your controls.

14. Highlight all three TextBlock controls. In the Properties panel, set the following properties:

    • FontFamily: Verdana

    • FontSize: 16

    • FontWeight: Bold

    • Margin: 5,5,5,5

15. Select the three TextBox controls, and set the following properties:

    • FontFamily: Verdana

- FontSize: 14

- FontWeight: Bold

- Foreground: #FF0008FF

- Background: #FFF9F57D

- VerticalAlignment: Top

- Margin: 5,5,5,5

16. Highlight the three Button controls, and set the following properties:

- FontFamily: Verdana

- FontSize: 11

- Width: 75

- Margin: 5,5,5,5

17. Switch to split-view mode. Within the XAML, place your cursor within one of the RowDefinition items. Then, in the Properties panel, set the Height property to Auto. Repeat this for all of the RowDefinition items in the Grid. When you are finished setting the Height properties on the RowDefinition items, the XAML for the application should be as follows:

```
<Grid x:Name="LayoutRoot" Background="White" >
    <Grid.RowDefinitions>
        <RowDefinition Height="Auto"/>
        <RowDefinition Height="Auto"/>
        <RowDefinition Height="Auto"/>
        <RowDefinition Height="Auto"/>
    </Grid.RowDefinitions>
    <Grid.ColumnDefinitions>
        <ColumnDefinition Width="150"/>
        <ColumnDefinition/>
    </Grid.ColumnDefinitions>
    <TextBlock Text="First Name" FontFamily="Verdana"
        FontSize="16" FontWeight="Bold" Margin="5,5,5,5"/>
    <TextBlock Text="Last Name" Grid.Row="1" FontFamily="Verdana"
        FontSize="16" FontWeight="Bold" Margin="5,5,5,5"/>
    <TextBlock Text="Age" Grid.Row="2" FontFamily="Verdana"
        FontSize="16" FontWeight="Bold" Margin="5,5,5,5"/>
    <TextBox Text="" Grid.Row="0" Grid.Column="1"
        FontFamily="Verdana" FontSize="14" FontWeight="Bold"
        Foreground="#FF0008FF" Background="#FFF9F57D"
        VerticalAlignment="Top" Margin="5,5,5,5"/>
    <TextBox Text="" Grid.Row="1" Grid.Column="1"
        FontFamily="Verdana" FontSize="14" FontWeight="Bold"
        Foreground="#FF0008FF" Background="#FFF9F57D"
        VerticalAlignment="Top" Margin="5,5,5,5"/>
    <TextBox Text="" Grid.Row="2" Grid.Column="1"
        FontFamily="Verdana" FontSize="14" FontWeight="Bold"
```

```
            Foreground="#FF0008FF" Background="#FFF9F57D"
            VerticalAlignment="Top" Margin="5,5,5,5"/>
        <StackPanel Grid.Row="3" Grid.Column="1" Orientation="Horizontal">
            <Button Content="Save" Margin="5,5,5,5"
                Width="75" FontFamily="Verdana"/>
            <Button Content="Next" Margin="5,5,5,5"
                Width="75" FontFamily="Verdana"/>
            <Button Content="Delete" Margin="5,5,5,5"
                Width="75" FontFamily="Verdana"/>
        </StackPanel>
    </Grid>
```

18. Your application will appear something like what is shown in Figure 12-12.
    When you run the application, it should look very similar to the application at
    the end of the previous exercise (which was shown in Figure 12-6).

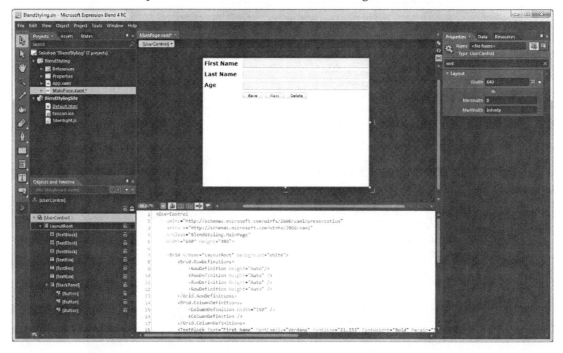

Figure 12-12. *Final project in Expression Blend*

Getting the code perfect is not the point of this exercise. It's OK if your application doesn't look exactly like my screen shot. The main objective was to get you familiar with setting and resetting inline properties in Expression Blend.

In these two exercises, you saw how to change the appearance of your Silverlight applications using inline properties in Visual Studio 2010 and Expression Blend. Although this method is very straightforward, in a normal application with a lot of controls, setting all of the properties can become tedious. And if you need to change the appearance of some elements throughout the application, it will not be an easy task. This is where Silverlight styles come in.

Silverlight Styles

In the previous section, you saw how you can change the appearance of a Silverlight application by setting inline properties. This works perfectly fine, but it presents maintenance problems. From a maintenance perspective, it's better to separate the style properties from the control definitions. For example, consider the following TextBlock definition:

```
<TextBlock
    Grid.Row="0"
    Grid.Column="0"
    Text="First Name"
    FontFamily="Verdana"
    FontSize="16"
    FontWeight="Bold"
    Margin="5" />
```

Suppose you defined all your TextBlock controls this way, throughout your application. Then, if you wanted to update the look of your application's text boxes, you would need to modify the TextBox definitions one by one. To save time and avoid errors, it's preferable to be able to make updates to properties related to the control's appearance in one central location, rather than in each instance of the control.

This problem is certainly not new to Silverlight. Developers and designers have faced this challenge for years with HTML-based pages. HTML solves the problem with a technology known as Cascading Style Sheets (CSS). Instead of specifying the different attributes of HTML controls directly, developers can simply specify a style for the control that corresponds to a style in a style sheet. The style sheet, not the HTML, defines all of the different appearance attributes for all controls. This way, if developers want to adjust an attribute of a control in an application, they can change it in the style sheet one time, and that change will be automatically reflected in every control in the application that references that style.

Silverlight offers a similar solution. Silverlight allows you to create style resources, in much the same way you define styles in a CSS style sheet. In Silverlight, style resources are hierarchical and can be defined at either the page level or the application level. If defined at the page level, the styles will be available only to controls on that page. Styles defined at the application level can be utilized by controls on all pages across the entire application. The "Silverlight Style Hierarchy" section later in this chapter provides more information about the style hierarchy.

A Silverlight style is defined using the <Style> element, which requires two attributes: the Key attribute represents the name of the style, and the TargetType attribute tells Silverlight which type of control gets the style. Within the <Style> element, the style is made up of one or more <Setter> elements, which define a Property attribute and a Value attribute. As an example, the preceding TextBlock control's appearance properties could be defined in the following Silverlight style definition:

```
<Style x:Key="FormLabel" TargetType="TextBlock">
    <Setter Property="FontFamily" Value="Verdana"/>
    <Setter Property="FontSize" Value="16"/>
    <Setter Property="FontWeight" Value="Bold"/>
    <Setter Property="Margin" Value="5,5,5,5"/>
</Style>
```

In HTML, to reference a style from a control, you simply set the style attribute. In Silverlight, this syntax looks a little different. Silverlight styles are referenced in a control using an XAML markup extension. You saw markup extensions in use in Chapter 5—when working with data binding in Silverlight, you set a control's property using the form {Binding, <path>. To reference the sample FormLabel style from your TextBlock, the syntax looks as follows:

```
<TextBlock Text="Age" Grid.Row="2" Style="{StaticResource FormLabel}"/>
```

Let's give styles a try, starting with defining styles at the page level.

Try It Out: Using Styles As Static Resources

In this exercise, you will define the styles as a static resource at the page level, using Expression Blend. The application will have a very simple UI, so you can focus on styles.

1. In Expression Blend, create a new Silverlight Application + Website named Styles.

2. Double-click the StackPanel control in the Toolbox to add a StackPanel. With the StackPanel selected, reset the Width and Height properties so that the StackPanel will automatically resize. Next, double-click the StackPanel in the Objects And Timeline panel so that it is selected. (You should see the border change around the StackPanel item.) With the StackPanel selected, add two TextBox and two Button controls to the StackPanel. The Objects And Timeline panel should appear as shown in Figure 12-13.

Figure 12-13. The controls for the application in the Objects And Timeline panel

3. The XAML at this point should appear as follows:

```
<Grid x:Name="LayoutRoot" Background="White" >
    <StackPanel HorizontalAlignment="Left" VerticalAlignment="Top">
        <TextBox Text="TextBox" TextWrapping="Wrap"/>
        <TextBox Text="TextBox" TextWrapping="Wrap"/>
        <Button Content="Button"/>
        <Button Content="Button"/>
    </StackPanel>
</Grid>
```

4. Run the application. As shown in Figure 12-14, at this point, it really is nothing special. Now you'll use Silverlight styles to spice up its appearance.

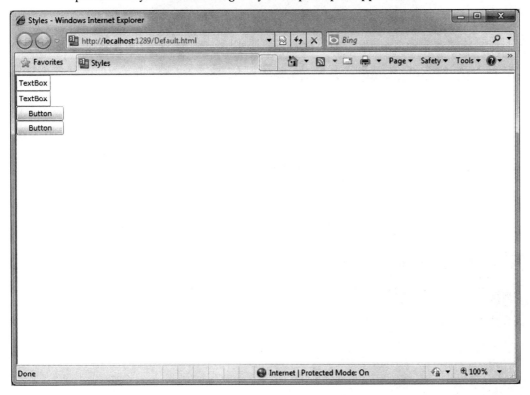

Figure 12-14. Initial Silverlight application without styles

5. First, you need to build your Silverlight styles. Select the first TextBox in the Objects And Timeline panel, and select Object ➤ Edit Style ➤ Create Empty from the main menu. This brings up the Create Style Resource dialog box. Enter TextBoxStyle in the Name text box, and stick with the default Define In option, which will define the style in the current document. Your dialog box should look like Figure 12-15. Click OK.

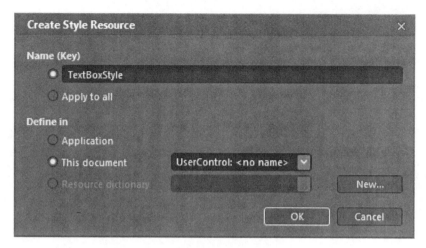

Figure 12-15. *The Create Style Resource dialog box*

6. At this point, you might notice a few changes:

    •   The Objects And Timeline panel now contains the style object, but all of the
        form objects are no longer visible. At the top of the Objects And Timeline
        panel, you will see an up arrow with the text TextBoxStyle (TextBox Style) to
        its right. If you hover the mouse over the arrow, you will see a message that
        reads "Return scope to [UserControl]," as shown in Figure 12-16. Clicking
        this arrow returns you to the Objects And Timeline panel you have grown
        used to, with the different form objects showing.

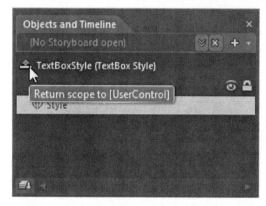

Figure 12-16. *Clicking the arrow next to the style name to see the controls in the UserControl's scope listed
in the Objects And Timeline panel*

    •   A new breadcrumb appears at the top of the artboard, as shown in Figure
        12-17. The breadcrumb provides another way for you to navigate back to
        normal design mode.

Figure 12-17. A new breadcrumb that allows you to navigate back to normal design mode

- The XAML has changed. A new `<UserControl.Resources>` section has been added, and the first `TextBox` has an added `Style="{StaticResource TextBoxStyle}"` attribute, as follows:

```xaml
<UserControl.Resources>
    <Style x:Key="TextBoxStyle" TargetType="TextBox"/>
</UserControl.Resources>

<Grid x:Name="LayoutRoot" Background="White" >
    <StackPanel HorizontalAlignment="Left" VerticalAlignment="Top">
        <TextBox Text="TextBox" TextWrapping="Wrap"
            Style="{StaticResource TextBoxStyle}"/>
        <TextBox Text="TextBox" TextWrapping="Wrap"/>
        <Button Content="Button"/>
        <Button Content="Button"/>
    </StackPanel>
</Grid>
```

7. Next, you will set the different style attributes for your TextBoxStyle. Make certain that the TextBoxStyle is still in the Objects And Timeline panel, and from the Properties panel, set the following properties:

- FontSize: 22

- FontFamily: Trebuchet MS

- Foreground: #FFFF0000

- Margin: 5

8. If you now examine the XAML, you will see that Expression Blend has added a number of Setter elements to the TextBoxStyle, as follows:

```xaml
<UserControl.Resources>
    <Style x:Key="TextBoxStyle" TargetType="TextBox">
        <Setter Property="FontSize" Value="22"/>
        <Setter Property="FontFamily" Value="Trebuchet MS"/>
        <Setter Property="Foreground" Value="#FFFF0000"/>
        <Setter Property="Margin" Value="5"/>
    </Style>
</UserControl.Resources>
```

9. Click the up arrow in the Objects And Timeline panel to return to the UserControl, and highlight the first Button control you added. With it selected, choose Object ➤ Edit Style ➤ Create Empty from the main menu. Name the style ButtonStyle, and leave it as defined in this document.

10. This creates the new style ButtonStyle of TargetType Button and adds the Style attribute to the first button on your form. With the ButtonStyle selected, set the following properties:

   - FontSize: 20

   - FontFamily: Trebuchet MS

   - FontWeight: Bold

   - Width: 200

   - Margin: 5

   - Foreground: #FF0000FF

11. With these properties set, your XAML will be updated to add the new Setter elements to the ButtonStyle style, as follows:

```
<UserControl.Resources>
    <Style x:Key="TextBoxStyle" TargetType="TextBox">
        <Setter Property="FontSize" Value="22"/>
        <Setter Property="FontFamily" Value="Trebuchet MS"/>
        <Setter Property="Foreground" Value="#FFFF0000"/>
        <Setter Property="Margin" Value="5"/>
    </Style>
    <Style x:Key="ButtonStyle" TargetType="Button">
        <Setter Property="FontSize" Value="20"/>
        <Setter Property="FontFamily" Value="Trebuchet MS"/>
        <Setter Property="FontWeight" Value="Bold"/>
        <Setter Property="Width" Value="200"/>
        <Setter Property="Foreground" Value="#FF0000FF"/>
        <Setter Property="Margin" Value="5"/>
    </Style>
</UserControl.Resources>
```

12. Now you have two styles defined, and two of your controls are set to these styles. Next, you need to set the style for your other controls.

13. Return to the UserControl in the Objects and Timeline panel and select the second TextBox control. Select Object ➤ Edit Style ➤ Apply A Resource ➤ TextBoxStyle from the main menu. This adds the Style="{StaticResource TextBoxStyle}" attribute to the second TextBox.

14. Select the second Button control, and select Object ➤ Edit Style ➤ Apply A Resource ➤ ButtonStyle.

15. Your XAML should now look as follows:

```
<UserControl.Resources>
    <Style x:Key="TextBoxStyle" TargetType="TextBox">
        <Setter Property="FontSize" Value="22"/>
        <Setter Property="FontFamily" Value="Trebuchet MS"/>
        <Setter Property="Foreground" Value="#FFFF0000"/>
        <Setter Property="Margin" Value="5"/>
```

```
        </Style>
        <Style x:Key="ButtonStyle" TargetType="Button">
            <Setter Property="FontSize" Value="20"/>
            <Setter Property="FontFamily" Value="Trebuchet MS"/>
            <Setter Property="FontWeight" Value="Bold"/>
            <Setter Property="Width" Value="200"/>
            <Setter Property="Foreground" Value="#FF0000FF"/>
            <Setter Property="Margin" Value="5"/>
        </Style>
    </UserControl.Resources>

    <Grid x:Name="LayoutRoot" Background="White" >
        <StackPanel HorizontalAlignment="Left" VerticalAlignment="Top">
            <TextBox Text="TextBox" TextWrapping="Wrap"
                Style="{StaticResource TextBoxStyle}"/>
            <TextBox Text="TextBox" TextWrapping="Wrap"
                Style="{StaticResource TextBoxStyle}"/>
            <Button Content="Button" Style="{StaticResource ButtonStyle}"/>
            <Button Content="Button" Style="{StaticResource ButtonStyle}"/>
        </StackPanel>
    </Grid>
```

16. Run the application. The form now appears as shown in Figure 12-18.

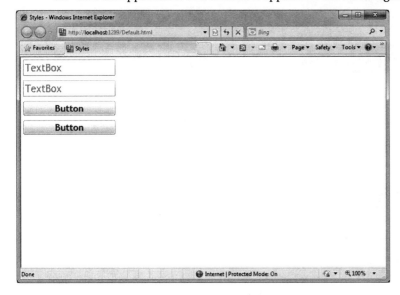

Figure 12-18. Silverlight application with styles applied

17. Now, let's say that you want to change the width of the text boxes in your application. Currently, their width is automatically set, but you would like to change them to a fixed width of 400 pixels. If you were using inline properties, as in the first two exercises in this chapter, you would need to set the property for each TextBox control in your application. However, because you are using

Silverlight styles, you can simply change the TextBoxStyle, and all TextBox controls assigned to that style will be updated automatically. Let's see how this works.

18. To modify the TextBoxStyle property from Expression Blend, click the Resources panel. When you expand the UserControl item, you will see your two styles listed. To the right of TextBoxStyle, you will see an Edit Resource button, as shown in Figure 12-19. Click this button, and you will see that you have returned to the TextBoxStyle's design scope.

Figure 12-19. Resources panel showing the TextBoxStyle

19. In the Properties panel, set the Width property of the TextBoxStyle to 400. Then click the up arrow in the Objects And Timeline panel to return to the UserControls scope.

20. Your XAML should now look as follows:

```
<Style x:Key="TextBoxStyle" TargetType="TextBox">
    <Setter Property="FontSize" Value="22"/>
    <Setter Property="FontFamily" Value="Trebuchet MS"/>
    <Setter Property="Foreground" Value="#FFFF0000"/>
    <Setter Property="Margin" Value="5"/>
    <Setter Property="Width" Value="400"/>
</Style>
```

21. Run the application to confirm that the width of both text boxes has been updated, as shown in Figure 12-20.

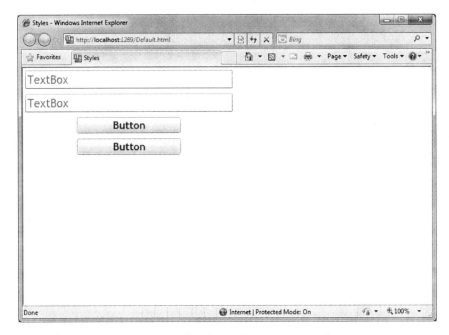

Figure 12-20. The application with the updated TextBoxStyle

This exercise showed how Silverlight styles can be used as an alternative to defining styles inline. As you can see, this approach provides for much cleaner XAML and also greatly improves the ease of maintaining your application.

Defining Styles at the Application Level

In the previous example, you defined the styles locally, within your `UserControl`. If you have multiple `UserControl` components that you would like to share styles, you can define the styles at the application level. As far as the controls are concerned, there is absolutely no difference. You still indicate the style for the control using the `Style="{StaticResource StyleName}"` extended attribute. What does change is where the styles are defined.

In the preceding example, your styles were defined within the `<UserControl.Resources>` element on the `UserControl` itself, as follows:

```
<UserControl.Resources>
   <Style x:Key="TextBoxStyle" TargetType="TextBox">
      <Setter Property="FontSize" Value="22"/>
      <Setter Property="FontFamily" Value="Trebuchet MS"/>
      <Setter Property="Foreground" Value="#FFFF0000"/>
      <Setter Property="Margin" Value="5"/>
      <Setter Property="Width" Value="400"/>
   </Style>
   <Style x:Key="ButtonStyle" TargetType="Button">
      <Setter Property="FontSize" Value="20"/>
      <Setter Property="FontFamily" Value="Trebuchet MS"/>
```

```xml
            <Setter Property="FontWeight" Value="Bold"/>
            <Setter Property="Width" Value="200"/>
            <Setter Property="Foreground" Value="#FF0000FF"/>
            <Setter Property="Margin" Value="5"/>
        </Style>
    </UserControl.Resources>

    <Grid x:Name="LayoutRoot" Background="White" >
        <StackPanel HorizontalAlignment="Left" VerticalAlignment="Top">
            <TextBox Text="TextBox" TextWrapping="Wrap"
                Style="{StaticResource TextBoxStyle}"/>
            <TextBox Text="TextBox" TextWrapping="Wrap"
                Style="{StaticResource TextBoxStyle}"/>
            <Button Content="Button" Style="{StaticResource ButtonStyle}"/>
            <Button Content="Button" Style="{StaticResource ButtonStyle}"/>
        </StackPanel>
    </Grid>
```

To define the styles at the application level, instead of defining the styles in the `<UserControl.Resources>`, you move them to the App.xaml file within the element `<Application.Resources>`, as follows:

```xml
<Application.Resources>
    <Style x:Key="TextBoxStyle" TargetType="TextBox">
        <Setter Property="FontSize" Value="22"/>
        <Setter Property="FontFamily" Value="Trebuchet MS"/>
        <Setter Property="Foreground" Value="#FFFF0000"/>
        <Setter Property="Margin" Value="5"/>
        <Setter Property="Width" Value="400"/>
    </Style>
    <Style x:Key="ButtonStyle" TargetType="Button">
        <Setter Property="FontSize" Value="20"/>
        <Setter Property="FontFamily" Value="Trebuchet MS"/>
        <Setter Property="FontWeight" Value="Bold"/>
        <Setter Property="Width" Value="200"/>
        <Setter Property="Foreground" Value="#FF0000FF"/>
        <Setter Property="Margin" Value="5"/>
    </Style>
</Application.Resources>
```

That is all there is to it. Again, there are no changes at all to the controls themselves. For example, to use these styles on your UserControl, the XAML would still look like the following:

```xml
<Grid x:Name="LayoutRoot" Background="White" >
    <StackPanel HorizontalAlignment="Left" VerticalAlignment="Top">
        <TextBox Text="TextBox" TextWrapping="Wrap"
            Style="{StaticResource TextBoxStyle}"/>
        <TextBox Text="TextBox" TextWrapping="Wrap"
            Style="{StaticResource TextBoxStyle}"/>
        <Button Content="Button" Style="{StaticResource ButtonStyle}"/>
        <Button Content="Button" Style="{StaticResource ButtonStyle}"/>
    </StackPanel>
</Grid>
```

Merged Resource Dictionaries

Another feature of Silverlight is the ability to place your style definitions in external files called Merged Resource Dictionaries. As I have discussed in this chapter, you can define styles at the document or application level. If defining in the application level, your styles must be placed in the App.xaml file. This can result in a very large App.xaml. Instead, you can now place your style definitions in external files and simply reference them in your application. An additional benefit from this change is that you can now create styles that can be easily reused between your applications, by simply copying the style resource files to your new solution. An example of using Merged Resource Dictionaries is seen the code in this section.

You can add a Resource Dictionary to a Silverlight application in Visual Studio by right-clicking on your project in the Solution Explorer and selecting Add ➤ New Item. On the Add New Item screen, select the template named Silverlight Resource Dictionary and enter a name for the dictionary as shown in Figure 12-21.

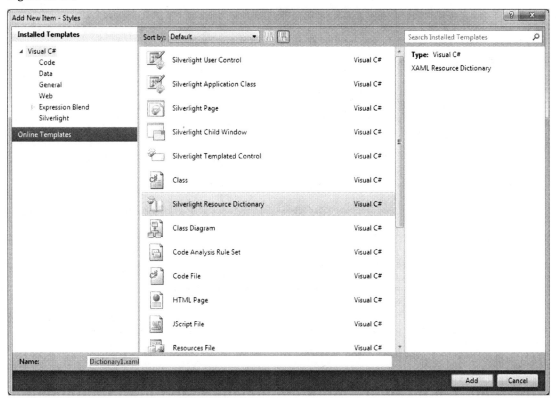

Figure 12-21. *Adding a Resource Dictionary*

You can then add your style information to the resource dictionary as the following code displays:

```xml
<ResourceDictionary
    xmlns="http://schemas.microsoft.com/winfx/2006/xaml/presentation"
    xmlns:x="http://schemas.microsoft.com/winfx/2006/xaml">

    <Style x:Key="Heading1" TargetType="TextBlock">
        <Setter Property="FontSize" Value="22" />
        <Setter Property="Foreground" Value="Silver" />
    </Style>

    <Style x:Key="Heading2" TargetType="TextBlock">
        <Setter Property="FontSize" Value="18" />
    </Style>

</ResourceDictionary>
```

Finally, to use the resource dictionary in your application, you need to add an entry in the ResourceDictionary.MergedDictionaries section, as shown in the following code. Once you have added the entry for the ResourceDictionary, you can then use the styles as normal.

```xml
<UserControl.Resources>
    <ResourceDictionary>
        <ResourceDictionary.MergedDictionaries>
            <ResourceDictionary Source="Dictionary1.xaml" />
        </ResourceDictionary.MergedDictionaries>
    </ResourceDictionary>
</UserControl.Resources>
<StackPanel x:Name="LayoutRoot">
  <TextBlock Text="Heading 1" Style="{StaticResource Heading1}" />
  <TextBlock Text="Heading 2" Style="{StaticResource Heading2}" />
</StackPanel>
```

Silverlight Style Hierarchy

As I mentioned earlier in the chapter, Silverlight styles are hierarchical. When a control has a style set, Silverlight first looks for the style at the local level, within the document's <UserControl.Resources>. If the style is found, Silverlight looks no further. If the style is not found locally, it looks at the application level. If the style is not found there, an XamlParseException is thrown.

In addition to locally defined styles overriding application-level styles, any properties that are defined inline in the control element itself will override properties within the style. For example, consider the following XAML:

```xml
<UserControl.Resources>
    <Style x:Key="TextBoxStyle" TargetType="TextBox">
        <Setter Property="FontSize" Value="22"/>
        <Setter Property="FontFamily" Value="Trebuchet MS"/>
        <Setter Property="Foreground" Value="#FFFF0000"/>
        <Setter Property="Margin" Value="5"/>
        <Setter Property="Width" Value="400"/>
    </Style>
    <Style x:Key="ButtonStyle" TargetType="Button">
        <Setter Property="FontSize" Value="20"/>
```

```
        <Setter Property="FontFamily" Value="Trebuchet MS"/>
        <Setter Property="FontWeight" Value="Bold"/>
        <Setter Property="Width" Value="200"/>
        <Setter Property="Foreground" Value="#FF0000FF"/>
        <Setter Property="Margin" Value="5 "/>
    </Style>
</UserControl.Resources>

<Grid x:Name="LayoutRoot" Background="White" >
    <StackPanel HorizontalAlignment="Left" VerticalAlignment="Top">
        <TextBox Text="TextBox" TextWrapping="Wrap"
            Style="{StaticResource TextBoxStyle}" FontSize="10"/>
        <TextBox Text="TextBox" TextWrapping="Wrap"
            Style="{StaticResource TextBoxStyle}"/>
        <Button Content="Button" Style="{StaticResource ButtonStyle}"/>
        <Button Content="Button" Style="{StaticResource ButtonStyle}"/>
    </StackPanel>
</Grid>
```

Both TextBox controls are set to the TextBoxStyle style; however, the first TextBox has an inline property defined for FontSize. Therefore, when you run the XAML, it will appear as shown in Figure 12-22.

Figure 12-22. *An example of inline properties overriding style properties*

Notice that even though FontSize was defined inline, the control still picked up the remaining properties from TextBoxStyle. However, a locally defined style will prevent any properties from being applied from an application-level style.

Inheriting Styles Using BasedOn

A feature that first showed up in Silverlight 3 is the ability to create styles that are based on another style. This allows you to create base styles that can help organize and maintain your styles across your application. As an example, consider the following source. Notice there are three styles that are defined. BaseButtonStyle defines the base style, and RedButton derives from BaseButtonStyle, inheriting all properties from the base style—including the FontSize, FontFamily, and Margin—and additionally sets the Foreground to Red. There is also a third style, RedButtonBigFont, that derives from the RedButton style and overrides the FontSize.

```
<UserControl.Resources>
    <Style x:Key="BaseButtonStyle" TargetType="Button">
        <Setter Property="FontSize" Value="22" />
        <Setter Property="FontFamily" Value="Trebuchet MS" />
        <Setter Property="Margin" Value="5" />
    </Style>

    <Style x:Key="RedButton" TargetType="Button"
            BasedOn="{StaticResource BaseButtonStyle}">
        <Setter Property="Foreground" Value="Red" />
    </Style>

    <Style x:Key="RedButtonBigFont" TargetType="Button"
            BasedOn="{StaticResource RedButton}">
        <Setter Property="FontSize" Value="28" />
    </Style>

</UserControl.Resources>
<StackPanel x:Name="LayoutRoot">

    <Button Style="{StaticResource BaseButtonStyle}"
            Content="Base Button" />
    <Button Style="{StaticResource RedButton}"
            Content="Red Button" />
    <Button Style="{StaticResource RedButtonBigFont}"
            Content="Red Button Big Font" />

</StackPanel>
```

If you run this source, you get the results shown in Figure 12-23. Notice that the Red Button has all of the attributes of the Base Button, but additionally it has the font color red. Similarly, the Red Button Big Font button has all the attributes of the Red Button but overrides the FontSize to have a larger font.

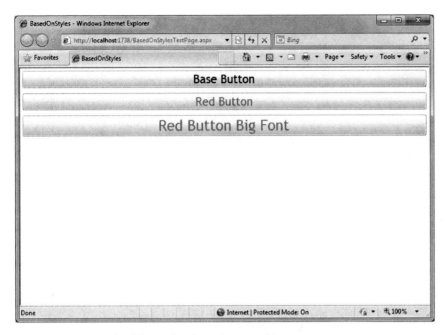

Figure 12-23. Result of derived styles using BasedOn

Implicit Styles

Another feature present in Silverlight is the ability to create an implicit style that will be applied to all controls of a given TargetType automatically. This means that if you know that you want the default look of all your Button controls, you can create an implicit style that will be applied to all buttons without having to set the Style property on the actual Button control definitions.

Consider the following example of a StackPanel that contains five buttons. The first four buttons simply have the base <Button /> definition, where the last Button also includes a style reference. Because the first four buttons do not have a style specified, they will all use the implicit Button style defined in UserControl.Resources. The last Button will not use any of the Style properties defined in the implicit style, however, because it has an explicit style specified. Instead, it will get its style from the OverrideStyle style. The result of the following example is shown in Figure 12-24.

```
<UserControl.Resources>
    <Style TargetType="Button">
        <Setter Property="FontSize" Value="10" />
        <Setter Property="Width" Value="200" />
        <Setter Property="Foreground" Value="Red" />
        <Setter Property="Content" Value="Default Style" />
        <Setter Property="Margin" Value="5" />
    </Style>
    <Style x:Key="OverrideStyle" TargetType="Button">
        <Setter Property="FontSize" Value="14" />
        <Setter Property="Width" Value="300" />
        <Setter Property="FontWeight" Value="Bold" />
```

```
            <Setter Property="Content" Value="Overridden Style" />
        </Style>
</UserControl.Resources>

<StackPanel x:Name="LayoutRoot" Background="White">
    <Button />
    <Button />
    <Button />
    <Button />
    <Button Style="{StaticResource OverrideStyle}"  />
</StackPanel>
```

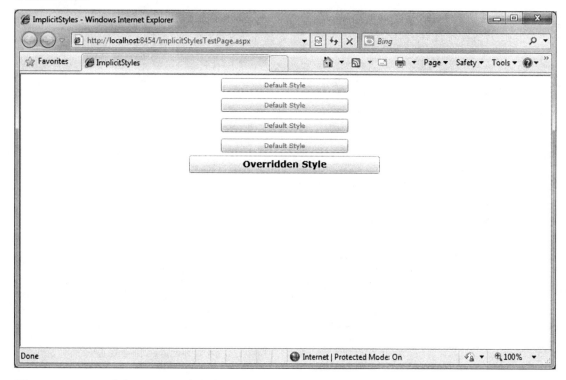

Figure 12-24. *Result from usage of implicit styles*

Summary

In this chapter, you looked at options for styling your Silverlight applications. You saw how to define style properties inline using both Visual Studio and Expression Blend. Then you explored defining styles with Silverlight styles, both at the document level and the application level. In the next chapter, you will look at using Expression Blend to define Silverlight transformations and animations.

CHAPTER 13

Transformations and Animations

Incorporating animation of objects in a web application can really enhance the UI. In the past, to implement this type of animation in a web site, you would most likely turn to Adobe Flash. The cool thing for Microsoft .NET developers is that now you can do it all within the technologies you know and, better yet, code it using .NET. Personally, I consider this the most exciting aspect of Silverlight. For years, I have been struggling with the desire to put animations into my applications but haven't done so because I did not want to jump over to Flash. But that's no longer necessary. You can now do it all within .NET, my friends! This chapter will show you just how that's done.

Introduction to Silverlight Animation

The term *animation* usually brings to mind cartoons or animated features like those that Disney has brought to life on the big screen. Artists create a number of images with slight variations that, when shown in rapid sequence, appear as fluid movement. Fundamental to any type of animation is the changing of some attribute of an object over time.

For Silverlight, the implementation of an animation is very straightforward. You change a property of an object gradually over time in such a way that you have the appearance of that object moving smoothly from one point to the next.

As an example, Figure 13-1 shows an icon bar I created for one of my Silverlight applications. As your mouse rolls over an icon in the bar, the icon grows; as the mouse leaves the icon, it shrinks back to its initial size. When you click one of the icons, the icon bounces, just as it does on the Mac OS X Dock.

Figure 13-1. *An animated application bar created with Silverlight*

In the example in Figure 13-1, for one of the icons, the animation that was created when the mouse was placed over the icon had two basic positions: at timestamp 0.00, the icon's Width and Height properties were set to 50 pixels; at timestamp 0.25, the Width and Height properties were set to 75 pixels. To make the transition smooth from timestamp 0.00 to 0.25, Silverlight creates a *spline*, which will generate all of the "frames" along the way to make the movement appear fluid to the human eye.

Silverlight Storyboards

In movies or cartoon animations, a *storyboard* is a sequence of sketches that depict changes of action over the duration of the film or cartoon. So, essentially, a storyboard is a timeline. In the same way, storyboards in Silverlight are timelines. As an example, Figure 13-2 shows a storyboard for an application that animates the transformation of a circle and two rectangles.

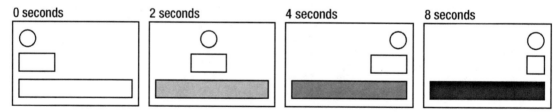

Figure 13-2. *Example of a storyboard*

In the storyboard in Figure 13-2, three objects are represented: a circle, a small rectangle, and a large rectangle. At the start of the storyboard's timeline, all three objects are on the left side of the document. After 2 seconds, the circle and smaller rectangle start to move toward the right side of the document. The larger rectangle starts to change its background from white to black. At 4 seconds into the timeline, the circle and the smaller rectangle will have reached the right side of the document. At that time, the smaller rectangle will begin to turn into a square. At 8 seconds, the smaller rectangle will have turned into a square, and the larger rectangle will have turned fully black.

If you translate this storyboard into Silverlight animations, you will have four animations:

- Two animations that cause the circle and the smaller square to move from the left to the right side of the document

- An animation that changes the background of the larger rectangle from white to black

- An animation to change the smaller rectangle into a square

Next, you will look at the different types of animations in Silverlight.

Types of Animations in Silverlight

There are two basic types of animations in Silverlight:

- *Linear interpolation animation*: This type of animation smoothly and continuously varies property values over time.

- *Keyframe animation*: With this type of animation, values change based on keyframes that have been added to a given point in the timeline.

Most commonly, keyframe animations are used in conjunction with a form of interpolation to smooth animations.

All types of animation in Silverlight are derived from the `Timeline` class found in the `System.Windows.Media.Animation` namespace. The following types of animations are available:

- `ColorAnimation`

- `ColorAnimationUsingKeyFrames`

- `DoubleAnimation`

- `DoubleAnimationUsingKeyFrames`

- `ObjectAnimationUsingKeyFrames`

- `PointAnimation`

- `PointAnimationUsingKeyFrames`

Each of these animates a different type of object. For example, `ColorAnimation` animates the value of a `Color` property between two target values. Similarly, `DoubleAnimation` animates the value of a `Double` property, `PointAnimation` animates the value of a `Point` property, and `ObjectAnimation` animates the value of an `Object` property. Developers determine which animation type to use based on what they want to animate.

As an example, let's look at a simple animation where you increase the size of a rectangle over time, as shown in Figure 13-3. This example will allow us to dissect some of the properties involved with the animation.

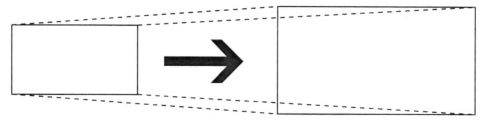

Figure 13-3. *Animation of growing a rectangle*

To perform this animation, you need to use a `DoubleAnimationUsingKeyFrames` animation because you are modifying the `Width` and `Height` properties of the rectangle, both of which are properties of type Double. Let's look at the XAML used to perform this animation:

```
<UserControl.Resources>
    <Storyboard x:Name="Storyboard1">
        <DoubleAnimationUsingKeyFrames
            BeginTime="00:00:00"
            Storyboard.TargetName="rectangle"
            Storyboard.TargetProperty="Width">
            <SplineDoubleKeyFrame KeyTime="00:00:02" Value="400"/>
        </DoubleAnimationUsingKeyFrames>
        <DoubleAnimationUsingKeyFrames
            BeginTime="00:00:00"
            Storyboard.TargetName="rectangle"
            Storyboard.TargetProperty="Height">
            <SplineDoubleKeyFrame KeyTime="00:00:02" Value="240"/>
        </DoubleAnimationUsingKeyFrames>
    </Storyboard>
</UserControl.Resources>

<Grid x:Name="LayoutRoot" Background="White" >
    <Rectangle
        Height="120"
        Width="200"
        HorizontalAlignment="Left"
        VerticalAlignment="Top"
        Stroke="#FF000000"
        x:Name="rectangle"/>
</Grid>
```

A number of elements are required. First, the rectangle itself has a name defined. This is required, as the animation needs to be able to refer to the rectangle by its name.

Next, in the storyboard, you have two animations: one to animate the width and one to animate the height.

The `BeginTime` property tells Silverlight at what time during the storyboard the animation should begin. In both cases, you are starting the animations as soon as the storyboard is initiated (`BeginTime="00:00:00"`).

The `TargetName` property tells the animation which control is being animated. In this case, both animations are targeting the rectangle.

The final property set is TargetProperty. This is an attached property that refers to the property that is being animated. In the case of the first animation, TargetProperty is set to the rectangle's Width property. As the animation's value is changed, the value will be set to the Width property of the rectangle.

Finally, because this is a keyframe animation, keyframes are defined within the animation. In your case, only one keyframe is defined, 2 seconds (KeyTime="00:00:02") into the storyboard. In the first animation, 2 seconds into the storyboard's timeline, the value of the Width property will be changed to 400:

```
<SplineDoubleKeyFrame KeyTime="00:00:02" Value="400"/>
```

Programmatically Controlling Animations

Once your animations have been created, Silverlight needs to know when to trigger a given animation or storyboard. Silverlight provides a number of functions that allow you to programmatically control your storyboard animations. Table 13-1 lists some common storyboard methods.

Table 13-1. Common Storyboard Animation Methods

Method	Description
Begin()	Initiates the storyboard
Pause()	Pauses the storyboard
Resume()	Resumes a paused storyboard
Stop	Stops the storyboard
Seek()	Skips to a specific part of the storyboard animation

As an example, consider a simple animation where a rectangle grows and shrinks, repeating forever. You want to allow the user to control the animation through a simple UI. Clicking the Start button starts the animation, and clicking the Stop button stops it. In addition, if the user clicks the rectangle, it will pause and resume the animation. Here's the XAML to set up the application:

```
<UserControl.Resources>
  <Storyboard x:Name="MoveRect" RepeatBehavior="Forever">
    <DoubleAnimationUsingKeyFrames BeginTime="00:00:00"
        Storyboard.TargetName="rectangle" Storyboard.TargetProperty="Width">
      <SplineDoubleKeyFrame KeyTime="00:00:00" Value="200"/>
      <SplineDoubleKeyFrame KeyTime="00:00:03" Value="600"/>
      <SplineDoubleKeyFrame KeyTime="00:00:06" Value="200"/>
    </DoubleAnimationUsingKeyFrames>
    <DoubleAnimationUsingKeyFrames BeginTime="00:00:00"
        Storyboard.TargetName="rectangle" Storyboard.TargetProperty="Height">
      <SplineDoubleKeyFrame KeyTime="00:00:00" Value="100"/>
      <SplineDoubleKeyFrame KeyTime="00:00:03" Value="300"/>
      <SplineDoubleKeyFrame KeyTime="00:00:06" Value="100"/>
    </DoubleAnimationUsingKeyFrames>
  </Storyboard>
```

```
</UserControl.Resources>

<Grid x:Name="LayoutRoot" Background="White" >
  <Rectangle Height="100" Width="200" Fill="#FF000AFF"
      Stroke="#FF000000" StrokeThickness="3" x:Name="rectangle" />
  <Button Height="24" Margin="200,416,340,40"
      Content="Start" Width="100" x:Name="btnStart" />
  <Button Height="24" Margin="340,416,200,40"
      Content="Stop" Width="100" x:Name="btnStop" />
</Grid>
```

The UI is shown in Figure 13-4.

To implement the desired behavior, you will wire up three event handlers in the Page constructor.

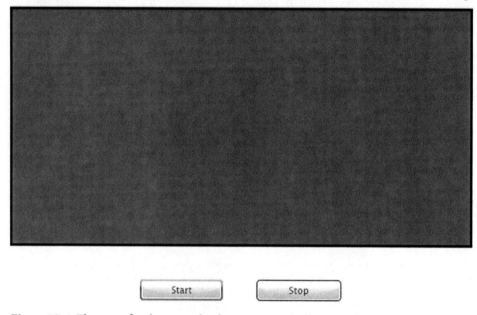

Figure 13-4. The setup for the example of programmatically controlling animation

To start the animation when the user clicks the Start button, you use the storyboard's Begin() method. To stop the animation, you use the storyboard's Stop() method. The pause/resume behavior, which you will trigger by clicking on the rectangle, is a bit trickier, but it's still not complicated. You include a private Boolean property called Paused, which you use to tell the code behind whether or not the animation is paused. To pause and resume the animation, you use the Pause() and Resume() methods. The code looks like this:

```
private bool Paused;
public Page()
{
    // Required to initialize variables
    InitializeComponent();
    this.btnStart.Click += new RoutedEventHandler(btnStart_Click);
    this.btnStop.Click += new RoutedEventHandler(btnStop_Click);
    this.rectangle.MouseLeftButtonUp +=
        new MouseButtonEventHandler(rectangle_MouseLeftButtonUp);
}

void rectangle_MouseLeftButtonUp(object sender, MouseButtonEventArgs e)
{
    if (Paused)
    {
        this.MoveRect.Resume();
        Paused = false;
    }
    else
    {
        this.MoveRect.Pause();
        Paused = true;
    }
}

void btnStop_Click(object sender, RoutedEventArgs e)
{

    this.MoveRect.Stop();

}

void btnStart_Click(object sender, RoutedEventArgs e)
{
    this.MoveRect.Begin();
}
```

That's all there is to it!

So far in this chapter, you have looked at some very simple animations. Of course, in reality, animations can get much more complex. One of the key advantages you have as a developer is that there are tools to assist you with these animations. Expression Blend is the tool to use when designing your Silverlight animations.

Using Expression Blend to Create Animations

Although you can use Visual Studio 2010 to create your animations in Silverlight, Visual Studio does not include designer tools to assist you. If you are going to build animations programmatically, Visual Studio is the way to go. But if you are creating your animations in design mode, Expression Blend has the tools that allow you to do this easily.

Viewing a Storyboard in the Expression Blend Timeline

The primary asset within Expression Blend for animations is the Objects And Timeline panel. Up to this point, you have focused on the object side of the Objects And Timeline panel. With animations, it is all about the timeline. With a storyboard selected, the timeline appears, as shown in Figure 13-5.

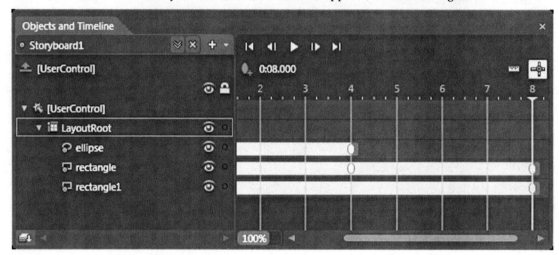

Figure 13-5. *Expression Blend's timeline for a storyboard*

The timeline in Figure 13-5 is actually the implemented timeline for the storyboard shown earlier in Figure 13-2. The three objects in the storyboard are listed in the Objects And Timeline panel. To the right of each of these objects, you see the timeline with just over 10 seconds showing horizontally. At time zero, there are three keyframes added, indicating that some animation action is taking place at that time. Then, at 4 seconds into the timeline, you see two keyframes providing the end point of the circle and smaller rectangle's movement from left to right. At 8 seconds through the timeline, there are two final keyframes: one providing an end point for the smaller rectangle turning into a square and one changing the larger rectangle to black.

To better understand how Expression Blend can help you build your animations, let's run through an exercise.

Try It Out: Creating an Animation with Expression Blend

In this exercise, you'll create the classic bouncing-ball animation using Expression Blend. You'll create an animation that will make a red ball drop and bounce on a black rectangle until it comes to rest. You'll start off with a very simple animation, and then add to it to make it progressively more realistic.

1. Create a new Silverlight application in Expression Blend named Ch13_BlendAnimations.

2. Add an Ellipse control with red fill and a black border near the top center of the grid. Next, add a Rectangle control to the very bottom of the grid and have it stretch all the way from left to right. Set the fill color and border color to black. Your application should appear similar to Figure 13-6.

Figure 13-6. Initial application layout

3. The first step in creating an animation is to create a new storyboard. On the Objects And Timeline panel, click the button with the plus sign, to the right of the text "(No Storyboard open)," as shown in Figure 13-7. This opens the Create Storyboard Resource dialog box.

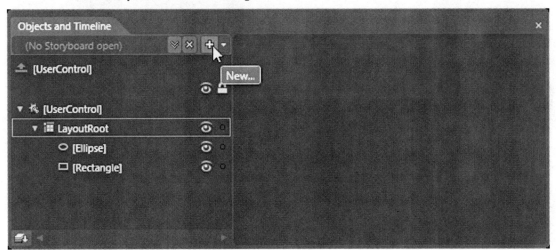

Figure 13-7. Click the plus button to create a new storyboard.

4. In the Create Storyboard Resource dialog box, enter BounceBall in the Name (Key) text box and click OK, as shown in Figure 13-8. This will be the name of your storyboard.

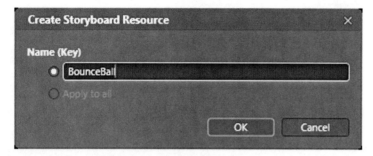

Figure 13-8. Name your storyboard in the Create Storyboard Resource dialog box.

5. When the storyboard is created, the timeline will be visible on the right side of the Objects And Timeline panel. To better see this, switch to the Animation workspace in Expression Blend by selecting Window Workspaces Animation Workspace. Your workspace should now look similar to Figure 13-9.

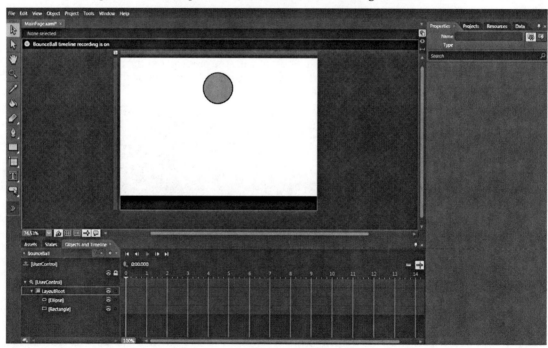

Figure 13-9. The Animation workspace in Expression Blend

6. Your animation will have many keyframes because the ball will be moving up and down as it "bounces" on the rectangle. To simplify things, every change of direction will cause the need for a new keyframe. For your first keyframe, you will simply take the ball and drop it onto the top of the rectangle. To do this,

you need to add a new keyframe and move the ball to its new position on the grid.

7. Make sure the artboard is surrounded in a red border with "Timeline recording is on" in the upper-left corner. If this is not the case, make certain that BounceBall is selected for the storyboard in the Object And Timeline panel, and you can click the red circle in the top-left corner to toggle between recording and not recording.

8. Move the playhead (the yellow vertical line on the timeline with the down arrow at the top) to position 3 (3 seconds), as shown in Figure 13-10.

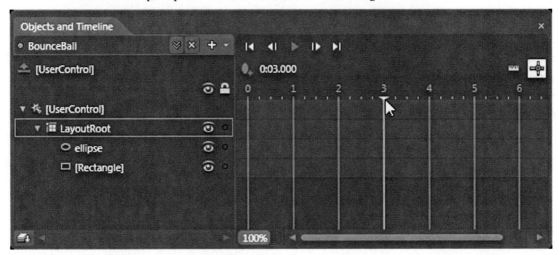

Figure 13-10. Moving the playhead on the timeline

9. With the playhead at 3 seconds, select the ellipse and move it down so that it is positioned directly below its starting point, but touching the black rectangle, as shown in Figure 13-11.

Figure 13-11. Repositioned ball on your grid

10. If you look carefully at the timeline, you'll notice that a red circle has shown up at the left of the Ellipse control in the Objects And Timeline panel, with a white arrow indicating that the object contains an animation. In addition, in the timeline, at position 3 seconds, a white ellipse has appeared to the right of the Ellipse control. This is how Expression Blend visually represents a keyframe.

11. At the top of the timeline, you will see buttons for navigating forward and backward between the frames in the animation. In addition, there is a play button that lets you view the animation.

12. Click the play button to view the animation. If you followed the steps properly, you will see the ball start at the top of the grid and slowly move downward to the top of the rectangle.

13. You just created your first animation! However, it isn't very realistic. In a real environment, the ball would accelerate as it fell toward the rectangle. So its movement would start out slow and speed up. You can mimic this behavior by modifying your keyframe and adding a spline.

14. Select the newly added keyframe in the timeline. (When the keyframe is selected, it will turn gray instead of being white.)

15. Once the keyframe is selected, in the Properties panel, you will see a section titled Easing. This section allows you to adjust the KeySpline property. By default, the interpolation between the two keyframes is linear. However, for this example, you want to speed up the ball as it gets closer to the second keyframe.

16. Click and drag the dot in the upper-right corner of the KeySpline grid (the end point of the right side of the line), and drag it down so that it appears as shown in Figure 13-12.

17. Click the play button at the top of the timeline. This time, you will see that the circle starts to drop slowly and then speeds up the closer it gets to the rectangle. This makes for a much more realistic animation.

18. Next, the circle is going to bounce back up after touching the rectangle. With recording still on, move the playhead to 6 seconds on the timeline, and then move the circle directly up from its current position to about three-fourths its initial starting point.

19. Select the new keyframe that is created, and navigate to the Easing section of the Properties panel. This time, you want the movement to start out fast and slow down as the circle reaches its apex. To get this effect, move the bottom-left dot up so that the KeySpline curve appears as shown in Figure 13-13.

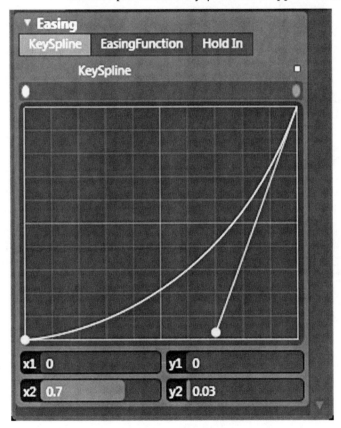

Figure 13-12. Adjusting the KeySpline property for the ball dropping

Figure 13-13. Adjusting the KeySpline property for the ball rising

20. Click the play button above the timeline to see the animation you have so far. The circle will fall with increasing speed, and then bounce back up with decreasing speed. So far so good, but what goes up must come down.

21. Move the playhead to 8 seconds, and move the circle up about one-fourth of its initial position and adjust the KeySpline property to match Figure 13-12. Sticking with the pattern, move the playhead to 10 seconds, and move the circle down to the top of the rectangle. The KeySpline curve should match Figure 13-13. Repeat this pattern at 11 seconds, and then 11.5 seconds.

22. Click the play button. You should see the circle bounce on the rectangle as you would expect. The final timeline will appear as shown in Figure 13-14.

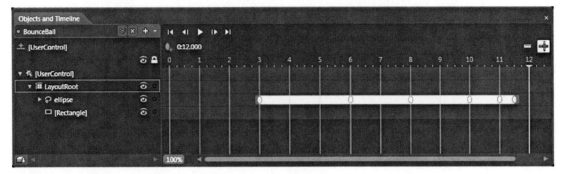

Figure 13-14. *Final timeline for bouncing ball*

23. Next, you need to tell Silverlight when the animation should take place. You will keep it simple and have the animation start when the page is loaded.

24. Navigate to the code behind for the `MainPage.xaml` file. In the `Page()` constructor, add the event handler for the `Loaded` event, as follows:

```
public MainPage()
{
    // Required to initialize variables
    InitializeComponent();
    this.Loaded += new RoutedEventHandler(Page_Loaded);
}

void Page_Loaded(object sender, RoutedEventArgs e)
{
    this.BounceBall.Begin();
}
```

25. Run the application. At this point, you should see the ball bounce on the rectangle. You might see something like what is shown in Figure 13-15.

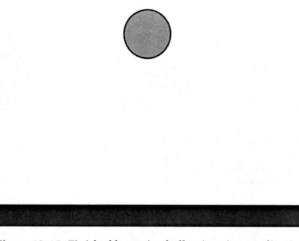

Figure 13-15. Finished bouncing ball animation application

In this section, you discussed animations in Silverlight. You should be comfortable creating new animations for your application in Expression Blend, and modifying and programming against those animations in Visual Studio 2010. The next section addresses transformations in Silverlight.

Creating Transformations in Silverlight

Silverlight includes a number of 2D *transforms*, which are used to change the appearance of objects. Transforms in Silverlight are defined using a transformation matrix, which is a mathematical construct for mapping points from one coordinate space to another. If this sounds a bit confusing, do not fear, Silverlight abstracts this matrix.

Silverlight supports four transformation types: rotation, scaling, skewing, and translation.

■ **Note** You can also define your own transformation matrix if you need to modify or combine the four transformation types. See *Pro Silverlight 5* by Matthew MacDonald (Apress, 2012) for details on how to do this.

Transformation Types

Figure 13-16 shows a Silverlight application that has been divided into four grid cells. Each cell contains two rectangles that have their width and height set to 100 pixels. One of the rectangles in each cell has a border with its width set to 1 pixel, and the other has a border with its width set to 5 pixels. The rectangle with the thicker border was then transformed so that you can see the result of each transformation.

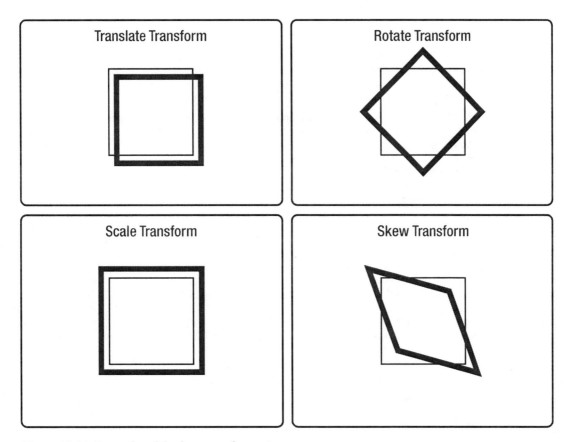

Figure 13-16. Examples of the four transformation types

ScaleTransform

The ScaleTransform type allows you to transform the size of a Silverlight object. The ScaleX property is used to scale the object on the horizontal axis, and the ScaleY property is used to scale the object on the vertical axis. The values of these properties are multiples of the object's original size. For example, setting the ScaleX property to 2 will double the size of the object on the horizontal axis. The following XAML was used to create the ScaleTransform in Figure 13-16:

```
<Rectangle Height="100" Width="100" Stroke="#FF000000" Grid.Row="1" Grid.Column="0"
    StrokeThickness="5" RenderTransformOrigin="0.5,0.5">
  <Rectangle.RenderTransform>
    <TransformGroup>
      <ScaleTransform ScaleX="1.25" ScaleY="1.25"/>
    </TransformGroup>
  </Rectangle.RenderTransform>
</Rectangle>
```

SkewTransform

The SkewTransform type allows you to skew a Silverlight object horizontally and vertically. The SkewTransform is used most commonly to create a 3D effect for an object. The AngleX property is used to skew the object horizontally, and AngleY is used to skew the object vertically. The following XAML was used to create the SkewTransform in Figure 13-16:

```
<Rectangle Height="100" Width="100" Stroke="#FF000000" Grid.Row="1" Grid.Column="1"
    StrokeThickness="5" RenderTransformOrigin="0.5,0.5">
  <Rectangle.RenderTransform>
    <TransformGroup>
      <SkewTransform AngleX="20" AngleY="15"/>
    </TransformGroup>
  </Rectangle.RenderTransform>
</Rectangle>
```

RotateTransform

The RotateTransform type allows you to rotate a Silverlight object by a specified angle around a specified center point. The angle is specified by the Angle property, and the center point is specified by the RenderTransformOrigin property. When you create a RotateTransform for a rectangle in Expression Blend, by default it will set RenderTransformOrigin to 0.5, 0.5, which is the center of the object. You can also specify the center point using the CenterX and CenterY properties on the RotateTransform element. The following is the XAML to produce the RotateTransform in Figure 13-16:

```
<Rectangle Height="100" Width="100" Stroke="#FF000000" Grid.Row="0" Grid.Column="1"
    StrokeThickness="5" RenderTransformOrigin="0.5,0.5">
  <Rectangle.RenderTransform>
    <TransformGroup>
      <RotateTransform Angle="45"/>
    </TransformGroup>
  </Rectangle.RenderTransform>
</Rectangle>
```

TranslateTransform

The TranslateTransform type allows you to change the position of a Silverlight object, both horizontally and vertically. The X property controls the position change on the horizontal axis, and the Y property controls the change to the vertical axis. The following XAML was used to create the TranslateTransform in Figure 13-16:

```
<Rectangle Height="100" Width="100" Stroke="#FF000000" Grid.Row="0" Grid.Column="0"
    StrokeThickness="5" RenderTransformOrigin="0.5,0.5">
  <Rectangle.RenderTransform>
    <TransformGroup>
      <TranslateTransform X="10" Y="10"/>
    </TransformGroup>
  </Rectangle.RenderTransform>
</Rectangle>
```

Now that you have covered the basics of transforms in Silverlight, let's run through a quick exercise that will give you a chance to try them out for yourself.

Try It Out: Using Expression Blend to Transform Silverlight Objects

In this exercise, you'll use Expression Blend to add and animate transformations.

1. Create a new Silverlight application in Expression Blend called Ch13_BlendTransforms. Add two ColumnDefinition elements and two RowDefinition elements so that the root Grid is equally divided into four cells, as follows:

```
<Grid x:Name="LayoutRoot" Background="White" >
  <Grid.RowDefinitions>
    <RowDefinition/>
    <RowDefinition/>
  </Grid.RowDefinitions>
  <Grid.ColumnDefinitions>
    <ColumnDefinition/>
    <ColumnDefinition/>
  </Grid.ColumnDefinitions>
</Grid>
```

2. Next, add two rectangles to each of the cells you just created. Create two sets of rectangles: one set with StrokeThickness="1" and another with StrokeThickness="5". Also, name the second set of rectangles recTrans. Add the following code:

```
<Grid x:Name="LayoutRoot" Background="White" >

  <Grid.RowDefinitions>
    <RowDefinition/>
    <RowDefinition/>
  </Grid.RowDefinitions>
  <Grid.ColumnDefinitions>
    <ColumnDefinition/>
    <ColumnDefinition/>
  </Grid.ColumnDefinitions>

    <Rectangle Grid.Row="0" Grid.Column="0" Height="100"
        Width="100" Stroke="#FF000000" StrokeThickness="1" />
    <Rectangle Grid.Row="0" Grid.Column="1" Height="100"
        Width="100" Stroke="#FF000000" StrokeThickness="1"  />
    <Rectangle Grid.Row="1" Grid.Column="0" Height="100"
        Width="100" Stroke="#FF000000" StrokeThickness="1"  />
    <Rectangle Grid.Row="1" Grid.Column="1" Height="100"
        Width="100" Stroke="#FF000000" StrokeThickness="1"  />

    <Rectangle Grid.Row="0" Grid.Column="0" Height="100"
        Width="100" Stroke="#FF000000" StrokeThickness="5" x:Name="recTrans" />
    <Rectangle Grid.Row="0" Grid.Column="1" Height="100"
        Width="100" Stroke="#FF000000" StrokeThickness="5" x:Name="recRotate" />
```

```
<Rectangle Grid.Row="1" Grid.Column="0" Height="100"
    Width="100" Stroke="#FF000000" StrokeThickness="5" x:Name="rectScale" />
<Rectangle Grid.Row="1" Grid.Column="1" Height="100"
    Width="100" Stroke="#FF000000" StrokeThickness="5" x:Name="rectSkew" />

</Grid>
```

3. At this point, your application should have four squares equally spaced in the four cells of your application. The next step is to introduce your transforms, but instead of just adding the transforms, you are going to animate the transformation taking place.

4. Using the techniques discussed earlier in this chapter, create a new storyboard called TransformElements.

5. You will perform the transformations over 2 seconds, so move the playhead on the timeline to 2 seconds. Select the rectangle named recTrans. In the Properties panel, find the Transform section. Click on the Translate tab. Set X and Y to 25. This causes the top-left square to move down and to the right, as shown in Figure 13-17.

6. Highlight the rectangle named recRotate. In the Transform section of the Properties panel, click on the Rotate tab. Set the Angle property to 45. The top-right square will rotate 45 degrees, as shown in Figure 13-18.

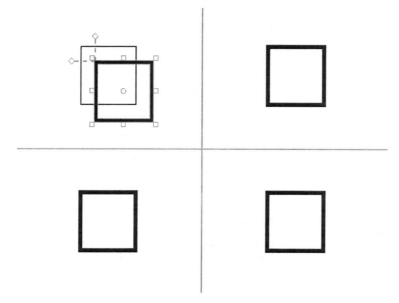

Figure 13-17. Adding the TranslateTransform

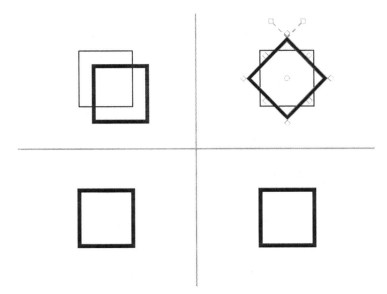

Figure 13-18. Adding the RotateTransform

7. Select the rectangle named rectScale. In the Transform section of the
    Properties panel, click on the Scale tab. Set the values of the X and Y properties
    to 1.5, which scales the bottom-left square 1.5x, or 150%, as shown in
    Figure 13-19.

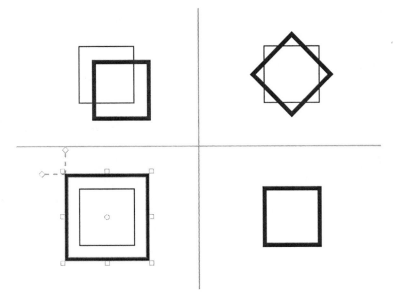

Figure 13-19. Adding the ScaleTransform

8. Select the rectangle named rectSkew. In the Transform section of the Properties panel, click on the Skew tab. Set the values of the X and Y properties to 20. This causes the square to skew into a diamond shape, as shown in Figure 13-20.

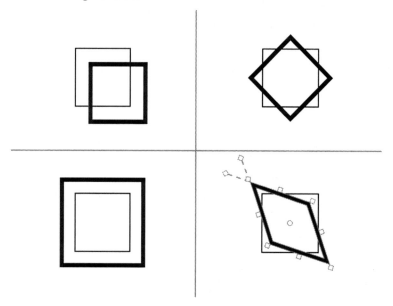

Figure 13-20. Adding the SkewTransform

9. Click the play button at the top of the timeline, and watch the objects transform from their original shapes and locations.

As you've seen in this exercise, applying transformations is pretty straightforward.

Summary

This chapter covered creating animations in Silverlight. You looked at animations from a high level, explored the different elements that make up an animation in Silverlight, and learned how to programmatically control animations in the code behind. You also looked at how Expression Blend helps you create complex animations. Then you shifted your focus to transformations in Silverlight. You looked at each of the four transform types and then created a simple Silverlight application utilizing transforms.

In the following chapter, you will look at the more advanced topic of creating your own Silverlight custom controls. Custom controls allow you to create Silverlight functionality that can be easily reused in different Silverlight applications.

CHAPTER 14

Custom Controls

So far in this book, you have learned about the many elements of Silverlight and how they can be used to build Rich Internet Applications (RIAs). But what if Silverlight doesn't offer the specific functionality you need for an application? In that case, you might want to create a custom control to provide that additional functionality.

The actual procedure for creating custom controls is not terribly difficult, but understanding the process can be. Under the hood, Silverlight performs some complex work, but most Silverlight developers do not need to know these details. However, to understand custom controls and the process used to build them, you must dive in and see how Silverlight ticks.

In this chapter, you will examine when it is appropriate to write custom controls in Silverlight and explore the different aspects of the Silverlight control model. You will then build a custom control for Silverlight.

When to Write Custom Controls

When you find that none of the existing Silverlight controls do exactly what you want, creating a custom control is not always the solution. In fact, in most cases, you should be able to get by without writing custom controls. Because of the flexibility built into the Silverlight controls, you can usually modify an existing one to suit your needs.

As a general rule, if your goal is to modify the appearance of a control, there is no need to write a custom control. Silverlight controls that are built properly, following Microsoft's best practices, will adopt the "Parts and States" model, which calls for complete separation of the logical and visual aspects of your control. As a result of this separation, developers can change the appearance of controls, and even change transitions of the controls between different states, without needing to write custom controls.

So, just when is creating a custom control the right way to go? Here are the primary reasons for writing custom controls:

- *Abstraction of functionality*. When developing your applications, you might need to implement some functionality that can be achieved using Silverlight's out-of-the-box support. However, if this functionality needs to be reused often in your application, you can choose to create a custom control that abstracts the functionality, in order to simplify the application. An example of this is if you wanted to have two text boxes next to each other for first and last names. Instead of always including two TextBox controls in your XAML, you could write a custom control that automatically includes both text boxes and abstracts the behavior surrounding the text boxes.

- *Modification of functionality.* If you would like to change the way a Silverlight control behaves, you can write a custom control that implements that behavior, perhaps inheriting it from an existing control. An example of this is if you want to create a button that pops up a menu instead of simply triggering a click method.

- *Creation of new functionality.* The most obvious reason for writing a custom control in Silverlight is to add functionality that does not currently exist in Silverlight. As an example, you could write a control that acts as a floating window that can be dragged and resized.

Although these are valid reasons for creating custom controls, there are two more resources you should check before you do so: the Silverlight Control Toolkit and third-party controls.

Silverlight Control Model

Before you start to build custom controls for Silverlight, you should understand the key concepts of the Silverlight control model. In this section, you will look at two of these concepts:

- The "Parts and States" model

- Dependency properties

"Parts and States" Model

Following Microsoft's best practices, Silverlight controls are built with a strict separation between the visual aspects of the control and the logic behind the control. This allows developers to create templates for existing controls that will dramatically change the visual appearance and the visual behaviors of a control, without needing to write any code. This separation is called for by the "Parts and States" model. The visual aspects of controls are managed by Silverlight's Visual State Manager (VSM).

■ **Note** You are not required to adhere to the "Parts and States" model when developing custom controls. However, developers are urged to do so in order to follow the best practices outlined by Microsoft.

The "Parts and States" model uses the following terminology:

- *Parts:* Named elements contained in a control template that are manipulated by code in some way are called *parts*. For example, a simple Button control could consist of a rectangle that is the body of the button and a text block that represents the text on the control.

- *States:* A control will always be in a *state*. For a Button control, different states include when the mouse is hovered over the button, when the mouse is pressed down on the button, and when neither is the case (its default or normal state). The visual look of a control is defined by its particular state.

- *Transitions*: When a control changes from one state to another—for example, when a Button control goes from its normal state to having the mouse hovered over it—its visual appearance might change. In some cases, this change might be animated to provide a smooth visual transition from the states. These animations are defined in the "Parts and States" model by *transitions*.

- *State group*: According to the "Parts and States" model, control states can be grouped into mutually exclusive groups. A control cannot be in more than one state within the same state group at the same time.

Dependency Properties

Properties are a common part of object-oriented programming and are familiar to .NET developers. Here is a typical property definition:

```
private string _name;
public string Name
{
    get { return _name; }
    set { _name = value; }
}
```

In Silverlight and Windows Presentation Foundation (WPF), Microsoft has added some functionality to the property system. This new system is referred to as the *Silverlight property system*. Properties created based on this new property system are called *dependency properties*.

In a nutshell, dependency properties allow Silverlight to determine the value of a property dynamically from a number of inputs, such as data binding or template binding. As a general rule, if you want to be able to style a property or to have it participate in data binding or template binding, it must be defined as a dependency property.

You define a property as a dependency property using the DependencyProperty object, as shown in the following code snippet:

```
public static readonly DependencyProperty NameProperty =
    DependencyProperty.Register(
        "Name",
        typeof(string),
        typeof(MyControl),
        null
        );

public string Name
{
    get
    {
        return (string)GetValue(NameProperty);
    }
    set
    {
        SetValue(NameProperty, value);
    }
}
```

This example defines the `Name` property as a dependency property. It declares a new object of type `DependencyProperty` called `NameProperty`, following the naming convention detailed by Microsoft. `NameProperty` is set equal to the return value of the `DependencyProperty.Register()` method, which registers a dependency property within the Silverlight property system.

The `DependencyProperty.Register()` method is passed a number of arguments:

- The name of the property that you are registering as a dependency property—`Name`, in this example.

- The data type of the property you are registering—`string`, in this example.

- The data type of the object that is registering the property—`MyControl`, in this example.

- Metadata that should be registered with the dependency property. Most of the time, this will be used to hook up a callback method that will be called whenever the property's value is changed. This example simply passes `null`. In the next section, you will see how this last argument is used.

Now that I have discussed custom controls in Silverlight from a high level, it's time to see how to build your own.

Creating Custom Controls in Silverlight

As I mentioned at the beginning of the chapter, creating a custom control does not need to be difficult. Of course, the work involved depends on how complex your control needs to be. As you'll see, the custom control you'll create in this chapter is relatively simple. Before you get to that exercise, let's take a quick look at the two options for creating custom controls.

Implementing Custom Functionality

You have two main options for creating custom functionality in Silverlight:

- *With a UserControl*: The simplest way to create a piece of custom functionality is to implement it with a `UserControl`. Once the `UserControl` is created, you can then reuse it across your application.

- *As a custom control*: The content that is rendered is built from scratch by the developer. This is by far the most complex option for creating a custom control. You would need to do this when you want to implement functionality that is unavailable with the existing controls in Silverlight.

In this chapter's exercise, you will take the custom control approach.

Try It Out: Building a Custom Control

In this exercise, you will build your own "cool-down" button. This button will be disabled for a set number of seconds—its cool-down duration—after it is clicked. If you set the cool-down period to be three seconds, after you click the button, you cannot click it again for three seconds.

For demonstration purposes, you will not use the standard Silverlight `Button` control as the base control. Instead, you will create a custom control that implements `Control`. This way, I can show you how to create a control with a number of states.

The cool-down button will have five states, implemented in two state groups: NormalStates and CoolDownStates. The NormalStates state group will have these states:

- *Pressed*: The button is being pressed. When it is in this state, the thickness of the button's border is reduced.

- *MouseOver*: The mouse is hovering over the button. When the button is in this state, the thickness of the button's border is increased.

- *Normal*: The button is in its normal state.

The cool-down button will also have a state group named CoolDownStates, which will contain two states:

- *Available*: The button is active and available to be clicked.

- *CoolDown*: The button is in its cool-down state, and therefore is not active. To indicate that the button is in this state, you will place a rectangle over top of the button that is of 75% opacity. In addition, you will disable all other events while the button is in this state.

Keep in mind that this is only an example, and it has many areas that could use improvement. The goal of the exercise is not to produce a control you will use in your applications, but rather to demonstrate the basic steps for creating a custom control in Silverlight.

Setting Up the Control Project

Let's get started by creating a new project for the custom control.

1. In Visual Studio 2010, create a new Silverlight application named CoolDownButtonTest and allow Visual Studio to create a Web Application project to host your application.

2. From Solution Explorer, right-click the solution and select Add ➤ New Project.

3. In the Add New Project dialog box, select the Silverlight Class Library template and name the library CoolDownButton, as shown in Figure 14-1. If prompted about which version of Silverlight to use, select Silverlight 5 and click OK, as shown in Figure 14-2.

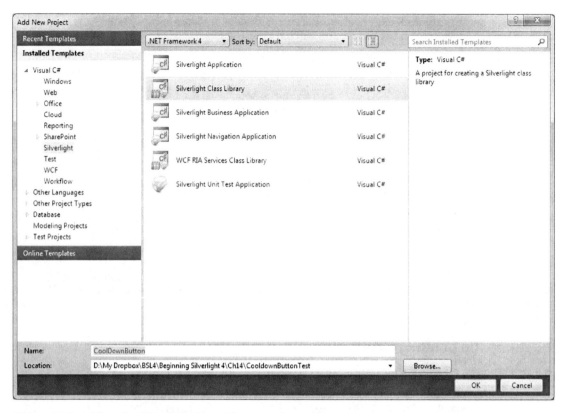

Figure 14-1. Adding the Silverlight Class Library to the project

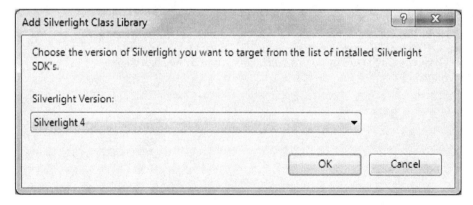

Figure 14-2. Silverlight version-selection screen

    4.   By default, Visual Studio creates a class named Class1.cs. Delete this file from the project.

5. Right-click the CoolDownButton project and select Add ➤ New Item.

6. In the Add New Item dialog box, select the Class template, name the class
    CoolDownButtonControl.cs, and click Add, as shown in Figure 14-3.

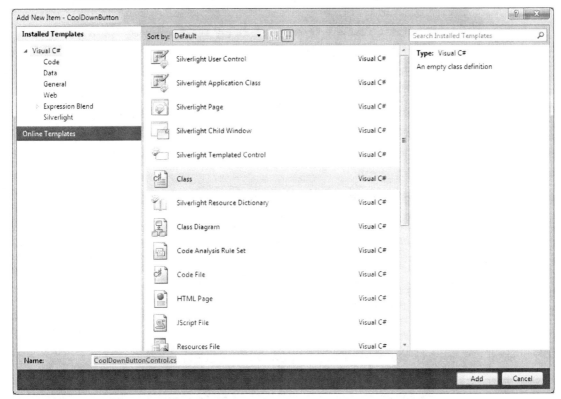

Figure 14-3. Adding the new class to the project

Defining Properties and States

Now you're ready to create the control. Let's begin by coding the properties and states.

1. Within the CoolDownButtonControl.cs file, set the control class to inherit from
    Control, in order to gain the base Silverlight control functionality, as follows:

```
namespace CoolDownButton
{
    public class CoolDownButtonControl : Control
    {

    }
}
```

2. Now add the control's public properties, as follows:

```
namespace CoolDownButton
{
    public class CoolDownButtonControl : Control
    {
        public static readonly DependencyProperty CoolDownSecondsProperty =
            DependencyProperty.Register(
            "CoolDownSeconds",
            typeof(int),
            typeof(CoolDownButtonControl),
            new PropertyMetadata(
            new PropertyChangedCallback(
                CoolDownButtonControl.OnCoolDownSecondsPropertyChanged
                )
            )
        );

        public int CoolDownSeconds
        {
            get
            {
                return (int)GetValue(CoolDownSecondsProperty);
            }
            set
            {
                SetValue(CoolDownSecondsProperty, value);
            }
        }

        private static void OnCoolDownSecondsPropertyChanged(
            DependencyObject d, DependencyPropertyChangedEventArgs e)
        {
            CoolDownButtonControl cdButton = d as CoolDownButtonControl;

            cdButton.OnCoolDownButtonChange(null);
        }

        public static readonly DependencyProperty ButtonTextProperty =
            DependencyProperty.Register(
                "ButtonText",
                typeof(string),
                typeof(CoolDownButtonControl),
                new PropertyMetadata(
                    new PropertyChangedCallback(
                        CoolDownButtonControl.OnButtonTextPropertyChanged
                        )
                    )
                );

        public string ButtonText
```

```
        {
            get
            {
                return (string)GetValue(ButtonTextProperty);
            }
            set
            {
                SetValue(ButtonTextProperty, value);
            }
        }

        private static void OnButtonTextPropertyChanged(
            DependencyObject d, DependencyPropertyChangedEventArgs e)
        {
            CoolDownButtonControl cdButton = d as CoolDownButtonControl;
            cdButton.OnCoolDownButtonChange(null);
        }

        protected virtual void OnCoolDownButtonChange(RoutedEventArgs e)
        {

        }
    }
}
```

3. As explained earlier in the chapter, for your properties to allow data binding, template binding, styling, and so on, they must be dependency properties. In addition to the dependency properties, you added two callback methods that will be called when the properties are updated. By naming convention, the CoolDownSeconds property has a DependencyProperty object named CoolDownSecondsProperty and a callback method of onCoolDownSecondsPropertyChanged(). So you need to watch out, or your names will end up being very long, as they are here.

4. Add some private members to contain state information, as follows:

```
namespace CoolDownButton
{
    public class CoolDownButtonControl : Control
    {
        private FrameworkElement corePart;
        private bool isPressed, isMouseOver, isCoolDown;
        private DateTime pressedTime;

        ...
    }
}
```

5. The corePart members are of type FrameworkElement and hold the instance of the main part, which responds to mouse events. The isPressed, isMouseOver, and isCoolDown Boolean members are used to help keep track of the current button state. And the pressedTime member records the time that the button

was clicked in order to determine when the cool-down state should be removed.

6. Add a helper method called GoToState(), which will assist in switching between the states of the control:

```
private void GoToState(bool useTransitions)
{
    // Go to states in NormalStates state group
    if (isPressed)
    {
        VisualStateManager.GoToState(this, "Pressed", useTransitions);
    }
    else if (isMouseOver)
    {
        VisualStateManager.GoToState(this, "MouseOver", useTransitions);
    }
    else
    {
        VisualStateManager.GoToState(this, "Normal", useTransitions);
    }

    // Go to states in CoolDownStates state group
    if (isCoolDown)
    {
        VisualStateManager.GoToState(this, "CoolDown", useTransitions);
    }
    else
    {
        VisualStateManager.GoToState(this, "Available", useTransitions);
    }
}
```

7. This method checks the private members you added in the previous step to determine in which state the control should be. When the proper state is determined, the VisualStateManager.GoToState() method is called, passing it the control, the name of the state, and whether or not the control should use transitions when switching from the current state to this new state (that is, whether or not an animation should be shown).

Now let's turn to the visual aspect of the control.

Defining the Control's Appearance

The default control template is placed in a file named generic.xaml, which is located in a folder named themes. These names are required. The generic.xaml is a resource dictionary that defines the built-in style for the control. You need to add the folder and file, make some adjustments to the file, and then add the XAML to set the control's appearance.

1. To add the required folder, right-click the CoolDownButton project and select Add ➤ New Folder. Name the folder themes.

2. Right-click the newly added themes folder and select Add ➤ New Item.

3. In the Add New Item dialog box, select the Silverlight Resource Dictionary template and name the file generic.xaml, as shown in Figure 14-4. Click Add, and confirm that the generic.xaml file was added within the themes folder.

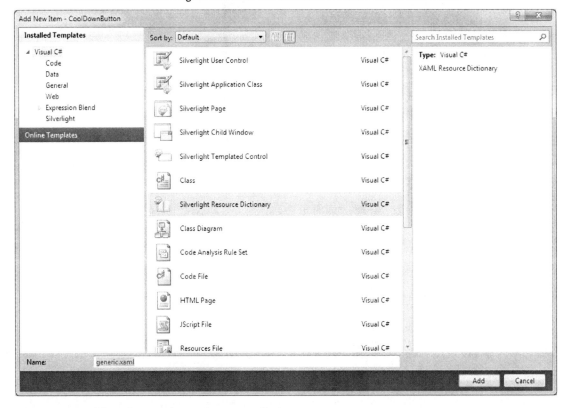

Figure 14-4. Adding the generic.xaml resource dictionary

4. Right-click the generic.xaml file and select Properties. Change the Build Action to Resource as shown in Figure 14-5.

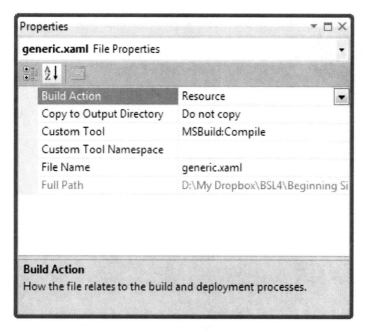

Figure 14-5. The Properties panel for generic.xaml

5. Open the generic.xaml file. You will see that, by default, the file has the following contents:

```
<ResourceDictionary
    xmlns="http://schemas.microsoft.com/winfx/2006/xaml/presentation"
    xmlns:x="http://schemas.microsoft.com/winfx/2006/xaml">

</ResourceDictionary>
```

6. Next you need to add a reference to the CoolDownButton namespace:

```
<ResourceDictionary
    xmlns="http://schemas.microsoft.com/winfx/2006/xaml/presentation"
    xmlns:x="http://schemas.microsoft.com/winfx/2006/xaml"
    xmlns:bsl="clr-namespace:CoolDownButton">

</ResourceDictionary>
```

7. Now you can add the actual XAML that will make up the control. First, add a Style tag, with the TargetType set to CoolDownButtonControl. Then add a Setter for the control template, and within that, add the ControlTemplate definition, again with TargetType set to CoolDownButtonControl. The control will consist of two Rectangle components: one for the button itself, named coreButton, and one for the 75% opacity overlay that will be displayed when the button is in its CoolDown state. It will also have a TextBlock component to contain the text of the button. This defines the control in the default state.

Therefore, the opacity of the overlay rectangle is set to 0% to start, because the overlay should not be visible by default. The additions are as follows:

```
<ResourceDictionary
    xmlns="http://schemas.microsoft.com/winfx/2006/xaml/presentation"
    xmlns:x="http://schemas.microsoft.com/winfx/2006/xaml"
    xmlns:bsl="clr-namespace:CoolDownButton">
    <Style TargetType="bsl:CoolDownButtonControl">
        <Setter Property="Template">
            <Setter.Value>
                <ControlTemplate TargetType=" bsl:CoolDownButtonControl">
                    <Grid x:Name="LayoutRoot">
                        <Rectangle
                            StrokeThickness="4"
                            Stroke="Navy"
                            Fill="AliceBlue"
                            RadiusX="4"
                            RadiusY="4"
                            x:Name="innerButton" />
                        <TextBlock
                            HorizontalAlignment="Center"
                            VerticalAlignment="Center"
                            Text="Test"
                            TextWrapping="Wrap"/>
                        <Rectangle
                            Opacity="0"
                            Fill="#FF000000"
                            Stroke="#FF000000"
                            RenderTransformOrigin="0.5,0.5"
                            RadiusY="4" RadiusX="4"
                            x:Name="corePart">
                            <Rectangle.RenderTransform>
                                <TransformGroup>
                                    <ScaleTransform
                                    ScaleX="1"
                                    ScaleY="1"/>
                                </TransformGroup>
                            </Rectangle.RenderTransform>
                        </Rectangle>
                    </Grid>
                </ControlTemplate>
            </Setter.Value>
        </Setter>
    </Style>
</ResourceDictionary>
```

8. Now that you have defined the default appearance of the control, you need to add the VisualStateGroups, along with the different states for the control. To do this, add the following code just before the first Rectangle. Notice that for each state, a Storyboard is used to define the state's visual appearance:

```
<VisualStateManager.VisualStateGroups>
    <VisualStateGroup Name="NormalStates">
        <VisualState Name="Normal"/>
        <VisualState Name="MouseOver" >
            <Storyboard >
                <DoubleAnimation
                    Storyboard.TargetName="innerButton"
                    Storyboard.TargetProperty="(UIElement.StrokeThickness)"
                    Duration="0" To="6"/>
            </Storyboard>
        </VisualState>
        <VisualState x:Name="Pressed">
            <Storyboard>
                <DoubleAnimation
                    Storyboard.TargetName="innerButton"
                    Storyboard.TargetProperty="(UIElement.StrokeThickness)"
                    Duration="0" To="2"/>
            </Storyboard>
        </VisualState>
    </VisualStateGroup>
    <VisualStateGroup Name="CoolDownStates">
        <VisualState Name="Available"/>
        <VisualState Name="CoolDown">
            <Storyboard>
                <DoubleAnimation
                    Storyboard.TargetName="corePart"
                    Storyboard.TargetProperty="(UIElement.Opacity)"
                    Duration="0" To=".75"/>
            </Storyboard>
        </VisualState>
    </VisualStateGroup>
</VisualStateManager.VisualStateGroups>
```

Now let's turn our attention back to the CoolDownButtonControl.cs file to finish up the logic behind the control.

Handling Control Events

To complete the control, you need to handle its events and define its control contract.

1. First, you must get an instance of the core part. Referring back to step 8 in the "Defining the Control's Appearance" section, you'll see that this is the overlay rectangle named corePart. This is the control on top of the other controls, so it is the one that accepts the mouse events. To get the instance of corePart, use the GetChildElement() method. Call this method in the OnApplyTemplate() method that is called whenever a template is applied to the control, as follows:

```
public override void OnApplyTemplate()
{
    base.OnApplyTemplate();

    CorePart = (FrameworkElement)GetTemplateChild("corePart");
```

```
        GoToState(false);
    }

    private FrameworkElement CorePart
    {
        get
        {
            return corePart;
        }

        set
        {
            corePart = value;
        }
    }
}
```

2. Notice that this method calls the base OnApplyTemplate() method, and then calls the GoToState() method, passing it false. This is the first time that the GoToState() method is called, and you are passing it false so that it does not use any transitions while changing the state. The initial view of the control should not have any animations to get it to the initial state.

3. At this point, you need to wire up event handlers to handle the mouse events. First, create the event handlers themselves, as follows:

```
void corePart_MouseEnter(object sender, MouseEventArgs e)
{
    isMouseOver = true;
    GoToState(true);
}

void corePart_MouseLeave(object sender, MouseEventArgs e)
{
    isMouseOver = false;
    GoToState(true);
}

void corePart_MouseLeftButtonDown(object sender, MouseButtonEventArgs e)
{
    isPressed = true;
    GoToState(true);
}

void corePart_MouseLeftButtonUp(object sender, MouseButtonEventArgs e)
{
    isPressed = false;
    isCoolDown = true;
    pressedTime = DateTime.Now;
    GoToState(true);
}
```

4. Next, wire up the handlers to the events. You can do this in the CorePart property's setter, as follows. Note that in the case where more than one template is applied, before wiring up the event handlers, you need to make sure to remove any existing event handlers.

```
private FrameworkElement CorePart
{
    get
    {
        return corePart;
    }

    set
    {
        FrameworkElement oldCorePart = corePart;

        if (oldCorePart != null)
        {
            oldCorePart.MouseEnter -=
                new MouseEventHandler(corePart_MouseEnter);
            oldCorePart.MouseLeave -=
                new MouseEventHandler(corePart_MouseLeave);
            oldCorePart.MouseLeftButtonDown -=
                new MouseButtonEventHandler(
                    corePart_MouseLeftButtonDown);
            oldCorePart.MouseLeftButtonUp -=
                new MouseButtonEventHandler(
                    corePart_MouseLeftButtonUp);
        }

        corePart = value;

        if (corePart != null)
        {
            corePart.MouseEnter +=
                new MouseEventHandler(corePart_MouseEnter);
            corePart.MouseLeave +=
                new MouseEventHandler(corePart_MouseLeave);
            corePart.MouseLeftButtonDown +=
                new MouseButtonEventHandler(
                    corePart_MouseLeftButtonDown);
            corePart.MouseLeftButtonUp +=
                new MouseButtonEventHandler(
                    corePart_MouseLeftButtonUp);
        }
    }
}
```

5. Recall that when the button is clicked, you need to make sure the button is disabled for however many seconds are set as the cool-down period. To do

this, first create a method that checks to see if the cool-down time has expired, as follows:

```
private bool CheckCoolDown()
{
    if (!isCoolDown)
    {
        return false;
    }
    else
    {
        if (DateTime.Now > pressedTime.AddSeconds(CoolDownSeconds))
        {
            isCoolDown = false;
            return false;
        }
        else
        {
            return true;
        }
    }
}
```

6. The logic behind this method is pretty simple. If the isCoolDown flag is true, you are simply checking to see if the current time is greater than the pressedTime added to the cool-down period. If so, you reset the isCoolDown flag and return false; otherwise, you return true.

7. Now you need to surround the code in each of the event handlers with a call to the CheckCoolDown() method, as follows. If the cool-down period has not yet expired, none of the event handlers should perform any action.

```
void corePart_MouseEnter(object sender, MouseEventArgs e)
{
    if (!CheckCoolDown())
    {
        isMouseOver = true;
        GoToState(true);
    }
}

void corePart_MouseLeave(object sender, MouseEventArgs e)
{
    if (!CheckCoolDown())
    {
        isMouseOver = false;
        GoToState(true);
    }
}

void corePart_MouseLeftButtonDown(object sender, MouseButtonEventArgs e)
{
```

```
        if (!CheckCoolDown())
        {
            isPressed = true;
            GoToState(true);
        }
    }

    void corePart_MouseLeftButtonUp(object sender, MouseButtonEventArgs e)
    {
        if (!CheckCoolDown())
        {
            isPressed = false;
            isCoolDown = true;
            pressedTime = DateTime.Now;
            GoToState(true);
        }
    }
```

8. Recall that in step 2 of the "Defining Properties and States" section you created
    a method called OnCoolDownButtonChange(). At that time, you did not place
    anything in this method. This is the method that is called whenever there is a
    notification change to a dependency property. When a change occurs, you
    need to call GoToState()so that the control can reflect the changes, as follows:

```
protected virtual void OnCoolDownButtonChange(RoutedEventArgs e)
{
    GoToState(true);
}
```

9. Next, create a constructor for your control and apply the default style key. In
    many cases, this will simply be the type of your control itself.

```
public CoolDownButtonControl()
{
    DefaultStyleKey = typeof(CoolDownButtonControl);
}
```

10. The final step in creating the control is to define a control contract that
    describes your control. This is required for your control to be modified by tools
    such as Expression Blend. This contract consists of a number of attributes that
    are placed directly in the control class, as follows. These attributes are used
    only by tools; they are not used by the runtime.

```
namespace CoolDownButton
{
    [TemplatePart(Name = "Core", Type = typeof(FrameworkElement))]
    [TemplateVisualState(Name = "Normal", GroupName = "NormalStates")]
    [TemplateVisualState(Name = "MouseOver", GroupName = " NormalStates")]
    [TemplateVisualState(Name = "Pressed", GroupName = " NormalStates")]
    [TemplateVisualState(Name = "CoolDown", GroupName = "CoolDownStates")]
    [TemplateVisualState(Name = "Available", GroupName = "CoolDownStates")]
    public class CoolDownButtonControl : Control
    {
```

```
            . . .
        }
    }
```

This completes the creation of the custom control.

Compiling and Testing the Control

Now you're ready to try out your new control.

1. Compile your control.

2. If everything compiles correctly, you need create an instance of your control in
    your CoolDownButtonTest project. To do this, right-click the
    CoolDownButtonTest project in Solution Explorer and select Add Reference. In
    the Add Reference dialog box, select the Projects tab and choose
    CoolDownButton, as shown in Figure 14-6. Then click OK.

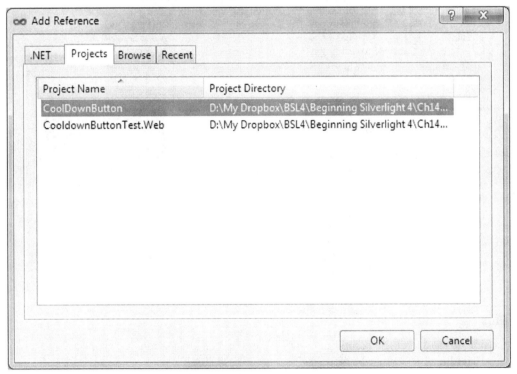

Figure 14-6. Adding a reference to your control

3. Navigate to your MainPage.xaml file within the CoolDownButtonTest project.
    First add a new xmlns to the UserControl definition, and then add an instance
    of your control, as follows:

```
<UserControl x:Class="CooldownButtonTest.MainPage"
    xmlns="http://schemas.microsoft.com/winfx/2006/xaml/presentation"
    xmlns:x="http://schemas.microsoft.com/winfx/2006/xaml"
    xmlns:d="http://schemas.microsoft.com/expression/blend/2008"
    xmlns:mc="http://schemas.openxmlformats.org/markup-compatibility/2006"
    xmlns:bsl="clr-namespace:CoolDownButton;assembly=CoolDownButton"
    mc:Ignorable="d"
    d:DesignHeight="300" d:DesignWidth="400">

    <Grid x:Name="LayoutRoot" Background="White">
        <bsl:CoolDownButtonControl
            CoolDownSeconds="3"
            Width="150" Height="60" />
    </Grid>
</UserControl>
```

4. Run the project. You should see your button.

5. Test the states of your button. When you move the mouse over the button, the border thickness will increase. Click the mouse on the button, and the border will decrease. When you release the mouse from the button, the border will go back to normal, and the overlay will appear. You can continue to move the mouse over the button, and you will notice that it does not respond to your events until three seconds have passed. Figure 14-7 shows the various control states.

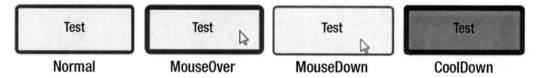

Figure 14-7. Button states

Clearly, this cool-down button has a lot of room for improvement. However, the goal was to show you the basic steps involved in creating a custom control. As you most certainly could tell, the process is pretty involved, but the rewards of following the best practices are worth it. When the control is built properly like this, you can apply custom templates to it to dramatically change its appearance, without needing to rewrite any of the code logic.

Summary

Without a doubt, this was the most complex content covered in this book so far. The goal was to give you a basic understanding of what is involved in creating custom controls the right way in Silverlight.

In this chapter, you looked at when you might want to create a custom control. Then you learned about some of the key concepts within the Silverlight control model, including the "Parts and States" model and dependency properties. Finally, you built your own custom control.

CHAPTER 15

Printing in Silverlight

One of the features most requested by the Silverlight community has been client-side printing support. Silverlight 5 includes a new printing API that allows developers to enable client printing from a Silverlight application. In this chapter, we will explore the new printing API and run through some exercises to see printing in action.

The Printing API

The primary class that controls printing from a Silverlight application is the PrintDocument class. Let's take a look at the PrintDocument class and its members.

PrintDocument Events

The action of opening the print dialog box and printing is initiated by the Print method. This method triggers three events in the following order: The BeginPrint event is fired when the print dialog box displays successfully and the user selects Print. Once the printing process begins, the PrintPage event is fired as each page prints. The EndPrint event is fired when the printing process is complete or when the printing job has been cancelled by the user. If there was an error while printing, the Error property of EndPrintEventArgs can be inspected.

Determining Print Content

When the PrintPage event fires, what will be printed is determined by the PrintPageEventArgs.PageVisual property. You can either set the PageVisual property to a UIElement contained within your XAML content, or you can construct your own XAML content dynamically and set that content to the PageVisual. Let's walk through two exercises, one for each of these options.

Try It Out: Implementing Simple Printing

In this example, you'll create a simple Silverlight application with a DataGrid that displays contacts, and you'll add printing functionality.

1. Create a new Silverlight application in Visual Studio 2010. Name it SimplePrinting, and allow Visual Studio to create an ASP.NET Web Application called SimplePrinting.Web.

2. When the project is created, you should be looking at the MainPage.xaml file. Change the LayoutRoot item to be a StackPanel, add a TextBlock with the Text

property set to "Contacts," and set the FontWeight property to Bold. Next, add a DataGrid named ContactGrid. Note that for the DataGrid you must have a reference to the Silverlight SDK as explained in Chapter 5. Below the DataGrid, add a nested horizontal StackPanel containing two buttons. The content should be "Print As-Is" for the first button and "Print Formatted" for the second:

```xml
<StackPanel x:Name="LayoutRoot" Background="White">
    <TextBlock Text="Contacts" FontWeight="Bold" />
    <sdk:DataGrid Name="ContactGrid" />
    <StackPanel Orientation="Horizontal">
        <Button Content="Print As-Is" />
        <Button Content="Print Formatted" />
    </StackPanel>
</StackPanel>
```

3. Next you'll add some styles to improve the look of the application. You'll add three implicit styles (as discussed in Chapter 12):

```xml
<UserControl x:Class="SimplePrinting.MainPage"
    xmlns="http://schemas.microsoft.com/winfx/2006/xaml/presentation"
    xmlns:x="http://schemas.microsoft.com/winfx/2006/xaml"
    xmlns:d="http://schemas.microsoft.com/expression/blend/2008"
    xmlns:mc="http://schemas.openxmlformats.org/markup-compatibility/2006"
    xmlns:sdk="http://schemas.microsoft.com/winfx/2006/xaml/presentation/sdk"
    mc:Ignorable="d"
    d:DesignHeight="300" d:DesignWidth="400">

    <UserControl.Resources>
        <Style TargetType="Button">
            <Setter Property="Margin" Value="5" />
        </Style>
        <Style TargetType="sdk:DataGrid">
            <Setter Property="Margin" Value="5" />
        </Style>
        <Style TargetType="TextBlock">
            <Setter Property="Margin" Value="5" />
            <Setter Property="FontSize" Value="18" />
        </Style>
    </UserControl.Resources>

    <StackPanel x:Name="LayoutRoot" Background="White">
        <TextBlock Text="Contacts" FontWeight="Bold" />
        <sdk:DataGrid Name="ContactGrid" />
        <StackPanel Orientation="Horizontal">
            <Button Content="Print As-Is" />
            <Button Content="Print Formatted" />
        </StackPanel>
    </StackPanel>
</UserControl>
```

4. At this point, the application should look like what's shown in Figure 15-1.

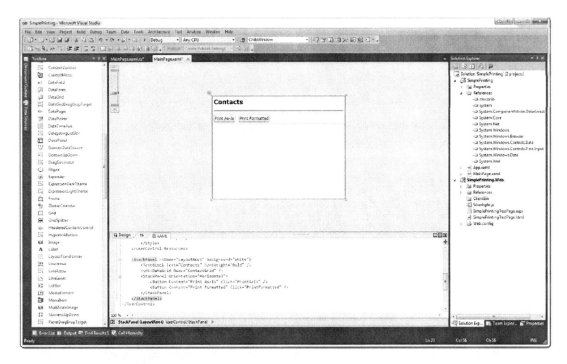

Figure 15-1. The SimplePrinting application

5.   Next you need to wire up an event handler for each button's Click event. First you'll set the Click event in the XAML. You will name the delegates PrintAsIs and PrintFormatted:

```
<StackPanel x:Name="LayoutRoot" Background="White">
    <TextBlock Text="Contacts" FontWeight="Bold" />
    <sdk:DataGrid Name="ContactGrid" />
    <StackPanel Orientation="Horizontal">
        <Button Content="Print As-Is" Click="PrintAsIs" />
        <Button Content="Print Formatted" Click="PrintFormatted" />
    </StackPanel>
</StackPanel>
```

6.   Next make certain the two event handlers are present in the code behind:

```
public partial class MainPage : UserControl
{
    public MainPage()
    {
        InitializeComponent();
    }

    private void Button_Click(object sender, RoutedEventArgs e)
    {
```

```
        }

        private void PrintAsIs(object sender, RoutedEventArgs e)
        {

        }

        private void PrintFormatted(object sender, RoutedEventArgs e)
        {

        }
    }
```

7. Now you need to define the data that you'll bind to your ContactGrid. First, create a simple class called Contact below the MainPage class that contains four simple string properties: Name, Address, CityStateZip, and Phone:

```
public class Contact
{
    public string Name { get; set; }
    public string Address{ get; set; }
    public string CityStateZip{ get; set; }
    public string Phone{ get; set; }
}
```

8. After the Contact class has been defined, you need to add the actual data to the DataGrid. You'll do this in the Loaded event, so first you need to create a delegate to handle the event. Then you can add your data:

```
public partial class MainPage : UserControl
{
    List<Contact> Contacts;

    public MainPage()
    {
        InitializeComponent();
        this.Loaded += new RoutedEventHandler(MainPage_Loaded);
    }

    void MainPage_Loaded(object sender, RoutedEventArgs e)
    {
        Contacts = new List<Contact>();

        Contacts.Add(new Contact() {
            Name = "John Doe",
            Address = "123 Driveway Road",
            CityStateZip = "SomeCity, OH 12345",
            Phone = "(123) 456-7890"
        });

        Contacts.Add(new Contact()
```

```
                {
                    Name = "Jane Doe",
                    Address = "456 Windy Road",
                    CityStateZip = "Cityville, FL 34566",
                    Phone = "(111) 222-3333"
                });

                ContactGrid.ItemsSource = Contacts;
            }

            private void Button_Click(object sender, RoutedEventArgs e)
            {

            }

            private void PrintAsIs(object sender, RoutedEventArgs e)
            {

            }

            private void PrintFormatted(object sender, RoutedEventArgs e)
            {

            }
        }

        public class Contact
        {
                public string Name { get; set; }
                public string Address{ get; set; }
                public string CityStateZip{ get; set; }
                public string Phone{ get; set; }
        }
```

9. Now test the application to make sure you have the data binding properly.
   Press F5 to debug the application; it should appear as shown in Figure 15-2.

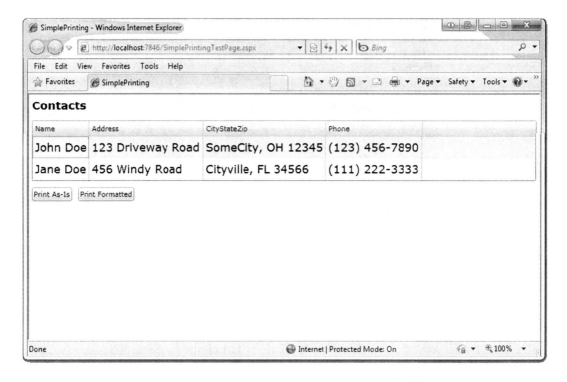

Figure 15-2. The SimplePrinting application with data bound

10. Now you need to add the printing logic to your application. In this example, you'll simply print what you see on the screen by setting the PageVisual to the LayoutRoot. To start, create an instance of the PrintDocument object in the PrintAsIs delegate. The PrintDocument object belongs to the System.Windows.Printing namespace, so you'll need to add the using System.Windows.Printing statement to the top of the MainPage.xaml.cs file, as shown in Figure 15-3.

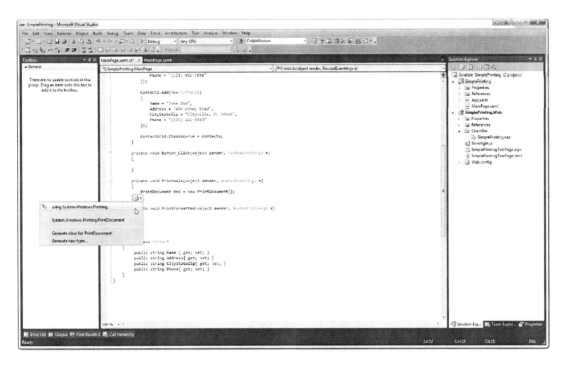

Figure 15-3. Referencing the System.Windows.Printing namespace

11. Next you'll wire up the PrintPage event. You can do this by defining a separate
    delegate, or you can use a lambda expression to define the delegate logic
    inline. In this example, you'll use the latter:

```
private void PrintAsIs(object sender, RoutedEventArgs e)
{
    PrintDocument doc = new PrintDocument();

    doc.PrintPage += (s, args) =>
        {

        };
}
```

12. After wiring up the PrintPage event, call the Print() method, which essentially
    calls the PrintPage logic. The Print() method requires a document name be
    passed, so pass in "As Is" as the name of the printed document:

```
 private void PrintAsIs(object sender, RoutedEventArgs e)
{
    PrintDocument doc = new PrintDocument();

    doc.PrintPage += (s, args) =>
        {
```

```
        };

    doc.Print("As Is");
}
```

13. Now you just need to add the logic to your PrintPage lambda expression. Because you're just printing the content as you see it on the screen, simply set the PageVisual property to the LayoutRoot to tell Silverlight to print all of the XAML content contained in the application. The PageVisual property belongs to the PrintPageEventArgs class and is passed into the PrintPage event delegate:

```
private void PrintAsIs(object sender, RoutedEventArgs e)
{
    PrintDocument doc = new PrintDocument();

    doc.PrintPage += (s, args) =>
        {
            args.PageVisual = LayoutRoot;
        };

    doc.Print("As Is");
}
```

14. Press F5 now to test the application. When the application is displayed, click the Print As-Is button, which displays the Print dialog as shown in Figure 15-4.

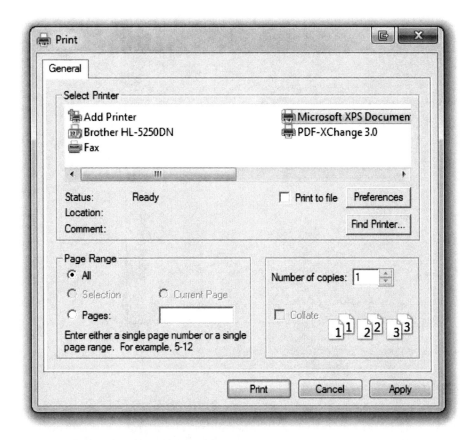

Figure 15-4. Print dialog box for the SimplePrinting application

15. Select the desired printer, and click Print. If all goes well, the content that is printed should be just as you see on the screen in Figure 15-5.

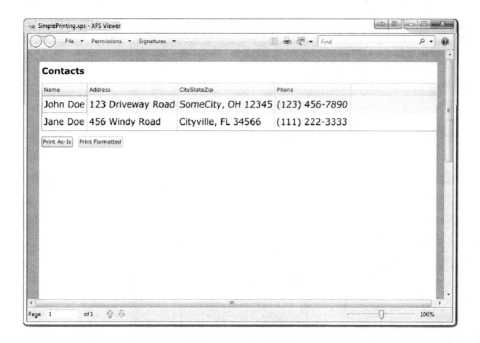

Figure 15-5. *Printed output from the SimplePrinting application*

Printing Custom Content

It might not always be ideal to print application content just as it's displayed on the screen. Fortunately, however, you can print custom content. Because you have to set the PageVisual property in order to print, you can simply set that to whatever content you'd like, including dynamically created content.

Try It Out: Implementing a Custom Print

1. You will continue working from the SimplePrinting project you created in the previous section. In the PrintFormatted delegate, add a new instance of the PrintDocument class, wire up the PrintPage event, and call the Print method:

```
private void PrintFormatted(object sender, RoutedEventArgs e)
{
    PrintDocument doc = new PrintDocument();

    doc.PrintPage += (s, args) =>
        {

        };

    doc.Print("Formatted Print");
}
```

2. Within the PrintPage event logic, you now need to wire up the PageVisual property. In the previous example, you simply set this to the LayoutRoot element, but in this case you want to customize the printed content. To do this, you'll dynamically create content to set to the PageVisual property. You will create a StackPanel at runtime and add content to that StackPanel for each Contact in your Contacts collection.

3. Add an instance of a StackPanel called customPrintPanel and then add a foreach statement that will step through each Contact in the Contacts collection. Then, within the foreach, create another StackPanel to contain the Contact information. Now add a Margin of 25 to surround the contact panel to prevent the content from appearing too close to the left margin of the printed page, as well as to keep the contacts from all stacking up together. Next insert the logic to add the contact panel to the customPrintPanel. Finally, outside the foreach, set the PageVisual to the customPrintPanel:

```
private void PrintFormatted(object sender, RoutedEventArgs e)
{
    PrintDocument doc = new PrintDocument();

    doc.PrintPage += (s, args) =>
        {
            StackPanel customPrintPanel = new StackPanel();

            foreach (Contact c in Contacts)
            {
                StackPanel contactPanel = new StackPanel();
                contactPanel.Margin = new Thickness(25);

                customPrintPanel.Children.Add(contactPanel);
            }

            args.PageVisual = customPrintPanel;
        };

    doc.Print("Formatted Print");
}
```

4. Next you need to add the contact information to the contact panel. In this example, you'll simply add a TextBlock for each of the contact attributes to display a plain text value:

```
private void PrintFormatted(object sender, RoutedEventArgs e)
{
    PrintDocument doc = new PrintDocument();

    doc.PrintPage += (s, args) =>
        {
            StackPanel customPrintPanel = new StackPanel();

            foreach (Contact c in Contacts)
            {
```

```
                    StackPanel contactPanel = new StackPanel();
                    contactPanel.Margin = new Thickness(25);

                    TextBlock name = new TextBlock();
                    name.Text = c.Name;
                    contactPanel.Children.Add(name);

                    TextBlock address = new TextBlock();
                    address.Text = c.Address;
                    contactPanel.Children.Add(address);

                    TextBlock city = new TextBlock();
                    city.Text = c.CityStateZip;
                    contactPanel.Children.Add(city);

                    TextBlock phone = new TextBlock();
                    phone.Text = c.Phone;
                    contactPanel.Children.Add(phone);

                    customPrintPanel.Children.Add(contactPanel);
                }

            args.PageVisual = customPrintPanel;
        };

    doc.Print("Formatted Print");
}
```

5. Now press F5 to test the application. When the application shows up, click the
    Print Formatted button; when you see the Print dialog, select your printer and
    click Print. If all goes well, the printed output should appear as shown in
    Figure 15-6.

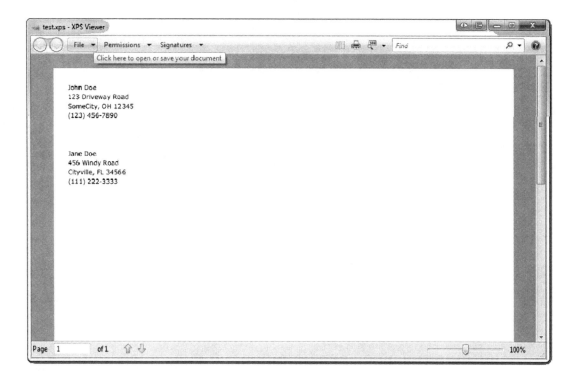

Figure 15-6. Custom print content

Additional Printing Customization

There might be times when you need even more control over the printing process. One such situation is when you want to provide a status notification to the user to indicate when the printing process is taking place, when it completes, and whether it was successful. Earlier in this chapter, we discussed two events, BeginPrint and EndPrint. You can use these events to create code that runs before and after the printing process takes place.

Try It Out: Handling the BeginPrint and EndPrint Events

You'll continue with the example you've been working with throughout this chapter and add handling for the BeginPrint and EndPrint events in order to display a message to the user about the status of the printing process.

1. Let's keep working with the SimplePrinting project you created earlier. Start by opening the XAML for MainPage.xaml.

2. Add a new TextBlock to the LayoutRoot StackPanel below the panel holding the buttons. Set the Foreground color to Red and the FontWeight to Bold. Name the TextBlock PrintStatus:

```xml
<StackPanel x:Name="LayoutRoot" Background="White">
    <TextBlock Text="Contacts" FontWeight="Bold" />
    <sdk:DataGrid Name="ContactGrid" />
    <StackPanel Orientation="Horizontal">
        <Button Content="Print As-Is" Click="PrintAsIs" />
        <Button Content="Print Formatted" Click="PrintFormatted" />
    </StackPanel>
    <TextBlock Foreground="Red" FontWeight="Bold" Text="" Name="PrintStatus" />
</StackPanel>
```

3. Move to the MainPage.xaml.cs file. You'll add to your Print Formatted functionality, so your coding will take place within the PrintFormatted event (the click event you added to your button). Below the PrintDocument instantiation, add two lambda expressions to handle the BeginPrint and EndPrint events:

```csharp
private void PrintFormatted(object sender, RoutedEventArgs e)
{
    PrintDocument doc = new PrintDocument();

    doc.BeginPrint += (s, args) =>
    {

    };

    doc.EndPrint += (s, args) =>
    {

    };

    doc.PrintPage += (s, args) =>
        {
            StackPanel customPrintPanel = new StackPanel();

            foreach (Contact c in Contacts)
            {
                StackPanel contactPanel = new StackPanel();
                contactPanel.Margin = new Thickness(25);

                TextBlock name = new TextBlock();
                name.Text = c.Name;
                contactPanel.Children.Add(name);

                TextBlock address = new TextBlock();
                address.Text = c.Address;
                contactPanel.Children.Add(address);

                TextBlock city = new TextBlock();
                city.Text = c.CityStateZip;
                contactPanel.Children.Add(city);

                TextBlock phone = new TextBlock();
```

```
                phone.Text = c.Phone;
                contactPanel.Children.Add(phone);

                customPrintPanel.Children.Add(contactPanel);
            }

            args.PageVisual = customPrintPanel;
        };

    doc.Print("Formatted Print");
}
```

4. Next you'll add code to these two lambda expressions. In the BeginPrint event, you'll change the Text of the PrintStatus TextBlock you added to "Printing" so that the user can see when the printing process began. In the EndPrint event, concatenate the phrase "Printing Finished!" to the end of the PrintStatus TextBlock. This will tell the user when the printing process is complete.

```
private void PrintFormatted(object sender, RoutedEventArgs e)
{
    PrintDocument doc = new PrintDocument();

    doc.BeginPrint += (s, args) =>
    {
        PrintStatus.Text = "Printing...";
    };

    doc.EndPrint += (s, args) =>
    {
        PrintStatus.Text += "Printing Finished!";
    };

    ...
}
```

5. Now press F5 to test the application. When the application opens, click the Print Formatted button. When the print dialog opens, select your printer and click Print. You'll see the status text displayed as shown in Figure 15-7.

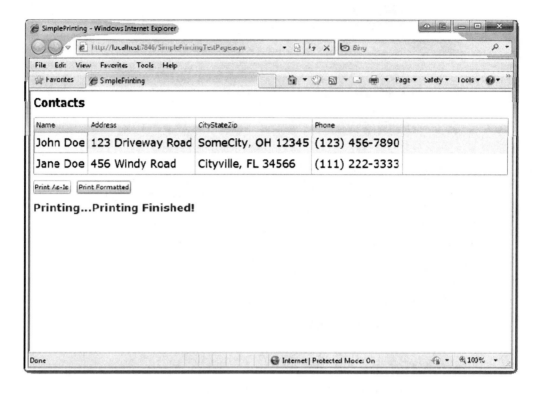

Figure 15-7. Handling the additional print events

Summary

In this chapter, you looked at the Silverlight printing API. You saw how to easily print content as it appears on the screen, as well as how to print custom content. As you saw, the new printing API lets you add rich printing functionality to your Silverlight applications. In the next chapter, we will take a look at deploying Silverlight applications.

CHAPTER 16

Deployment

Up to now in this book, I have discussed only the process of developing Silverlight applications. In this chapter, I turn your focus to post development and discuss the topic of deploying your Silverlight applications.

Deploying Silverlight Applications

Once you have finished developing your Silverlight application, you must then face the question of deployment. Luckily, Silverlight deployment is a trivial task that really involves only one concept: XAP files.

XAP Files

When you compile a Silverlight application, the application is packaged into a single file with the extension .XAP. This file is the only thing that needs to be sent to the client in order to run your application. The XAP file itself is really nothing special and is nothing more than a zip file with a special file extension. To prove this, you can simply change the file extension of a XAP file to give it a .ZIP extension. Once the file has been renamed, you can then view the contents of the compressed archive in the file explorer in Windows or in a zip archive tool such as WinZip.

　　The reason Silverlight uses XAP files to package applications is really to provide two benefits. First, by placing your files in a ZIP archive file, your files are compressed when they are deployed and sent to the client, which in turn reduces download times and improves the end-user experience. Second, by placing your entire Silverlight application in one file, it makes the process of deploying your application extremely simple.

Hosting Silverlight Content

To host Silverlight content on your web server, you do not need to be running a Windows server. In fact, just about any web server can serve Silverlight content, as long as it is set to serve up XAP files. In Internet Information Services 7 (IIS7) this is set up by default. So if you are running Windows 2008 Server, your web server is preconfigured to host your Silverlight content.

　　If you are running a version of IIS previous to IIS7 or if you are running on a non-Windows server, you must do some minor configuration to enable the MIME types for the Silverlight extensions. The two MIME types you need to add are described in Table 16-1.

Table 16-1. The Two MIME Types

Extension	MIME Type
.xaml	application/xaml+xml
.xap	application/x-silverlight-app

Because there are so many different servers out there, I won't attempt to show you how to set up this MIME type for each server possibility, so you will need to do some quick research on how to set up MIME types, though it is an extremely common task for server administration.

Application Library Caching

As the previous section described, when you deploy your Silverlight applications, all files for your application are included in a XAP package. This includes any assemblies that are required by your application. For example, your XAP file might look like Figure 16-1, where you can see that a number of assemblies are included in the package, such as System.Windows.Controls.Data.dll. This assembly alone is 128 KB in size, and this amount has to be downloaded to each and every client that runs your application. Furthermore, if there are multiple Silverlight applications that all require the use of the System.Windows.Controls.Data.dll assembly, each one by default will download their own copy of the assembly.

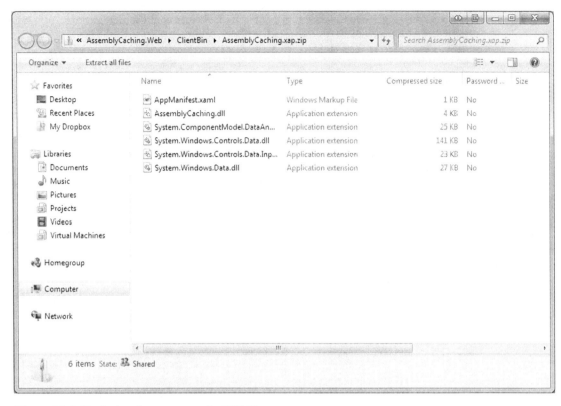

Figure 16-1. Exploring the contents of a XAP file

Application library caching is a new feature added since Silverlight 3 that allows you to cache assemblies locally and share them among different Silverlight applications running on a client machine. Once the files are separated from the application XAP file, their download location can be specified in the AppManifest.xml file.

Let's run through a very quick example to show how assembly caching works and how to activate it in your Silverlight applications.

Try It Out: Exploring Assembly Caching

In this exercise, you will create a simple Silverlight application that includes a number of assemblies. You will then look at the packaged XAP file before and after you activate assembly caching for the application. You will also explore the source changes that take place when using assembly caching. Let's get started!

1. In Visual Studio 2010, create a new Silverlight application named AssemblyCaching and allow Visual Studio to create a Web Application project to host your application.

2. In MainPage.xaml, make certain your cursor is positioned within the root Grid and double-click on the DataGrid from the toolbox. Note that for the DataGrid,

you must have a reference to the Silverlight Software Development Kit (SDK) as explained in Chapter 5. After the DataGrid has been added, right-click on it in the design view and select Reset Layout ➤ All. After this, your XAML should look like the following:

```
<Grid x:Name="LayoutRoot" Background="White">
    <sdk:DataGrid AutoGenerateColumns="False" Name="dataGrid1" />
</Grid>
```

3. Build the application by selecting Build ➤ Build Solution from the main menu.

4. Expand the ClientBin directory within the host web application's directory using Solution Explorer in Visual Studio. There you should find the AssemblyCaching.xap file, as shown in Figure 16-2.

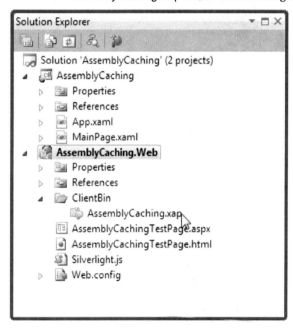

Figure 16-2. Locating your application's XAP file

5. Change the file name of this file to be AssemblyCaching.xap.zip from within Solution Explorer in Visual Studio to explore the contents. Once the file is renamed, double-click on the file name to open the compressed file in Windows Explorer. You will see the contents as shown in Figure 16-1. You will see that there are many assemblies contained in the *.xap file. Once you have finished inspecting the file, rename it back to AssemblyCaching.xap.

6. From Visual Studio, right-click on the Silverlight application in Solution Explorer and select Properties. On the properties dialog, you will see the Reduce XAP Size By Using Application Library Caching. Select this option, as shown in Figure 16-3, and save your changes.

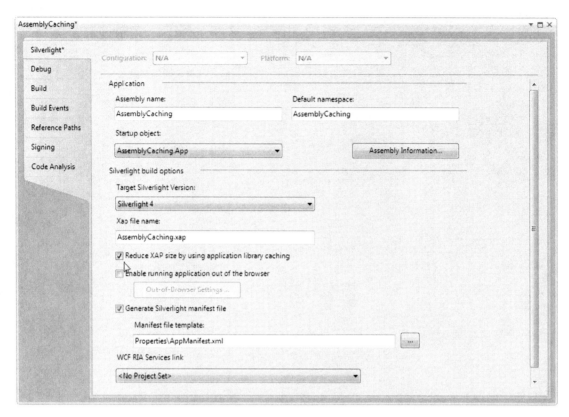

Figure 16-3. Enabling assembly caching

7. Rebuild the application and then navigate back to the ClientBin directory. Delete the AssemblyCaching.zip file from the previous step, and then once again, rename the AssemblyCaching.xap file to a *.zip file and open it in Windows Explorer. You will see that there are significantly fewer assemblies contained within the package, as shown in Figure 16-4.

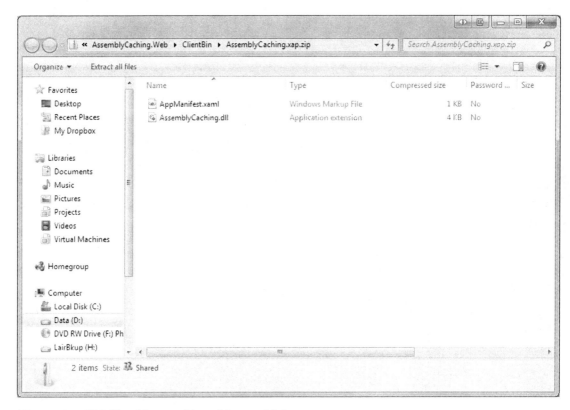

Figure 16-4. XAP file with assembly caching enabled

8. If you then refresh Solution Explorer and examine the `ClientBin` folder, you will see that a number of new .zip files have been added, as shown in Figure 16-5. These .zip files contain the assemblies that were removed from the *.xap file. When your Silverlight application needs the specific assemblies, they will download the assembly via the .zip file in the `ClientBin`.

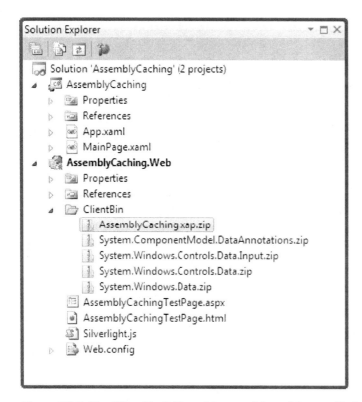

Figure 16-5. *The ClientBin folder with assembly caching enabled*

ENABLING ASSEMBLY CACHING SUPPORT FOR CUSTOM ASSEMBLIES

By default, custom assemblies do not support assembly caching. To quickly see this, add a control from the Silverlight toolkit and then build with assembly caching turned on. You will notice that the toolkit assemblies are not removed from the *.xap. To add support for assembly caching to your custom controls, a number of steps must be completed:

- First, you must assign your assembly using a public key token. This is done using the sn.exe utility.

- Next, you need to create an external part manifest for your assembly. This is an XML file with the extension <ASSEMBLY NAME>.extmap.xml. This manifest contains information that assembly caching needs in order to know where to retrieve the assembly when it is requested by the Silverlight application.

Once you have taken the preceding steps, your custom assembly can take advantage of assembly caching.

Full-Screen Pinning

Full-screen support has been available in Silverlight for quite some time, but if you are like me and you have multiple monitors, there has probably been a time when you put something in full screen and then changed the focus to another application on your system. If you have indeed tried this, you probably noticed that the Silverlight application that was shown in full screen was no longer in full screen.

Silverlight includes a feature called *full-screen pinning*, where developers can elect to keep their application in full screen, even when it loses focus. If they have enabled this feature for their application, when the user selects full screen the application prompts them with a consent dialog asking if it is OK to remain in full screen, as shown in Figure 16-6. Assuming the user clicks Yes, the application remains in full screen until the user presses escape while focused on the application or until the application removes itself from full screen.

Figure 16-6. Consent dialog for full-screen mode

As a developer, to enable full-screen pinning for your application, you simply need to add one line of code to your application, shown in the following code listing. Notice the property FullScreenOptions is set to StaysFullScreenWhenUnFocused. That is all there is to it!

```
public partial class MainPage : UserControl
{
    public MainPage()
    {
        InitializeComponent();
        App.Current.Host.Content.FullScreenOptions =
            System.Windows.Interop.FullScreenOptions.StaysFullScreenWhenUnfocused;
    }

    private void Button_Click(object sender, RoutedEventArgs e)
    {
        App.Current.Host.Content.IsFullScreen =
            !App.Current.Host.Content.IsFullScreen;
    }
}
```

Out-of-Browser Support

Another feature in Silverlight is the ability to run your Silverlight applications outside the browser. The feature allows users to right-click on a Silverlight application, install it locally to their machine, and execute it without opening their browser. Out-of-browser support is also just as safe and secure as running Silverlight within the browser, as applications that run out of the browser still live within the sandbox.

For developers, running an application out of the browser has a number of benefits. The most obvious is that the same XAP runs both in the browser as well as out of the browser. That means you can now develop an application that has identical user experiences in any browser, in any platform, and even outside the browser on any platform. In addition, out-of-browser functionality supports automatic updating of applications, which means even when a user installs the Silverlight application for out-of-browser execution, updates still are automatically sent to the user. Developers also have access to an API that allows them to determine when their applications are run out of the browser and modify the behavior of their app however they wish.

To enable out-of-browser support for your Silverlight application, the first step is to view the properties of the Silverlight application and select the Enable Running Application Out Of The Browser check box, as shown in Figure 16-7. Note that if you have enabled assembly caching, you will have to disable it to enable out-of-browser functionality.

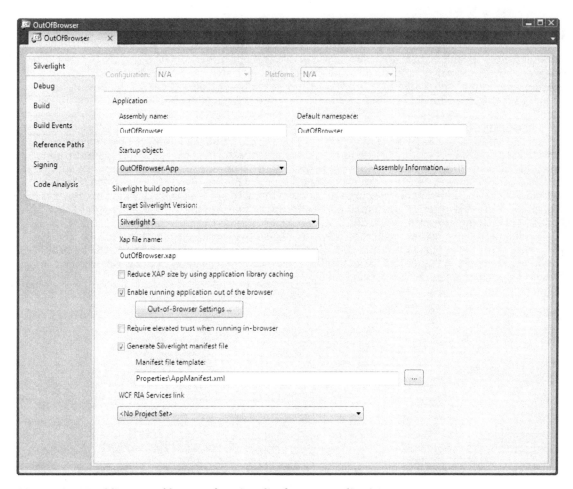

Figure 16-7. Enabling out-of-browser functionality for your application

When you select the Enable Running Application Out Of The Browser check box, Visual Studio will also change the debug start action to Out-Of-Browser Application. If it does not, you need to do that step manually, by clicking the Debug tab from the project settings and selecting the Out-Of-Browser Application radio button in the Start Action area, as shown in Figure 16-8. Now, when you run your application, you will see that it starts up out of the browser in its own window.

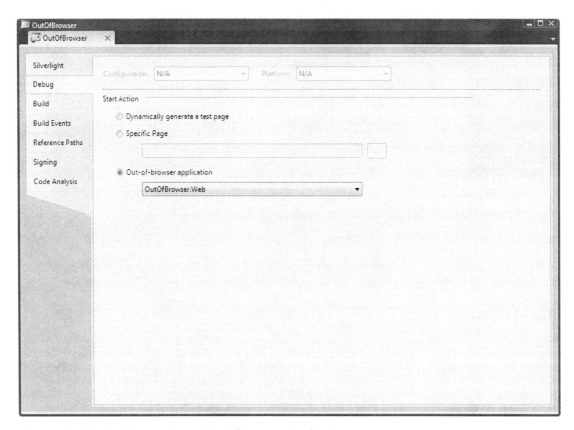

Figure 16-8. Setting Start Action to Out-Of-Browser Application

If you want to see what the end user will see when installing your application locally from the Web, change the Start Action back to Dynamically Generate A Test Page. Then run your application. When the application is displayed inside the web browser, right-click and select Install OutOfBrowser Application Onto This Computer. You will be presented with the default Install Application dialog shown in Figure 16-9. The user has the option to create shortcuts on either the Start menu, Desktop, or both.

Figure 16-9. *Default Install Application dialog*

After the installation is complete, the application relaunches outside the browser. At this point, the user can reopen the application at any time via the shortcuts she chooses during the installation.

Out-of-Browser API

As mentioned, in Silverlight, applications running out of the browser are running the exact same XAP as the application running in the browser. This is great for developers because you know the user will have the same experience in both situations. However, what if you wanted to change that experience? What if you wanted to change the behavior of some elements of your application in the event that users were running the application out of the browser? In Silverlight, you can work with a number of API methods, properties, and events to customize your application based on its state. One of these properties is the IsRunningOutOfBrowser property. This property returns true if application is running out of the browser and false if it is running within the browser. You can easily add code that looks at this property and executes accordingly:

```
private void Button_Click(object sender, RoutedEventArgs e)
{
    if (Application.Current.IsRunningOutOfBrowser)
    {
        OOBStatus.Text = "Application Running Out of Browser!";
    }
    else
    {
        OOBStatus.Text = "Application Running In Browser";
    }
}
```

By adding this code, you can run the application within the browser (as you can see in Figure 16-10) and out of the browser (as shown in Figure 16-11) to see that your application behaves differently depending on its state.

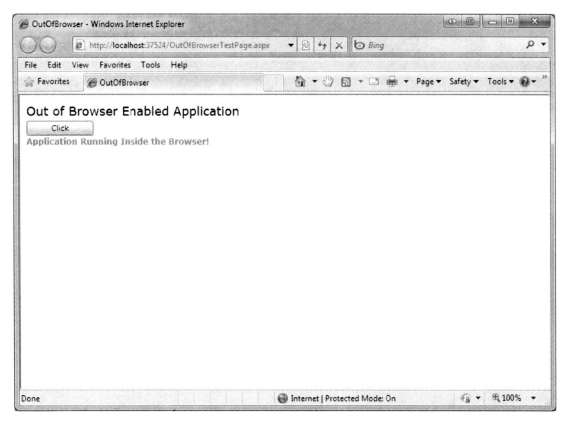

Figure 16-10. Application running within the browser

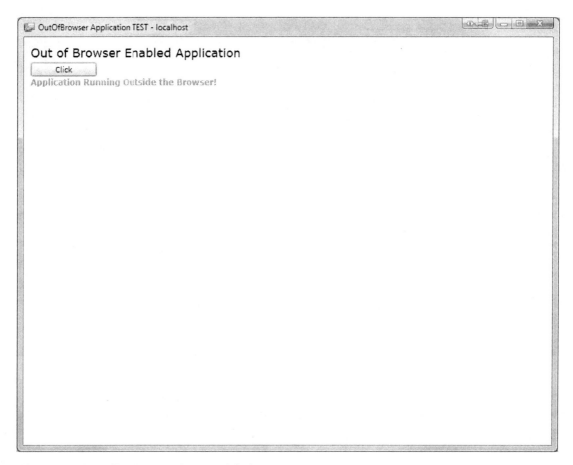

Figure 16-11. Application running out of the browser

Removing Installed Applications

You might be wondering how you can uninstall the Silverlight applications you installed locally. With Silverlight, you can uninstall your applications from Add/Remove programs within Windows, as shown in Figure 16-12. That is all there is to it!

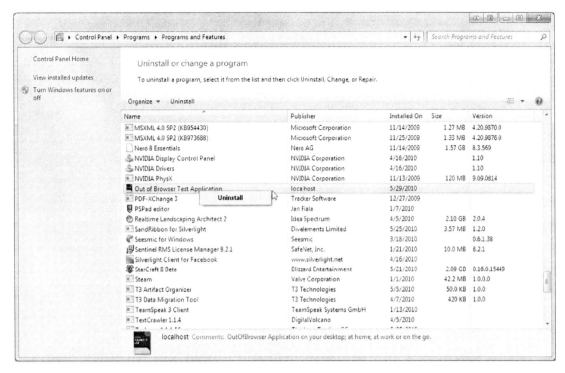

Figure 16-12. *Removing a Silverlight application from Add/Remove programs*

In addition to using Add/Remove programs, you can also uninstall your application from within the application itself. Uninstalling this way involves only one very simple step. Open the application, right-click on it, and select Remove This Application, as shown in Figure 16-13. That is all there is to it!

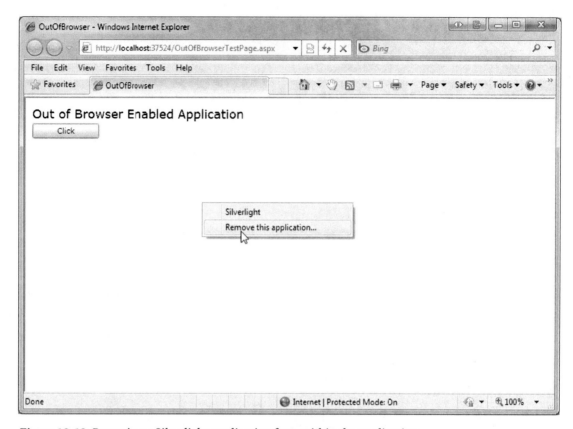

Figure 16-13. Removing a Silverlight application from within the application

Elevated Trust Applications

The addition of out-of-browser support in Silverlight 3 was among the most popular of the new features in Silverlight. However, many developers asked for more access to client desktops, including device support and hard-drive access. In Silverlight, developers can create applications that request elevated permissions, which provide the client support developers were seeking. For more information on taking advantage of elevated permissions, see Chapter 10, "System Integration and Device Support."

To enable elevated trust for your application, first enable out-of-browser functionality for your application, as shown in Figure 16-14.

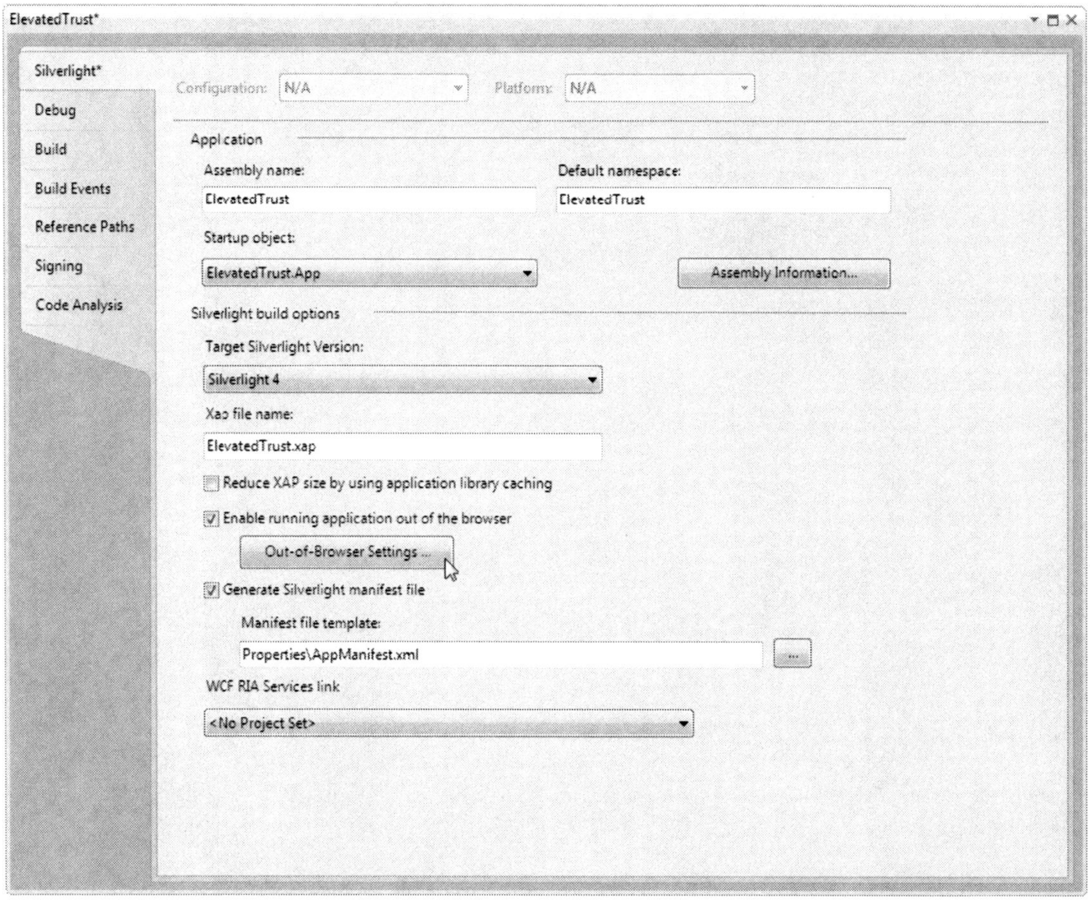

Figure 16-14. Enabling out-of-browser support

Next you need to select the Require Elevated Trust When Running Outside The Browser check box, as shown in Figure 16-15.

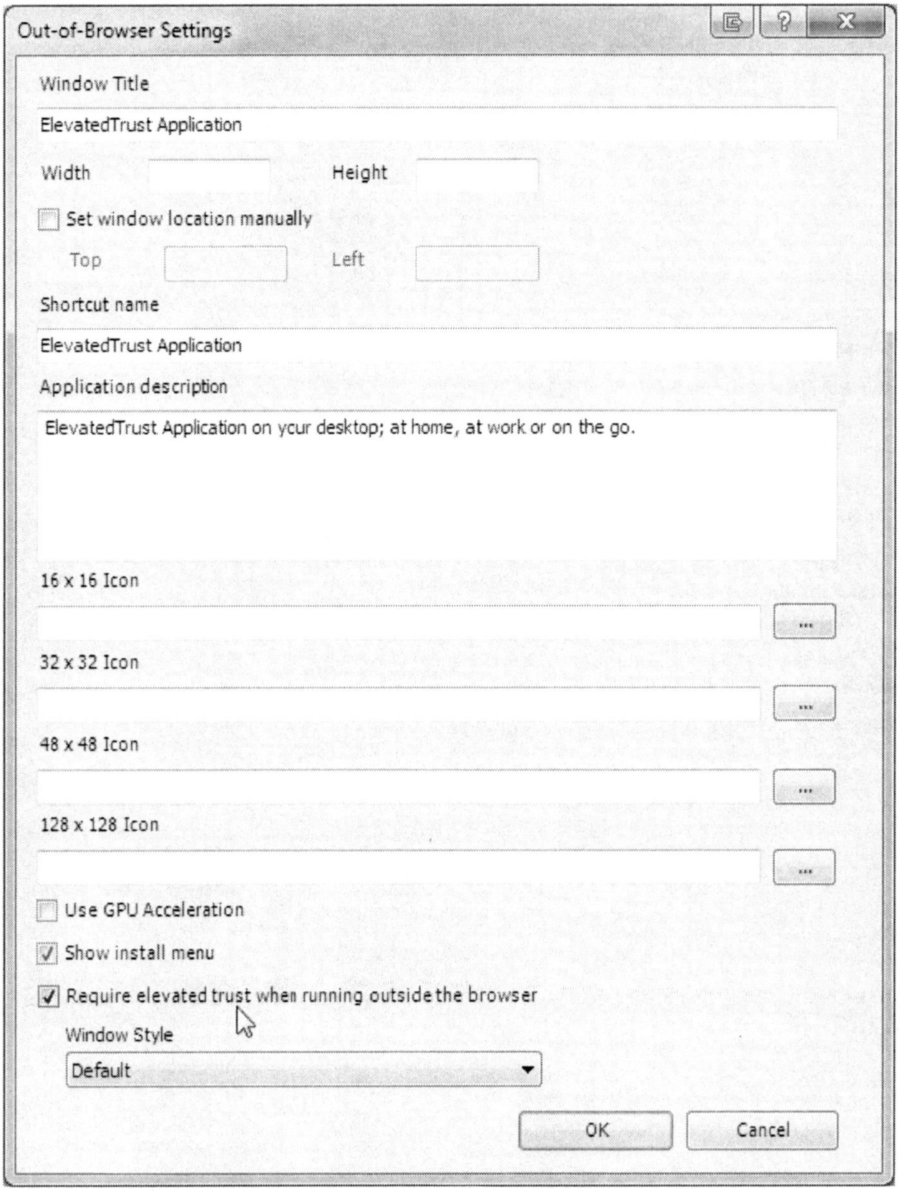

Figure 16-15. Enabling elevated trust

When users access your application and run it out of browser, they will be prompted with a consent dialog, shown in Figure 16-16., that will ask them if they are OK with granting your application the elevated permissions.

Figure 16-16. Elevated trust consent dialog

■ **Note** You are able to provide a much friendlier version of the elevated permission consent screen by signing your application with a code-signing certificate. The certificates start at around $100 per year and you can obtain them through many services, such as Go Daddy, Thawte, VeriSign, and Comodo.

Summary

In this chapter, you explored deploying Silverlight applications. As you have seen, deployment in Silverlight is straightforward and trivial, which is yet another benefit of Silverlight applications. You now are able to build your own Silverlight applications from start to finish and deploy them for the entire world to appreciate! Happy Silverlighting!

Index

CPSIA information can be obtained at www.ICGtesting.com
Printed in the USA
LVOW050426200412

278416LV00004B/1/P